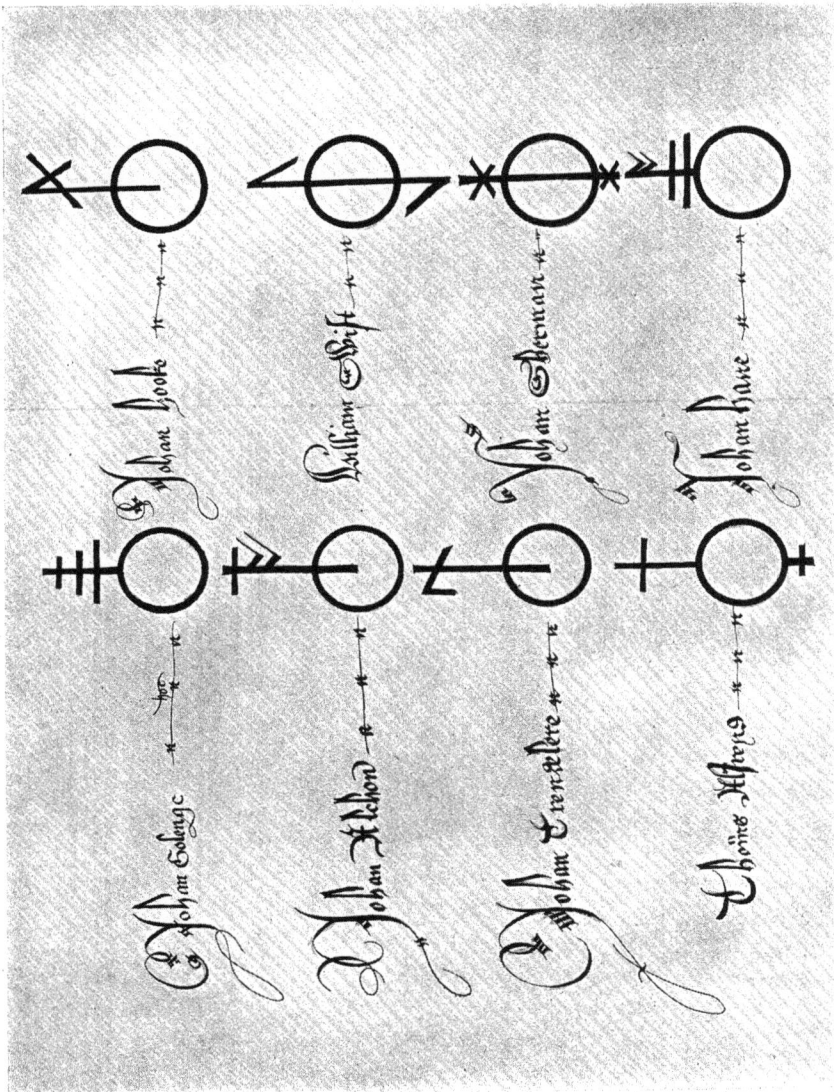

COOPERS' MARKS ENROLLED AT THE GUILD HALL, LONDON, IN 1420.

THE
HISTORICAL FOUNDATIONS OF
THE LAW RELATING TO
TRADE-MARKS

BY
FRANK I. SCHECHTER, A.M., J.D.
OF THE NEW YORK BAR

WITH FOREWORD BY
MUNROE SMITH, J.U.D., LL.D., J.D.
BRYCE PROFESSOR EMERITUS OF EUROPEAN LEGAL HISTORY
COLUMBIA UNIVERSITY

THE LAWBOOK EXCHANGE, LTD.
Clark, New Jersey

ISBN 9781584770350

Lawbook Exchange edition 1999, 2012

The quality of this reprint is equivalent to the quality of the original work.

THE LAWBOOK EXCHANGE, LTD.
33 Terminal Avenue
Clark, New Jersey 07066-1321

*Please see our website for a selection of our other publications
and fine facsimile reprints of classic works of legal history:*
www.lawbookexchange.com

Library of Congress Cataloging-in-Publication Data

Schechter, Frank I. (Frank Isaac), 1890-1937
    The historical foundations of the law relating to trade-marks /
by   Frank I. Schechter ; with foreword by Munroe Smith.
        p. cm.
    Originally published : New York : Columbia University Press,
1925.
    Includes bibliographical references and index.
    ISBN 1-58477-035-X (cloth : alk. paper)
      1. Trademarks—Law and legislation—United States—History.
2. Trademarks—Law and legislation—Great Britain—History.
I. Title.
KF3180.S3   1999
346.7304'88—dc21   99-41673
                                              CIP

Printed in the United States of America on acid-free paper

THE
HISTORICAL FOUNDATIONS OF
THE LAW RELATING TO
TRADE-MARKS

BY

FRANK I. SCHECHTER, A.M., J.D.

OF THE NEW YORK BAR

WITH FOREWORD BY

MUNROE SMITH, J.U.D., LL.D., J.D.

BRYCE PROFESSOR EMERITUS OF EUROPEAN LEGAL HISTORY
COLUMBIA UNIVERSITY

New York

COLUMBIA UNIVERSITY PRESS

1925

TO THE MEMORY

OF

My Mother

COLUMBIA LEGAL STUDIES

EDITED BY THE

FACULTY OF LAW OF COLUMBIA UNIVERSITY

EDITORIAL COMMITTEE

MUNROE SMITH, J.U.D., LL.D., J.D., Bryce Professor
Emeritus of European Legal History, General Editor.
HUGER W. JERVEY, A.M., LL.B., D.C.L., Professor of
Law and Dean of the Faculty of Law. UNDERHILL
MOORE, A.M., LL.B., Professor of Law. HESSEL E.
YNTEMA, PH.D., S.J.D., Associate Professor of Roman
Law and Comparative Jurisprudence.

FOREWORD

THE establishment of a doctorate in law, obtainable in course, has been under consideration in Columbia University for almost half a century. In 1880, when a Faculty of Political Science was established, and when it was provided that students completing a course of graduate study under this Faculty and presenting an acceptable printed dissertation should receive the degree of doctor of philosophy, Professor John W. Burgess proposed that students who had previously obtained the bachelor's degree in law and had also fulfilled the requirements for the doctor's degree under the Faculty of Political Science, should receive, in lieu of a doctorate of philosophy, a doctorate in law. This recommendation was not accepted. In 1905 a plan was formulated by the Faculty of Political Science for the establishment of a doctorate in law under the joint control of the Faculties of Law and of Political Science. This plan was accepted by the University Council but rejected by the Faculty of Law. Five years later it was proposed by a committee representing both Faculties, that such a degree should be established in the School of Law and under the primary jurisdiction of the Law Faculty. This degree was to be awarded only to students who had obtained the LL.B. degree and only after one year's further study of law and the presentation of an acceptable printed dissertation. This plan was unanimously accepted by both Faculties and by the University Council but failed to secure the assent of the Board of Trustees. A similar plan presented in 1922 was accepted by the Trustees.

In the Faculty of Political Science, from its establishment in 1880, provision was made for instruction in every branch of public law and in legal history and comparative jurisprudence — subjects at that time not included, or not ade-

quately presented, in the School of Law. It was therefore
possible for students of law to obtain the Ph.D. degree on
work essentially legal in character. Between 1883 and 1910
fifty-two students received this degree on the presentation
of strictly juristic dissertations. Of these students twenty-
six had previously obtained the degree of LL.D. Of the
fifty-two legal dissertations only eleven dealt with private-
law topics. After 1910 the number of legal dissertations presented by students in political science and also the proportion
of such dissertations dealing with private-law topics showed
a slight decrease. These results show clearly that a doctorate
of philosophy did not appeal to law students as an appropriate degree, and was in fact not an appropriate degree, for
advanced work and research in those fields of law which are
of special professional interest. It is perhaps significant that
the dissertation here presented, which is the first accepted
for the Columbia doctorate in law, represents research in
such a field and in a subject of a highly technical character.

In all the plans for a doctorate in law formulated at Columbia since 1880, as also in the plans now in operation, stress
has been and is laid on the presentation of an acceptable
dissertation. In the final successful appeal for the establishment of the degree, it was stated that it was not expected
that an accepted dissertation would often be an important
contribution to legal science, but that it was believed that the
preparation of a dissertation under the guidance of competent
instructors was the best possible training in investigation and
that it was confidently hoped that some of the students thus
trained would eventually, in their maturer years, do much to
raise the standard of American legal literature.

In the various plans presented since 1880 the degree proposed was that of *Juris Doctor*. In consequence of the fact
that since 1902 this degree had been awarded by the University of Chicago on a strictly professional course of study,
replacing the traditional degree of LL.B., and that this innovation had been accepted by several other American universities, the question naturally arose, in Columbia as elsewhere,

whether it were not desirable to award some other degree for advanced work and research in law. At Yale University the D.C.L. degree has been awarded since 1880 for advanced work and investigation in law. In Harvard University, when provision was made, some fifteen years ago, for a fourth-year course in law, a wholly new degree, that of S.J.D. was established. At Yale University a J.S.D. degree is awarded on the same basis. At Columbia the D.C.L. and the LL.D. degrees were rejected, because these degrees had so long been granted both in England and in the United States largely *honoris causa*. After long consideration Columbia decided to award the J.D. degree for advanced work and research in law, in spite of the fact that this degree has, perhaps over hastily, been recognized by the Association of American Law Schools and by the Association of American Universities as a purely professional degree. This decision was based upon the fact that outside of English-speaking countries this degree has been awarded for centuries and is still awarded not as a professional degree, nor to any considerable proportion of university students who have pursued the studies required for admission to the bar, but on the same condition of demonstrated capacity for research which is required by Columbia. Columbia has chosen to follow the tradition and practice of the civilized world at large rather than the different and somewhat discordant policies adopted by a limited number of American universities. As the value of a trade-mark depends upon the quality of the product, so also, it is believed, will the worth of an academic degree granted by any university be estimated, in the long run, by the amount and character of the work for which it is awarded.

In the study of the development of the law of trade-marks here presented, the author notes, at the outset, the tardy recognition by the English royal courts of the rules established centuries earlier by gilds and by towns and applied in the customary courts. This, as every student of English legal history knows, was the attitude of the royal common-law courts towards the entire body of commercial law when they drew under their jurisdiction those commercial cases which had previously been decided in the communal courts. The customs of merchants, however uniformly administered, were not recognized as English common law. Even less was it recognized that the commercial rules applied for centuries in the English common-law courts were in reality European law. It seemed incompatible with the independence of England and the sovereignty of its crown that foreign law should have any force save in so far as it was accepted by Parliament or by the royal courts.

In tracing the development of the law of trade-marks the author is therefore obliged to use "unorthodox" sources of information. Distinctive marks upon chattels were, as he points out, originally *indicia* of ownership — a purpose still subserved on our western cattle ranches by the distinctive brand of each ranch. Throughout the middle ages, the marks placed by merchants upon goods which they had bought for shipment served the same purpose. Quite a different purpose was subserved by marks placed upon wares by their makers. These, as the author shows, were not at first generally adopted by the makers in their own interest but were imposed upon them in the interest of the public, in order to locate responsibility for short weight, inferior material or poor workmanship. Like the finger prints taken today by the police, they established a liability rather than a right. But since this liability tended to secure honest and efficient workmanship, the trade-mark came to be regarded as an assurance of quality, and the confidence of the public in the quality of wares bearing a trade-mark of good repute became an asset. This asset grew in value when wares, at first produced only for local consumption, gained wider markets.

This gradual development was only tardily recognized in the law. To the liability imposed upon the maker of inferior goods was added, at an early period, the liability of the maker who used without right or who deceptively imitated a reputable trade-mark. This later liability, like the earlier, was at first imposed in the interest of the public and was based upon fraud committed against purchasers. The value of a trade-mark to its rightful user was more tardily protected. The development of remedies of which he might avail himself was impeded by prejudice against "monopoly." Even the remedies ultimately provided were colored by the earlier notion of deceit practiced upon purchasers. They were largely based upon "disloyal competition." And even when a trade-mark came to be recognized as an interest that could be transferred *inter vivos* or might pass to a widow or a child *mortis causa*, courts and writers hesitated, and still hesitate, to describe trade-marks as property rights, since their protection is still based on the ground of actual or constructive fraud.

This entire development finds many parallels in the history of other branches of private law. Interests rarely receive legal protection until they become of substantial economic value. Private rights have always been developed by the establishment of increasingly adequate remedies, and not only is the extent of a right measured by the remedies available for its protection, but also the conception of the nature of the right is colored by the character of the remedies.

The author apparently holds, and the data he gives will probably convince most readers, that trade-marks are today property rights. Whether they should be so classed, however, he regards as an academic rather than a practical question, since the rightful possessor of a trade-mark may claim protection in equity.

In the projected series of "Columbia Legal Studies," of which this dissertation is presented as the first volume, it is not intended to include all dissertations accepted for the doctorate, but, as in the Columbia "Studies in History, Economics and Public Law," only those that are regarded as valuable contributions to legal science. Nor is it expected or desired that the dissertations included should each form a volume. Shorter contributions will be issued as pamphlets and will later be included in bound volumes.

It is not intended that the "Columbia Legal Studies" shall consist wholly of doctor dissertations. It is expected, on the contrary, that they will include books and pamphlets written by members of the Columbia Faculty of Law and by alumni of the Columbia School of Law, and contributions from law teachers in other universities and from members of the bar will be welcomed. It is believed that this series will afford a convenient and desirable medium for the publication of studies that cannot well be compressed to the degree necessary for acceptance by law journals but do not need to be expanded into volumes.

MUNROE SMITH

PREFACE

THIS volume is not an attempt to add to the many manuals of current trade-mark law that are now available to the Bench and Bar. Its aim is to illumine the hitherto "dim historic trails" to the sources of trade-mark law and to analyze critically the present state and tendencies of trade-mark law in the light of its history. Bearing in mind Mr. Justice Holmes' warning against the enchanting "pitfall of antiquarianism," I have endeavored to present historical material solely for the purpose of seeing whence the present law has come and what should be the basis of its development in the future. If at times I may have been tempted from the main highway by the fascination of a particularly attractive by-path, as in the case of printers' and publishers' devices, my researches have been incorporated in a note or appendix in such a way as not to break the thread of the primary line of investigation. In the course of a survey of six centuries of the uses and piracy of trade symbols, I have necessarily been led into all sorts of byways in medieval law and in gild life and discipline from which has been extracted material that may, I venture to think, prove of interest not only to the legal profession, but to the economic historian and also to those concerned in a non-legal capacity with trade-marks and trade-marked articles.

In the preparation of a work of this kind, touching as it must upon so many phases and ages of law, economics and social history, the roll of those to whom I am indebted for assistance is necessarily exceedingly lengthy. Librarians, scholars, archivists and officials of archæological societies in England, who have been most courteous and helpful in answering inquiries, are too numerous for mention by name in this preface. As typical instances of their kindness I may cite that of Mr. A. E. Stamp, Secretary of the Public Record Office, and Mr. A. H. Thomas, Clerk of the Records, Guild Hall, London, who transcribed for me many passages from records in their respective archives. Acknowledgments for assistance in particular phases of my subject are made at the appropriate places in the work. However, certain indebtedness should be recorded here. On the very threshold of my researches I was led out of the impasse of purely legal records such as the Year Books, to the literature of the gilds and other archæological material by Dean Orrin K. McMurray of the Law School of the University of California during his year of residence at Columbia University. While I do not wish to appear to offer this work under the august ægis of Sir Paul Vinogradoff, it would, on the other hand, be improper for me to fail to mention that it was he who, during his visit to Columbia University in 1923, first pointed out to me the great significance for my subject of the administrative records of the Privy Council and of the Star Chamber of the sixteenth and seventeenth centuries.

For encouragement and for the suggestion that my work be submitted for inclusion in the series of Columbia Legal Studies, I am indebted to Associate Justice (formerly Dean) Harlan F. Stone. During the progress of this work I have had the privilege of consultation with Professors H. E. Yntema, H. Oliphant, N. Dowling and A. P. Evans of Columbia University. I am under special obligation to Professor Yntema, not only for valuable suggestions during the writing of this book, but also for his reading of the proofs. From Miss I. Mudge, the Reference Librarian of Columbia University, and from my friend, Professor Alexander Marx, I have received guidance and references in my study of printers' and publishers' devices which was submitted as a paper at the 1924 meeting of the American Bibliographical Society. To the officials of the Columbia University Library, and particularly to Mr. Frederic C. Erb, the Supervisor of the Loan Division, as well as to Professor Frederick C. Hicks, the Librarian of the School of Law, Columbia University, and to Mr. Lawrence H. Schmehl, the genial Assistant Librarian, I am deeply indebted for their unfailing liberality in the loan of books. I should also mention here the courtesies of the Library of Congress, Harvard Law Library, the Free Library of Philadelphia, the Library of the United States Trade-Mark Association of New York City and the Library of the Bar Association of the City of New York.

Mr. Edward S. Rogers of the Chicago Bar, and Mr. Hans v. Briesen, of the New York Bar, have aided me by their stimulating discussions of various problems of trade-mark law and by helpful citations. The latter has also kindly read the proofs. To my wife I am indebted for assistance during the writing of this volume and in the preparation of the bibliography and index. My thanks are due to Miss Belle de Costa Greene, the Librarian of the J. Pierpont Morgan Library, for the reproduction, in Chapter III, of the printers' device of Peter Short, from the 1609 edition of Spenser's *Faerie Queene*, to the Duke of Northumberland for a photograph of the imprint of the proceedings of the Privy Council against Thomas Jupp, reproduced in the appendix to Chapter IV, and to the Worshipful Company of the Cutlers of London for permission to reproduce the plate of cutlers' marks in Chapter V. Finally, there should be recorded here my appreciation of the courteous co-operation and interest of Mr. Sidney C. Erlanger which greatly facilitated the writing of this volume.

FRANK I. SCHECHTER

March 30, 1925

CONTENTS

xviii   CONTENTS

LIST OF ILLUSTRATIONS

TABLE OF CASES

TABLE OF STATUTES

[1] Attributed in some MSS. to 13 Edw. I (see *Stat. of the Realm*, i, 202, asterisked note).

CHAPTER I

INTRODUCTION

THE PROBLEM AND THE SOURCES

"There is, upon some subjects, a touching absence of curiosity among English lawyers. Institutions which are the very heart of modern business life, the fountain-heads of not ungrateful streams of litigation, are accepted as though, like the image of Ephesus, they fell direct from heaven for the benefit of a deserving profession. The legal questions to which they give rise are studied with minute care, the legal relationships which they create are made the occasion of microscopic analysis. But the subject itself, the really interesting and important matter, is left untouched." These words of the English legal historian, Edward Jenks, writing of the early history of negotiable instruments,[1] apply with equal force to practically all phases of commercial law. The lawyer who, for some unusual reason, has found it necessary to probe for origins in the particular field of law wherein his problem lies has, in more or less desultory fashion, scanned such early common law sources as may have been at hand. Finding nothing there, he has been quite content to cease his quest and to report the roots of the law in question as lying very near the surface. In the history of promissory notes, of bills of lading, of charter parties and of policies of insurance, their appearance in the development of the common law is uniformly of comparatively recent date, and the realization that, as a matter of fact, these commercial institutions have an ancient and complicated history of their own and a law that developed quite independently and outside of the sphere of influence of the common law is still "new learning" to many of those who, in their daily practice,

---

[1] *Select Essays in Anglo-American Legal History*, iii, 51.

are confronted with problems involving promissory notes, bills
of lading, charter parties and insurance.[1]

But nowhere is the obscurity of the origins and at the
same time the "touching absence of curiosity" concerning
these origins more apparent than in the field of the law of
trade-marks. When we consider how great a factor trade-
marks and good-will represent in commercial life today and
when we remember that out of the so-called law of technical
trade-marks has grown the law of unfair competition or
concurrence déloyale,[2] circumscribing at a hundred different
points the predatory and overreaching instincts of the mercantile mind, the comparative brevity of the history of that
law in the royal courts is remarkable indeed.

It may perhaps be not amiss to point out at this juncture
that the investigation of the historical development of our
trade-mark law is not merely of academic interest. Two problems of trade-mark law and of the law of unfair competition,
which has been developed largely by analogies to the law involving cases of technical trade-marks, perplex the minds of
both British and American courts, and conflicting theories
with regard to these problems are materially affecting the
decisions of these courts in cases that are constantly being
presented to them. In the first place, in both British and
American courts, the very nature of the right in a trade-mark
is still unfixed. Sir Frederick Pollock has pointed out[3] that

the protection of trademarks and trade names was originally
undertaken by the courts on the ground of preventing fraud.
The right to a trademark, after being more and more assimi-
lated to proprietary rights, has become a statutory franchise
analogous to patent rights and copyright, and the wrong to

[1] See for this whole subject: Holdsworth, *History of English Law*, i (3rd ed.),
544; v. 144: and the following essays in *Select Essays in Anglo-American Legal
History*, volume iii: T. E. Scrutton, "General Survey of the History of the Law
Merchant"; W. R. Vance, "The Early History of Insurance"; S. Brodhurst,
"The Merchants of the Staple"; W. Mitchell, *The Law Merchant*, pp. 77–78.
[2] See *Coty, Inc.* v. *Parfums de Grande Luxe, Inc.* (U.S. C.C.A., 2nd Cir.), 298
Fed. 865, 877; *United Drug Company* v. *Rectanus Company* 248 U.S. 90, 97;
Rogers, *Good Will, Trade Marks and Unfair Trading*, p. 127.
[3] Pollock on *Torts* (12th ed., 1923) 312–313.

be redressed is now, in cases within the statute, conceived no longer as a species of fraud, but as being to an incorporeal franchise what trespass is to the possession, or right to possession, of the corporeal subjects of property. . . .

In the second place, aside from the determination of the somewhat metaphysical question as to the exact nature of a right in a trade-mark and of injury to trade-marks, there is the very practical consideration as to the basis of relief in trade-mark cases and, more particularly, in cases of unfair competition. "There was no property in any trademark or trade name which the (common) law recognized. . . . The ground of the court's interference to prevent such fraudulent use was to save the public from a fraud."[1] In England and, to a much greater degree, in this country[2] courts are endeavoring to reach a conclusion as to whether, in such cases, the true basis of relief is the deception of the public or whether, on the other hand, it is the injury to the owner of the trade-mark involved. This precise issue was recently considered by the United States Circuit Court of Appeals for the Second Circuit, which said, "In cases of trade names and the like, outside the law of trade-marks proper, there has been a kind of oscillation between the notions of quasi-proprietary right and of the personal right not to be injured by fraudulent competition. But the latest decisions have come back to the ground of the earlier ones."[3] Furthermore, the tendency to insist upon deception of the public as not merely a *test* of a violation of a trade-mark right but as the *basis* of relief against such violation is still discernible in the opinions of the courts of this country.[4] Judge Hough, in dissenting from the opinion of the court just quoted, viz. that, because the plaintiff had not proven deception of the public, hence he

[1] Stephens, *Commentaries on the Laws of England* (16th ed. 1914) ii, 58.
[2] C. G. Haines, "Efforts to Define Unfair Competition," 29 *Yale Law Journal* 27.
[3] *A. Bourjois & Co., Inc.* v. *Katzel* 275 Fed. 539. *Cf. Standard Oil Co.* v. *Federal Trade Commission* 282 Fed. 82, 85.
[4] See *Florence Mfg. Co.* v. *J. C. Dowd & Co.* 178 Fed. 73; *Union Fishermen's Cooperative Packing Co.* v. *Point Adams Packing Co.* 108 Ore. 535, 548, and cases cited *infra*, pp. 162–163.

was not entitled to protection, pointed out that "it is not yet settled whether a trade-mark is to be primarily regarded as protecting the trade-mark owner's business from a species of unfair competition or protecting the public from imitations."[1] When this case came before the Supreme Court of the United States, however, that court, reversing the opinion of the Circuit Court, emphasized the investment by the plaintiff and the injury to the plaintiff's property right, disregarding entirely the lower court's emphasis on the absence of deception of the public.[2]

The hope is ventured that this study of the origins of trade-mark law may throw some light on the reason for the existence of this difference of opinion as to the basis of relief that should be applied and may aid in clarifying the confusion still admittedly prevailing in many jurisdictions as to the proper basis of relief.[3] This difference of opinion and confusion amid which courts are admittedly groping towards an adequate theory of relief are attributable not only to their failure to keep pace with the functional evolution of trade-marks, of which we shall see repeated evidences in later phases of this study, but to the mystery and uncertainty surrounding the initial entry of the common law courts into the fray against trade-mark piracy.

The first reference to trade-marks in the king's courts is an irrelevant reminiscent dictum first reported in 1656 to have been dropped, in the case of *Southern* v. *How*, by a Common Pleas judge, Dodderidge, in 1618, concerning the infringement of a clothier's mark in the reign of Elizabeth. The authority and longevity of Justice Dodderidge's dictum have been so extraordinary and unwarranted and they present so interesting a manifestation of "the judicial process" that we shall be obliged to dwell upon the many reports of *Southern*

---

[1] 275 Fed. at p. 543.
[2] 260 U. S. 689, Mr. Justice Holmes writing the opinion for the Court.
[3] See J. L. Gold, "Equity: Trademarks: Nature of Infringement" in 7 *Cornell Law Quarterly* 373. *Cf.* note to the decision by the Circuit Court of Appeals, 35 *Harvard Law Review* 624, concurring with the majority view that "safeguarding the public from deception" is "the primary purpose of trademarks." See also *infra*, ch. vii.

v. *How* and the various versions of the dictum itself at some length, — even at the risk of repeating what may be partly old learning to the practitioner of trade-mark law. The reasons for the utterance of the dictum are obscure and the very fact of its utterance is barely established by but one out of five extant reports of the case. *Southern* v. *How* was a King's Bench action on the case for the sale of counterfeit jewels to plaintiff by defendant through the latter's servant. The case, which is first reported in *Popham's Reports*, published in 1656, and stated therein as having been decided at the Trinity Term, 15 Jac. I, had no relation whatsoever to trade-mark law, but the report nevertheless states:[1]

Doderidge (*sic*) said, that 22 Eliz. the action upon the case was brought in the Common Pleas by a clothier, that whereas he had gained great reputation for his making of his cloth by reason whereof he had great utterance to his benefit and profit, and that he used to set his mark on his cloth whereby it should be known to be his cloth: and another clothier, observing it, used the same mark to his ill-made cloth on purpose to deceive him, and it was resolved that the action did well lie.

It should be noted that *Southern* v. *How*, while appearing in *Popham's Reports*, was not actually reported by Popham himself, but was included in the volume among "Some Remarkable Cases Reported by other learned Pens since his death." There are four later reports of *Southern* v. *How:* — *J. Bridgeman's Reports* (1659)[2] ascribes *Southern* v. *How* to the Hilary Term, 13 Jac. I, and does not mention Dodderidge's dictum. *Croke's Reports*[3] (also 1659) sets the Hilary Term, 15 Jac. I, as the date of the case, and contains an entirely different version of Dodderidge's dictum concerning the case of the clothier, squarely stating the action to have been brought not by the clothier whose mark had been misused, but by the defrauded purchaser:

Dodderidge cited a case to be adjudged 33 Eliz. in the Common Pleas: a clothier of Gloucestershire sold very good

[1] p. 144.   [2] p. 125.   [3] Cro. Jac. 469.

cloth, so that in London if they saw any cloth of his mark they would buy it without searching thereof; and another who made ill cloth put his mark upon it without his privity; and an action upon the case was brought by him who bought the cloth, for this deceit; and adjudged maintainable.

Volume 2 of *Rolle's Reports*, published in 1676, contains two conflicting accounts of *Southern* v. *How*. The first of these[1] reports the case as having been decided 15 Jac. I, Hilary Term, and, like *Bridgeman's Reports* above referred to, makes no mention of Dodderidge's dictum concerning the clothier's case. The second report,[2] ascribing the case to 16 Jac. I, Trinity Term, states,

> Dodridge (*sic*) Justice in 23 Eliz. in le Common Banke le case fuit, que un cloathier de Gloucester fait cloathes queux fueront pluis deere, & pluis vendable que les cloathes d'ascun auter, & il mist special marke sur eux que null auter cloathier avoit devant, & apres un cloathier avoir counterfeit le dit marke, & mitte ceo sur ces cloathes, queux ne fueront cy-bien, mes uncore il vend eux cy chare come lauter per cest deceipt fuit adjudge que action sur le case gist vers luy, mes Mr. Justice Dodridge ne dit per quel deux ceo gist lou per le cloathier que primerment avoit le dit marke, ou pur le vendee, mais semble que gist pur le vendee. . . .

To sum up the remarkable discrepancies occurring in the reports of this case: (1) Three of the five reports contain no reference whatsoever to the clothier's case in Elizabeth. (2) Of these three reports only one (*Popham*) definitely states the action to have been by the clothier whose mark had been infringed. Of the two others, one (*Croke*) is equally definite that the action was by the defrauded purchaser, and the other (*2 Rolle* 26), while not perhaps so positive in this regard, likewise believes that the action was by the vendee. (3) Popham reports Dodderidge to have remembered that the clothier's action occurred in *22* Elizabeth, *2 Rolle* says *23* Elizabeth, while Croke's report states *33* Elizabeth. (4) Only two of the five reports (*Popham* and *2 Rolle* 5) agree that *Southern*

---

[1] 2 Rolle 5.   [2] *Ibid.*, p. 28.

v. *How* was decided in 15 Jac. I, the other three reports giving other and different dates for the decision.

Despite the fact that Dodderidge's reminiscence, — whatever it was — was pure dictum, and despite the conflict of evidence as to what that dictum was, *Southern* v. *How* appears to have acquired considerable weight as authority for the proposition that the unauthorized use of a trade-mark is unlawful and may be the subject of an action in deceit. It is so classified in the abridgements and digests.[1] Chancellor Kent also states that *Southern* v. *How* was an "action against a clothier by another clothier."[2]

The English Courts have unequivocally relied upon the authority of *Southern* v. *How* to establish the antiquity of their jurisdiction to prevent trade-mark piracy. In *Blanchard* v. *Hill* (1742)[3] Lord Hardwicke appears to have assumed on the authority of "Popham 151" that an action at law would lie by a clothier against another for the misuse of trade-marks. In *Crawshay* v. *Thompson* (1842)[4] Maule, J., cited *Southern* v. *How* as reported in both *Popham* and *Cro. Jac.* without committing himself to either version of the case. In *Burgess* v. *Burgess* (1853)[5] Knight Bruce, L.J., interrupted the argument of counsel to remark that "the law on the subject is as old as *Southern* v. *How* in *Popham's Reports.*" In *Hall* v. *Barrows* (1863)[6] Romilly, M.R., stated that "it was established as early as *Popham's Reports* that an action at law would lie for the piracy of a trade-mark." In *Hirst* v. *Denham* (1872)[7] Bacon, V.C., expressed his doubts as to *Southern* v. *How*, — not whether that case was an action of the owner of a trade-mark for its infringement, but whether it was the *first* such action.

Finally, only a quarter of a century ago, in *Magnolia Metal*

[1] See 1 Nelson's *Abr.* 38, §17; 3 Bacon's *Abr.* (3d ed.) 560 (K); 1 Viner's *Abr.* (2nd ed., London 1791) 574; 1 Comyn's *Dig.* (London 1780), 166: "Action Upon the Case for a Deceit" (A9).
[2] See 2 *Kent's Commentaries*, 7th ed., p. 446, note b.
[3] 2 Atkyns 484, at p. 485.
[4] 4 Man. & G. 357, at pp. 385–6.
[5] 3 De. G. M. & G. 896, at p. 902.
[6] 32 L.J.N.S., Equity, 548, at p. 551.
[7] L.R., 14 Eq. 542, at p. 549.

Company v. *Tandem Smelting Syndicate, Ltd.*, (1900),[1] Lord Chancellor Halsbury, in analyzing the plaintiff's pleadings in a "passing-off" action, stated that such an action "has been a well recognized cause of action, certainly for the last two hundred and fifty years."

"My Lords," [continued Lord Halsbury[2]] "that cause of action is, as I have said, a very old and a very familiar one . . . [After quoting Dodderidge J. in *Southern* v. *How*] Going back, therefore, as far as the reign of Elizabeth the form of action which the Statement of Claim adopts has undoubtedly been a form of action in which if the right of a man to have the reputation of selling that which is his manufacture as his manufacture, the right to prevent other people fraudulently stating that it is their manufacture when it is not — if that right is infringed there is a remedy. That has, as I have said, ever since the reign of Elizabeth, been established in our Courts as being a right of action upon which anybody may sue who has a ground for doing so."

From Lord Halsbury's opinion there was no dissent.

Our somewhat lengthy excursus into the history of Justice Dodderidge's dictum in *Southern* v. *How* has enabled us to see in its true light the actual validity and subsequent authority of that dictum which may or may not have been uttered in 1618 as to an action which may or may not have been given by a royal court somewhere in the middle or later years of the reign of Queen Elizabeth. After *Southern* v. *How* there appears to have been absolute silence in the king's courts on the subject of trade-mark protection for over a century, — until 1742 — when for the first time injunctive relief against trade-mark infringement was sought from a very learned Lord Chancellor, — who, in *Blanchard* v. *Hill*,[3] denied that relief on the ground that the protection of trade-marks would create or protect monopolies. In no branch of the law can we conceive a more striking example of what Sir Paul Vinogradoff has recently termed "the fictitious character of the latent completeness of the law."[4]

---

[1] 17 Rep. Pat. Cas. 477, at p. 483.   [2] *Ibid.*, at p. 484.   [3] 2 Atkyns 484.
[4] P. Vinogradoff, *Introduction to Historical Jurisprudence*, p. 27.

Nevertheless, those who have attained pre-eminence either as practitioners or as text-writers of trade-mark law have with few exceptions been quite content to regard that law as practically the creation of the nineteenth century, without attempting in any way to ascertain the extent to which trade-marks had been used prior to the nineteenth century, the functions or purposes which these trade-marks had served and the methods, if any, by which they came under any form of legal protection or surveillance. Thus it is stated in the most recent edition of Kerly's *Treatise on the Law of Trade-marks*,[1] "The law on this subject cannot be traced back further than the nineteenth century." Sebastian, another English authority on trade-marks, likewise states with regard to the protection of trade-marks: "It is possible that this right was recognized as early as the reign of Queen Elizabeth; it was at any rate established in 1833. . . ."[2] American writers are equally uninquisitive. Hopkins, in his otherwise comprehensive treatise on *Trademarks, Trade Names and Unfair Competition*, referring to the origin of trade-marks and trade-mark law, says with an eloquent "carelessness of exactitudes":

We walk in almost absolute darkness along these dim historic trails. On every hand are signs that show the coming importance of trademarks. But Rome is to reach her zenith and her debacle, the Middle Ages are to intervene, the new world beyond the Atlantic is to be discovered, modern Europe is to be reorganized by states and peoples, before we again reach traces of the use of identifying marks in trade. Even then, the laws of trademarks will not come into existence until generations of traders have come and gone. The history of the law of trademarks is pretty accurately at our service. The history of the early use of trademarks has never been written and most of its evidences have crumbled into dust. For those illuminating examples of ancient marks preserved to us, the labor of the archæologist alone is responsible and to him our appreciation is due.[3]

[1] 5th ed. (1923) p. 2.
[2] Sebastian, *Trade Mark Registration* (2nd ed. 1922) p. 3.
[3] 4th ed., (1924) p. 2.

The courts have been no less vague and uncertain in their discussion of this subject than the textwriters, but, as shown above with regard to *Southern* v. *How*, their natural tendency has been to extend their own jurisdiction over trade-marks retrospectively as far as possible, preferably, it would seem, even to the Year Books.[1] As recently as 1919 it was stated by the United States Circuit Court of Appeals for the Second Circuit:[2]

It has been said frequently that the doctrine of exclusive property in trademarks has prevailed from the time of the Year Books. But an examination of the record hardly justifies the statement in the opinion of Mr. Upton, who nevertheless declares that — "Property in trademarks, exclusive and absolute, has existed and been recognized as a legal possession, which may be bought and sold and transmitted, *from the earliest days of our recorded jurisprudence.*"[3]

Our recital of the adventures of Dodderidge's dictum may perhaps have raised some doubts as to the accuracy of Mr. Hopkin's statement that "the history of the law of trade-marks is pretty accurately at our service."[4] Furthermore, whatever we know of the history of trade-mark law is largely due not so much to Englishmen or to Americans but, as in so many other fields of legal history, to foreign scholars. Joseph Kohler's *Das Recht des Markenschutzes* must be the foundation and starting point of our researches. Gustav Lastig's *Markenrecht und Zeichenregister*, Alexandre Braun's "Introduction Historique" to Braun and Capitaine's *Les marques de fabrique et de commerce* and Philippe Dunant's *Traité des marques de fabrique et de commerce en Suisse* contain further contributions to the subject. These writers have laboriously

[1] In *Knott* v. *Morgan* (1836) 2 Keen 218, counsel, *arguendo*, declared the law of passing-off to have "been settled, from the Year Books downwards." In *Amoskeag Mfg. Co.* v. *Spear* (1849) 2 Sandf. 599 at p. 604, Judge Duer cites "2 Keen 218" as stating that "the doctrine of exclusive property in trade-marks has prevailed from the time of the Year Books, implying the antiquity of the legal, in contradistinction to the equitable protection of marks."
[2] *Scandinavia Belting Co.* v. *Asbestos Rubber Works of America Inc.*, 257 Fed., pp. 937, 941, per Rogers, Cir. J.
[3] Citing Upton on *Trademarks*, p. 10. (Italics the writer's.)
[4] Hopkins, *op. cit.*, p. 2.

explored the "dim historic trails" and brought back with them a wealth of material that throws much light not only upon the early history of trade-marks and trade-mark law in their own countries, but upon the universal tendencies of the development of that law. An indication of the neglect of this subject by English and American writers may be found in the fact that the *Select Essays in Anglo-American Legal History*, intended by the Editors to constitute "a mosaic showing the general pattern of our law for the last six centuries" [1] contains no reference to the subject of trade-marks and unfair competition, although dealing with such equally isolated and specialized topics as the early history of patent law and insurance law and the carrier's liability. American writers on trade-mark law, drawing more or less upon the researches of European scholars, have only nibbled at the historical problem from time to time.[2] There has been hitherto no systematic endeavor to trace the history of trade-mark law in England up to the time of its administration by the King's Courts or to consider modern trade-mark law in the light of its history.

Any approach to such a study must be through channels and from sources that will be regarded as most unorthodox from a legal standpoint. The Year Books, to which judicial commentators on the "antiquity" of trade-mark law have been apt to resort,[3] are concerned mainly with land tenures, feudal dues, crimes of violence and defamation, — not with commerce — and do not aid us in our quest. The treatises of the medieval[4] English jurists, Bracton, Glanvil, Britton and Fleta, in contrast with those of Continental Europe,[5] display no interest in the subject.

[1] Preface to vol. ii, p. v.
[2] See W. H. Browne, *Treatise on the Law of Trademarks*, (2nd ed. 1898) Introd.: E. S. Rogers, "Some Historical Matter Concerning Trademarks," 9 *Michigan Law Review* 29; L. E. Daniels, "History of the Trademark," 7 *Bulletin U. S. Trademark Assn.*, New Ser., 239; E. S. Rogers, *Good Will, Trademarks and Unfair Trading* (1919 reprint) ch. iii.
[3] See *supra*, p. 12.
[4] In this essay the writer has used the terms "medieval" and "Middle Ages" to include a period extending into the seventeenth century. He has, however, sought to mitigate this freedom of phraseology by references to specific dates, wherever generalizations would be inaccurate.
[5] See C. Dietzel, *Das Handelszeichen und die Firma*, in *Jahrbuch des Gemeinen*

Nor do the proceedings of the local Courts furnish us with any clues as to the beginning of trade-mark law. The Leet Courts were anxious — much to the disgust of the legal profession — to redress private grievances and to settle private disputes.[1] However, as far as their records thus far published indicate, until the sixteenth century, with a single exception, the interest of the Leet Courts in trade-marks was confined to a more or less feeble enforcement by periodic fines of the statutes providing for the compulsory affixing or imprinting of marks by bakers and coopers.[2] The single exception just referred to is that of the granting of marks to the cutlers of Hallamshire by the Manor Court of the Earl of Salop in 1564,[3] which has a bearing upon the development of a unique system of trade-mark law by cutlery trades and which will be referred to in a later chapter dealing with those trades.[4] The Borough Court records, though they note actions for deceit in the sale of cloth[5] and food,[6] will be searched in vain for cases of trade-mark infringement or of unfair competition.

The records of the fair and market courts and of the Borough Piepowder Courts, administering the Law Merchant, might reasonably be expected to make valuable contributions to the history of trade-mark law. But although these courts

Deutschen Rechts, iv, p. 230 passim; Albert Braun, op. cit., pp. xxv et seq.; G. Lastig, op. cit., pp. 185 et seq.; P. Dunant op. cit., p. 31. Most medieval writers sought to trace the origin of trademark law to a provision of the Lex Cornelia concerning false seals, (De falsis, D. Book XLVIII, tit. X), but it is evident that the law in question referred to the forgery of seals on wills (see Kohler, op. cit., p. 39; D. R. Pella, Marcas de Fábrica y de Comercio en España (1911), p. 15.   Cf. infra, p. 129.

[1] See F. J. C. Hearnshaw, Leet Jurisdiction in England, pp. 218–219; William Hudson, Leet Jurisdiction in the City of Norwich (Selden Soc., vol. 5) pp. xxxiv, 8.

[2] Under date of October 30, 1923, the writer was advised by Professor Hearnshaw that "there are not any cases in any of the Leet Court Records which I have examined that suggest any conflicts between merchants or craftsmen concerning the use of marks." But for instances of punishment by the Leet Court for failure to affix compulsory marks under police regulations, see infra, pp. 51–52 (bakers' marks), p. 59 (coopers' marks); cf. infra, pp. 82–83 (Coventry cloth seal).

[3] R. E. Leader, History of the Cutlers of Hallamshire, i, p. 7.

[4] See infra, p. 120.

[5] W. H. Stevenson, Records of the Borough of Nottingham, ii, p. 71, No. XXXI.

[6] Ibid., p. 131.

dealt with a variety of commercial causes,[1] arising at the fair
to which flocked merchants from all over England as well
as from abroad, no case therein has thus far come to light
involving the misuse of trade-marks.[2] The Maritime Courts,
which concerned themselves with the causes and controversies
of traders arising at the seaport towns and at London, frequently, as we shall see in a later chapter,[3] especially in the
sixteenth century, had occasion to decide cases involving
merchants' marks, but such allusions in the records of these
courts clearly refer to such marks as indicative of ownership
of the goods to which they were affixed and have no relation
to conflicts of interest in the merchants' marks themselves.[4]

We have referred above[5] to the statutes requiring the
coopers and bakers, in the interest of consumers, to set their
marks upon their wares. We shall have occasion to refer to

---

[1] See *Select Cases on the Law Merchant*, i (Selden Soc. vol. 23) pp. 102 (breach
of covenant for failure to deliver goods according to sample), 91 (forfeiture of
goods not corresponding to sample), 110 (enforcement of girdlers' ordinance
against garnishment of girdles with lead), 85 (defamation of credit), 97 (trespass
for depriving a seller of his bargain for the sale of salmon, — "*de dicto barganio
ejecit*"); see also W. S. Holdsworth, *History of English Law*, v, pp. 109–113.

[2] Vol. I of the "Select Cases on the Law Merchant," edited by Gross
(Selden Soc. vol. 23), contains nothing on this subject, nor will Vol. II, the
writer is informed by Mrs. E. E. Watkins, who is now editing it for the Selden
Society. For a recent summary of the various matters of which the Law
Merchant took cognizance, see W. A. Bewes, *The Romance of the Law Merchant*,
pp. 19–25. It is difficult to find authority for the statement in the article on
the Law Merchant in the *Encyclopædia Britannica* (11th ed., vol. xvi, p. 300)
that "to the law merchant modern English law owes the fundamental principles in the law of trademarks."

[3] See *infra*, pp. 31 *et seq.*

[4] Until the fifteenth century, as pointed out by Gross (*Gild Merchant*, i,
p. 107), "the line of demarcation between the merchant and craftsman was
not yet sharply defined." However, from the subject matter of the branches
of the law developed in the Admiralty Courts, — such as charter-parties, bills
of lading, insurance, bills and notes, contracts made abroad, etc. — (See
Reginald G. Marsden, *Select Pleas in the Court of Admiralty*, Vol. I (Selden
Soc. vol. 6) Introd. p. lxvii; *ibid*. Vol. II (Selden Soc. vol. 11) Introd. pp. lxxix–
lxxx) it would appear that this law affected and concerned itinerant middle-
men or traders rather than the actual producers or craftsmen who were required by law to affix production marks to their goods. Malynes in his *Lex
Mercatoria* (1622, p. 5) defined a merchant as "he that continually dealeth in
buying and selling of commodities, or by way of permutation of wares both
at home and abroad in forreine parts." Molloy in his *De Jure Maritimo* (1676,
Book iii, ch. xiii, p. 436) follows substantially the same definition of a merchant
and states, "but those that buy Goods to reduce them by their own art or
industry into other forms than formerly there were of, are properly called
Artificers, not Merchants. . . ."

[5] See *supra*, p. 14.

these statutes again,[1] and also to consider similar statutes compelling the affixing of marks identifying the producer of the wares of goldsmiths,[2] arrowhead-makers,[3] clothiers,[4] pewterers[5] and wax-workers.[6] However, while the preambles and recitals of these statutes throw considerable light upon the functions and uses of the individual marks involved, they will not in themselves indicate the evolution of a system of trade-mark law, but will rather record or confirm the especial necessity for the use of a mark for a particular purpose at the time of their enactment.

Where, then, shall we find the germs of our modern trade-mark? We shall find the answer in the great mass of records of the organizations of merchants and craftsmen themselves, supplemented by the researches of antiquarian and archæological bodies, concerning these mercantile elements, wherein we shall see the first indications of the uses, abuses, and legal significance of the marks and symbols used in medieval commerce.

The first glance at the medieval economic structure and methods of production will furnish us with a very simple reason for the absence of any evidence of trade-mark litigation in the early records of the king's courts. Medieval trade was largely conducted through gilds or "misteries" and an integral part of the whole scheme of organization into gilds or "misteries" was the prevention of litigation among gildsmen in any tribunal save the court held by the gild officials or gild members themselves and the punishment of all efforts to seek redress "at law" for wrongs perpetrated by a gildsman against his fellow-gildsman, without the consent of the gilds. The nature and functions of the gilds will be discussed in a later chapter,[7] but the point may be emphasized here that arbitration among gildsmen was a primary duty of the master and wardens of practically every British gild and livery company, and resort to litigation was the gravest

[1] See *infra*, pp. 57 (coopers), 51 *et seq.* (bakers).
[2] See *infra*, p. 59.   [5] See *infra*, p. 102
[3] See *infra*, p. 105.   [6] See *infra*, p. 128.
[4] See *infra*, pp. 84, 86.   [7] See *infra*, ch. iii.

kind of an offense. Among the early "Ordinances of the Brotherhood of Our Lady of Bethlehem" appears the following typical provision:

Also they are agreed that if any dispute arise between any of the said Brotherhood, that he who shall feel himself aggrieved shall complain to the said Brotherhood so that the trespass may be redressed between the parties without making a disturbance, and that no one shall complain in any other place nor in any other manner; and if any one be a rebel (*soit rebell*) and will not be reformed by the said Brotherhood, that he be ousted from the Company forever.[1]

The records of the Grocers Company of London contain the following entry for the year 1379:

These are the tares of different wares ordained and assented to by the old company the eighteenth day of August, the year aforesaid, to stop and prevent all disputes which might arise between the mystery of Grocers in the case where the purchaser and vendor are of the same company or where the purchaser be of the company of Grocers and where no express agreement has been made in express terms at the time of the bargain.[2]

[1] A. H. Johnson, *History of the Worshipful Company of the Drapers of London* i, 200. This ordinance was evidently regarded as of sufficient importance to be marked "*lege*" (*ibid.* i, 262), *i.e.*, that it was to be read at certain stated, periodic "assemblies" of the Company.

[2] *Ms. Archives of the Company of Grocers of London* (ed. J. A. Kingdon), pt. i, p. 56. For similar ordinances punishing extra-gild litigation and providing methods of arbitration, and for illustration of gild arbitration and discipline, see *Cooper's Company, London* (ed. J. F. Firth), pp. 42, (1456) 85; Goldsmiths' Records in Herbert, *Livery Companies of London*, ii, p. 171 (1462); *Annals of the Barber-Surgeons of London* (ed. S. Young), pp. 33 (before 1388), 201 (1606); C. Welch, *History of the . . . Paviors of London*, p. 9 (1479) *History of the Saddlers of London* (ed. J. W. Sherwell), pp. 169–171 (*passim*) (1606–39); *Some Account of the Worshipful Company of Ironmongers of London* (ed. J. Nicholl), pp. 118, 120–21 (1504); *Annals of the Founders' Company of London* (ed. W. M. Williams), pp. 87–8; Coventry Smith's Records in *Coventry Leet Book* (ed. M. D. Harris, ii, p. 744 (1540); "Company of Stitchmen of Ludlow" (ed. G. M. Hills), in *Journ. Brit. Archaeol. Assn.*, vol. 24, p. 329 (1569); Ordinances of Listers of York in *York Memorandum Book* (Surtees Soc. Pub. vol. 125), pp. 211–12 (1472); "Shrewsbury Gild of Barber-Chirurgeons," in *Trans. Shropshire Archæol. & Nat. Hist. Soc.*, vol. 5, p. 265 (1432); Aberdeen Gildsmen in E. Bain, *Merchant and Craft Gilds*, p. 129 (1599); Dublin Carpenters, Millers, Masons, etc. in *Journ. Royal Assn. of Antiquaries of Ireland*, vol. 35 (vol. XV, 5th Series), p. 321 (1537); Dublin Merchants, *ibid.*, vol. 30 (vol. X, 5th Series), p. 44 (1438).

In reading the above mentioned ordinances prescribing arbitration among gildsmen as well as all other gild ordinances it is well to remember that many

Despite an Act of Parliament in 1504[1] prohibiting non-litigation ordinances, they continued steadily to be enacted and enforced for over a century thereafter.[2] In the light of such ordinances the reason for the absence of cases involving commercial disputes in the early common-law reports becomes apparent. Before seeking, however, in the gild records for the genesis of our modern trade-mark law, it will be necessary to consider in our next chapter how it came about that merchants and craftsmen, aside from the requirements of their gilds and of statute law, began to use certain marks known and above referred to as "merchants' marks" and what were the legal implications of those marks.

such gild ordinances are "only a reiteration, not an innovation" (see Sellars, Introd. to *York Memorandum Book*, pt. ii, (Surtees Soc. Pub. vol. cxxv), p. li), — in other words, that these ordinances are merely a confirmation or evidence of the pre-existing trade regulation or custom, or a repetition or later version of an earlier ordinance. For instance, in Bristol in 1346, "all the ordinances of the trade guilds in use at that time were rehearsed before the Mayor, Recorder and forty-eight councillors and in some respects amended; they were then entered in the present volume [The Red Book of Bristol] to stand as of record . . ." (See Francis F. Bickley, Introd. to *The Little Red Book of Bristol*, i, p. xxi. For similar instances see Toulmin Smith, *English Gilds*, pp. 293 and 430 (Bristol gilds); *ibid.*, p. 363 (Usages of Winchester); *ibid.*, pp. 411–412 (Worcester); also L. Toulmin Smith "The Bakers of York and Their Ancient Ordinary," *Archaeol. Rev.*, vol. i at p. 125.

[1] 19 Hen. VII c. 7, *Stat. of the Realm*, ii, p. 653.
[2] E. Lipson, *Economic Hist. of England*, i, pp. 309–310, and *supra*, p. 17, n. 2.

CHAPTER II

MERCHANTS' PERSONAL AND PROPRIETARY MARKS IN THE MIDDLE AGES

A TRADE-MARK is frequently defined by the courts as a mark, sign or symbol, "the primary and proper function" of which is, as the Courts say, "to identify origin or ownership of the goods to which it is affixed."[1] This definition of the function of the trade-mark has been in use with almost unvarying uniformity throughout the formative period of trade-mark law up to the present day.[2] In the course of this essay, we shall have occasion to consider the present accuracy and propriety of this definition in the light of recent developments in the methods of production and distribution of goods;[3] at present it is sufficient to note that from the standpoint of *historical* origins at any rate the definition is sound, describing as it does the two relations — "origin or ownership" — which, in the inception of trade-mark law, the mark implied.

The history of trade-mark law is of course inextricably associated with the history of the trade-marks themselves. Joseph Kohler, with his wide range of scholarship, utilized a great deal of the then available archæological material in his reconstruction of the early history of trade-marks and trade-mark law.[4] The great achievements of archæology in the forty years that have elapsed since the publication of

---

[1] See *Hanover Milling Co.* v. *Metcalf* 240 U. S. 403, 412.

[2] Cf. *Hanover Milling Co.* v. *Metcalf supra*, a leading case decided in 1915, with the first trademark decision of the same court, *Canal Company* v. *Clark* (1871), 13 Wall. 311, 322. Likewise the early decisions in *Amoskeag Manufacturing Company* v. *Spear* (1849) 2 Sandf. (N. Y.) 599, 606, and in *Boardman* v. *Meriden Britannia Company* (1868) 35 Conn. 402, 413, should be compared with *Patton Paint Co.* v. *Sunset Paint Co.* (1923) 290 Fed. 323, 325. See also Hopkins, *op. cit.*, sec. 3, collating judicial definitions of a trade-mark.

[3] See *infra*, pp. 147–150.

[4] *Das Recht des Markenschutzes*, pp. 30–51.

Kohler's work have added much to our knowledge of the early use of trade-marks. The ruins of the prehistoric settlement at Korakou near Corinth have yielded up saucers and bowls bearing potters' marks at least four thousand years old;[1] the recently published catalogue of the Yale University collection of Greek and Italian vases reproduces potters' factory marks imprinted in the fifth[2] and fourth[3] centuries B.C., and a Greek terracotta vase of the same period just acquired by the Metropolitan Museum of Art, New York City, is likewise reported to be marked with what is "probably the potter's stamp."[4]   However, in this present study of the history of trade-mark law no endeavor has been made to rewrite the history of trade-marks themselves prior to their appearance in England or to refer to their use either in England or contemporaneously on the continent, except in so far as such uses and parallels may serve to throw some light on the universality or development of some principle of trade-mark law.

The judicial conception of the alternative functions of a trade-mark, — the designation of "origin or ownership" of goods, — rests upon the uses to which marks were put in the Middle Ages.   Strictly speaking, marks designating ownership are not trade-marks at all but merely proprietary marks, which may or may not incidentally serve to designate the origin or source of the goods to which they are affixed.[5] However, the Courts of the twentieth century appear to be

[1] See C. W. Blegen, *Korakou, A Prehistoric Settlement Near Corinth* (American School of Classical Studies at Athens 1921) Fig. 3, No. 6, pp. 5, 11.

[2] See P. V. C. Baur, *Catalogue of the Rebecca Darlington Stoddard Collection* . . . (Yale Oriental Ser. Researches: vol. viii, 1922) No. 445, p. 225.

[3] *Ibid.*, No. 468, p. 230; *cf.* Nos. 516, p. 243; 647, p. 286.

[4] See *Bulletin of The Metropolitan Museum of Art*, vol. xix, No. 5, May 1924, p. 128.   For marks on Roman lamps discovered subsequent to Kohler's researches, see H. B. Watters, *History of Ancient Pottery* (Based on the Work of Samuel Birch, 1905) vol. ii, p. 423 *et seq.* See also E. Hannover, *Pottery and Porcelain* (tr. Rackham, 1925) i, ch. I and II.

After this book had gone to press it was reported by the leader of the "De Prorok Exploration Expedition" that in pottery kilns on the site of ancient Utica, Tunis, "eighty potters' marks" had been discovered, "several of which were hitherto unknown in Punic North Africa.   The oldest lamp so far found in the kilns is a lamp thought to be of the ninth century B.C." (*New York Times*, March 15, 1925).

[5] W. H. Browne, *op. cit.*, p. 14, n. 1.

no more careful to observe the distinction between technical trade-marks and proprietary marks than were their predecessors of the nineteenth century or the commentators and lexicographers of the eighteenth and seventeenth centuries to whom we shall refer later on.[1] It has therefore been deemed desirable to include proprietary marks in this study of the metamorphosis of the modern trade-mark and of the development of trade-mark law.

We have drawn the distinction above[2] between merchants' marks, such as those regarded by the Admiralty and other courts as proof of ownership of goods, and called "merchants' personal and proprietary marks," and the production marks indicating the source or origin of goods. In the present chapter we shall deal with marks of ownership, in the three succeeding chapters with production marks or marks of origin. But it should be noted at the outset that the same mark might and did often serve the dual function of personal or proprietary mark[3] and production mark. As we have said above,[4] until the fifteenth century the craftsman and merchant were often one and the same person. As craftsman he might be compelled by statute law or gild regulations to affix his mark to his goods,[5] — as merchant he would desire to affix a mark to the bale or wrapping of the same goods in order to identify them for the illiterate warehouse clerk and also for the Admiralty Court to which they might be brought after capture on the high seas or wreck on the English coast.

That individual merchants' marks were commonly used in medieval England is evident not only from the actual traces of these marks that still survive, but also from literary references of the period. A passage often quoted in this connection by English antiquarians is the description in

---

[1] See *infra*, pp. 124, 127–128, 147.

[2] See *supra*, pp. 15, 18, 20.

[3] The following pages discussing the social uses of merchants' marks will indicate the distinction between personal and proprietary marks. The former designated ownership, the latter expressed personality. It was the proprietary rather than the personal merchant's mark that acquired legal significance in the Middle Ages.

[4] *Supra*, p. 15, n. 4.   [5] See ch. iii.

Pierce the Ploughman's Crede (*ca.* 1394) of a church of the Friars Preachers:

> Wyde wyndowes y-wrought . y-written full thikke,
> Schynen with schapen scheldes . to schewen aboute
> With merkes of marchauntes . y-medled bytwene,
> Mo than twenty and two . twyes y-noumbred.[1]

A less well-known early English poem, *Wynnere and Wastoure*, antedating *Pierce the Ploughman's Crede* by over forty years, furnishes additional evidence of contemporary use of merchants' marks. *Wynnere and Wastoure*, an alliterative description of social and economic conditions in England in the year 1352, draws an elaborate picture of the various orders and estates that were assembled before the King (Edward III), with the Black Prince at his side, to listen to the debate between *Wynnere*, the representative of the wealth of merchants, of thrift and of skill on one side, and *Wastoure*, representing the lavish, reckless and unproductive self-indulgence of the military class on the other. Intermingled with the banners of the Pope, the lawyers and the Friars,, are displayed those of the merchants bearing their marks.

> And othere synes I see, sett appon lofte,
> Some witnesse of wolle, and some of wyne tounnes,
> [And other] of merchandes merke[s], so many and so thikke
> That I ne wote in my witt, for alle this werlde riche,
> What segge (man) vnder the sonne can the sowme rekken.[2]

Antiquarian researches in the towns and villages of England as well as Scotland corroborate the literary evidences of the extensive use of merchants' marks in the Middle Ages. These

---

[1] Ed. W. W. Skeat (Early English Text Soc. 1867) p. 7, lines 175–178.

[2] *A Good Short Debate Between Winner and Waster* (Selected Early English Poems, ed. Sir Israel Gollancz for Early English Text Soc., III) lines 188–192. The "merchandes merke[s]" of this poem are compared by the editor with those in *Pierce Ploughman's Crede*, and are evidently regarded by him as the marks of individual merchants in contradistinction to the collective emblems of the wine and wool trades. See his note to lines 189–190. See also *Reliquae Antiquae*, ed. T. Wright & J. O. Halliwell, vol. ii (London 1845), p. 280 (cited in Murray, *New Eng. Dict.* vol. 6, p. 168 as for the year 1450):
> "Thay salle be brynte on the hippe, chapmans *merke*,
> Bothe in froste and in snawe to go with lyarde."

marks not only were used commercially to designate the proprietor of the goods to which they were affixed, but also acquired a distinct social significance. It would appear that very early in the history of medieval commerce, merchants, as soon as they had arrived at any degree of prominence or substance, were anxious to perpetuate the marks which they had used to designate their products. They — especially the wealthy wool-staplers — signified their recognition of the Divine source of their prosperity by the erection or restoration of churches, and in those churches they or the grateful recipients of their benefactions placed the same marks that they used upon their bales and their goods. Almost two centuries ago Blomefield, the learned historian of Norfolk, speaking of the time of Edward III, wrote:

The use of these marks were (sic) found so beneficial that at that time all merchants of any note had their peculiar marks with which they marked all their wares, and bare in shields impaled with or instead of arms; witness the abundance of merchant-marks to be found in the houses, windows, and grave-stones, in all cities and great towns (sic), as Norwich, Lynn, etc., by which the memory of their owners is still preserved, it being very obvious to all that search into the records of those places, to find who used such a mark; and then, if we see it on a house, we may conclude it to have been that man's dwelling; if on a disrobed grave-stone, that it was his grave; if on a church-window, or any other publick building, that he was a benefactor thereto; and nothing is of greater use than ancient deeds to make out their marks by, for they are always sealed with them.[1]

[1] F. Blomefield, *History of Norfolk*, vol. i, p. 106 (ed. 1739), quoted from edition of 1805 (vol. i, p. 160, n. 5) by Edward Duke in his *Prolusiones Historicae* (Salisbury 1837) p. 83. The latter has collected (*ibid.* pp. 83–86) examples of the uses of merchants' marks in Lynn, Norwich, Salisbury, Southampton, etc. See William C. Ewing, "Notes of the Norwich Merchants' Marks" (*Pub. of Norfolk and Norwich Archæol. Soc.*, vol. iii, p. 177) for much valuable data and plates reproducing over three hundred marks of the thirteenth to sixteenth centuries; J. Paul Rylands, "*Merchants' Marks and Other Mediaeval Personal Marks*" (*Trans. Hist. Soc. of Lancashire and Cheshire*, vol. lxii, [New Ser. vol. xxvi], p. 1) reproducing eighty-seven such marks. *Cf.* Stow, *Survey of London* (ed. C. L. Kingsford, vol i, p. 274) "Concerning Arms of John Wells, Grocer"; R. R. Sharpe, *Cal. of Wills*, pt. i, p. 272, bequest of Thomas Carleton, "brouderer," for placing his "arms" upon a cross for his grave; *ibid.*, p. 544 bequests for tombstones with skinner's "arms" for decedent, his mother and his grandfather.

Since Blomefield's day, an additional source of information concerning medieval merchants' marks has been discovered in monumental brasses that were set up in churches by the gild or company to which the merchant may have belonged or by the church of which he had been a benefactor or by his surviving family. A large number of these brasses, such as that (dated 1525) of Thomas Pownder, merchant and "Bayley" of Ipswich, reproduced on the opposite page, bear a merchant's mark.[1] Merchants' marks usually consisted of crude lineal figures, such as the owner's monogram, or, often the reversed figure **4**, thought by antiquarians to be a variation of the crucifix or a modification of the *Agnus Dei*,[2] under the protection of which the merchant hoped for the success of his venture. Sometimes, as in the brass to Thomas Pownder, the monogram and reversed figure **4** were combined.

These marks would appear sometimes to have been hereditary and, in some cases, the various branches of a family retained the same mark, but with slight variations, to prevent mistakes.[3] By insisting on thus perpetuating their commercial conquests, the merchants soon found themselves in

[1] See W. H. Macklin, *The Brasses of England*, (2nd ed.) p. 97, for a description of this brass, also *ibid.*, pp. 166–73, for a list of wool-staplers' brasses in England. For other illustrations of or references to merchants' marks on monumental brasses, see *Trans. Monumental Brass Society*, vol. ii, p. 90, vol. vi, pp. 70, 332; H. Haines, *Manual of Monumental Brasses*, pt. i, pp. cxvii *et seq.;* J. S. Cotman, *Engravings of Sepulchral Brasses in Norfolk and Suffolk*, 2nd ed. vol. i, Plates 58 and 60; C. T. Davis, *Monumental Brasses of Gloucestershire*, pp. 56, 74, 95, 123, 136; E. H. W. Dunkin, *Monumental Brasses of Cornwall*, Plates LXI, Fig. 3, LXII, Fig. 3; J. L. Thorneley, *Monumental Brasses of Lancashire and Cheshire*, facing p. 286; J. M. Neale, *Illustrations of Monumental Brasses*, pp. 50 *et seq.;* T. F. Bumpus, *London Churches*, i, 165.
[2] For much valuable information concerning the history of the use of the reversed figure **4** as a merchant's mark, see David B. Morris, *The Stirling Merchant Gild*, pp. 160–170; J. P. Rylands, *op. cit.*, pp. 30–32.
[3] See illustrations in J. P. Rylands, *op. cit.*, pp. 8–9; *cf.* W. C. Ewing, *op. cit.*, p. 179. *Cf.* C. Ffoulkes, "The Craft of the Armourer" in *The Connoisseur*, vol. xxiv, at p. 102 and Plates V and VI, p. 103, showing variations in the armor marks of various members of the famous Colman family of armorers of Augsburg; also, by the same writer, "The Armourers of Italy," in *The Connoisseur*, vol. xxv, p. 31, plate VII, showing similar variations by members of the equally illustrious Missaglia family of armorers in Milan. The Missaglia's mark has been discovered on the capital of a column in the *Via degli Spadari* or Sword Makers' Street, in Milan (see W. Boeheim, "Werke Mailänder Waffenschmiede" in *Jahrbuch der Kunsthistorischen Sammlungen* (Vienna), vol. ix at p. 384; G. F. Laking, *European Arms and Armour*, i, pp. 198 *et seq.*).

MEMORIAL BRASS COMMEMORATING THOMAS POWNDER, MERCHANT OF IPSWICH, AND HIS WIFE, EMMA, 1525, SHOWING HIS MERCHANT'S MARK (IN SHIELD, UPPER CENTER) AND THE ARMS OF THE MERCHANT ADVENTURERS (UPPER RIGHT) AND OF THE TOWN OF IPSWICH (UPPER LEFT).

conflict with the Heralds who answered the question "whether trade extinguisheth gentry" in the affirmative and feared the encroachment of a new system of semi-heraldry or pseudo-heraldry, which would bring them neither *kudos* nor fees.[1] In the recital of "what the authority of a king of arms is in his province", Francis Thynne, Lancaster Herald, said in 1605: "He shall prohibit any merchant, or any other, to put their names, marks or devises in escutcheons or shields; which belong and only appertain to gentlemen bearing arms and to none others."[2]

. However, despite the fulminations of Heralds, the use of merchant's marks did not decrease. There is an interesting indication of how widespread was the distribution of these marks in the devices that appear upon the trade tokens which were issued in the seventeenth century in England, Wales and Ireland as an illegal "money of necessity," to take the place of copper coins, the issuance of which had ceased during the Commonwealth.[3] These tokens, issuance of which commenced in 1648 and was prohibited by royal proclamation in 1671, when the resumption of coinage of His Majesty's farthings and halfpence of copper was ordered,[4] frequently contained the merchant's mark on the one side and the name or initials of the issuer, together with those of his wife and the town or locality in which their business was located, on the obverse side.

We have thus far considered the social and commercial uses to which merchants' marks were put in England in the

[1] See Wm. Newton, *A Display of Heraldry*, pp. 394 *et seq.*; Duke, *op. cit.*, p. 82; Charles Boutell, *Heraldry*, pp. 117–118, pp. 367 *et seq.*

[2] Francis Thynne, *A Discourse of the Duty and Office of an Herald of Arms* reprinted in *A Collection of Curious Discourses*, by Thomas Hearne, 2nd ed., London 1775, i, at p. 153. Cf. *Northumbrian Monuments* (Newcastle-upon-Tyne Records Ser. vol. iv) p. 141, no. 293.

[3] For an excellent summary of the currency conditions necessitating the issuance of trade tokens see "Reasons Submitted by Thomas Violet of the Mint Committee to Prove the Necessity of Making Farthing Tokens" in *Cal. State Papers*, Dom., 1651, pp. 313–315, No. 23 (Aug. 10, 1651).

[4] Wm. Boyne, *Trade Tokens Issued in the 17th Century* (revised ed.) i, Introd. pp. xix *et seq.*; W. Gilbert, "Token Coinage in Essex in the 17th Century," in *Trans. Essex Archæol. Soc.*, New Ser., vol. xiii, pp. 184 *et seq.*; Gray and Symonds, "Somerset Trade Tokens, XVII Century," in *Proceedings Somersetshire Archæol. and Natural Hist. Soc.*, vol. lxi, pp. 115 *et seq.*

Middle Ages. We shall now examine the legal implications of these merchants' marks.

Dunant[1] and Braun[2] have shown the universality of the use of merchants' marks on the continent for the purpose of establishing property in goods that had gone astray through shipwreck, piracy or other mishap. Braun refers to the *Handelsbuch*, dated 1420, which was kept by a merchant of the city of Danzig[3] and which contains in the margin the marks of a great number of Dutch, English and Genoese merchants.[4]   In another document of the same period, the owners of three vessels bound from Riga to Flanders complained that the English had caused the loss of their ships. The cargo of flax is referred to as belonging to one hundred merchants, whose marks accompanied their respective names.[5] Dunant likewise calls attention to the function of the merchants' marks appearing on the goods and also entered on the registry of the ships carrying these goods, to establish at least a *prima facie* presumption of ownership in the goods,[6] and refers to a notarial instrument describing the steps which were taken in 1332 in the high court of Seville by merchants from the island of Majorca to recover certain balls of wax which had been thrown up on the coast of Flanders in a shipwreck. 'The Spanish bailiff in Flanders had refused to surrender these goods without surety that the proxy or agent (Bernardus Duran) of the owner (Bartholomeus Çagarra) could prove use of the mark appearing upon the wax ("*qualiter signum seu marca, de qua erant signate seu marcate dicte balle erat et est dicti Bartholomei Çagarra*"). [7] The instrument reproduces the mark of the claimant, Bartholomeus Çagarra, and

---

[1] *Traité des marques de fabrique*, pp. 10 et seq.

[2] Braun and Capitaine, *Les marques de fabrique*, Introd., p. xvii.

[3] For the relation of English merchants to Danzig in the Middle Ages see *York Memorandum Book*, vol. ii (*Surtees Soc. Pub.* vol. 125) Introd. pp. xix *et seq.*

[4] This document is the basis of a doctoral dissertation by W. von Slaski entitled *Danziger Handel in XVten Jahrhundert* (Heidelberg 1905).

[5] Braun and Capitaine, *op. cit.*, Introd. p. xvii.

[6] *Op. cit.*, pp. 12–13. For similar identification of goods strayed or stolen, in medieval German towns, see also Kohler, *op. cit.*, p. 27.

[7] The document referred to by Dunant, which is in the possession of the *Bibliothèque Nationale*, is described by E. T. Hamy in an article entitled "Un Naufrage en 1332," in *Études historiques et géographiques* (Paris 1896), pp. 95–

recites the decree of the judges and Alguazil of the Council
of Seville, requiring the bailiff to surrender the goods to
Çagarra without surety, for the reason that the latter had
satisfactorily proven by many witnesses his ownership and
long use of the mark appearing on the goods:
Et dicti testes dixerunt omnes et singuli quod per sacramen-
tum quod fecerant quod hoc signum seu marca, quod est
scriptum seu signatum in ista carta, quod est et erat dicti
Bartholomei Çagarra, et quod magnum tempus erat quod usus
fuerat hòc signo seu marca et nunc cotidie utitur eo . . .[1]

Just as the marks of English merchants were kept in foreign
registries, so those of foreign merchants were sometimes entered in English trade records. For instance, in the Book
of Entries of the Corporation of Great Yarmouth are many
foreign marks, principally of the merchants of Brabant, which
were regularly certified by foreign notaries.[2]

We shall find in English law in the fourteenth and following
centuries how unvaried and unbroken was the recognition
given to merchants' marks as affording practically conclusive
evidence of proprietary right in the articles to which they
were affixed or in connection with which they were used.
In the reign of Edward III "the most constant danger to
shipping was the ceaseless piracy that prevailed at sea, and
from the responsibility for this none of the sea-faring nations
of the age can be considered free."[3] For a considerable time
prior to Edward III, in cases where a ship was lost at sea
and the cargo thrown upon the land, the goods belonged to
the king as a "wreck" unless "a dog or other living animal
escaped, by which the owner might be discovered, or if the
goods was so marked, that they might be known."[4] Accord-

103, containing much interesting material concerning similar uses of merchants'
marks. Hamy publishes the whole document at pp. 444–447 of the same
volume, from which the Latin quotations above are made.
    [1] *Ibid.*, p. 445.
    [2] See Henry Harrod, *Notes on the Records of the Corporation of Great Yar-
mouth, Pub. of the Norwich and Norfolk Archæol. Soc.* vol. iv, pp. 258–9.
    [3] Frank Sargeant, "The Wine Trade with Gascony," in *Finance and Trade
under Edward III*, ed. George Unwin (Manchester University Historical
Ser., No. XXXII), p. 292.
    [4] T. L. Mears, "Admiralty Jurisdiction" in *Select Essays in Anglo-
American Legal History* ii, p. 333.

ingly in the epidemic of piracy during the reign of Edward III there was, as is disclosed by entries in the Close and Patent Rolls of the period, frequent occasion to resort to the merchants' marks upon goods for the purpose of establishing property rights in these goods.   There were, as we shall see, also other occasions, non-piratical in nature, on which for one reason or another, it was necessary to establish property rights in goods, and such identification was made by means of merchants' marks. A few instances of both kinds follow.

In 17 Edward III (1343) there is an order to the Sheriff of Southampton

to deliver to Conrad Covenache, Burgess of Bruges, 20 packs of cloth of different colours, . . . by indenture containing the number of packs and the signs that are there signed (*signa quibus signantur*) as Conrad has besought the king to order those packs to be restored to him for himself and the remaining 15 as the proctor of John de Peroun, Burgess of Bruges, and Giles de Hooft, Burgess of that town, as 5 packs of Conrad's cloth under his seal (*signo suo*), 6 packs of John's cloth under his seal (*signo ipsius Johannes*) and 9 packs of Giles's cloth under his seal (*signo ipsius Egidii*) . . .[1]

Likewise in 1346 Harvey Tirel, Sheriff of Devon, and the king's sergeant-at-arms, are ordered to obtain restitution for Sancius, a merchant of Spain, of certain tuns of wine lost in a piracy committed on the English coast, which tuns had been identified by Sancius and Tirel, who went "to the tavern of Richard Gordon of Dertemuth and there found two tuns of wine under Sancius's seal (*de signo predicti Sancii*)."[2] In the same year the Bailiffs of Ipswich are ordered to "cause 9 tuns and a pipe of woad to be restored to James called Urbaen, Burgess of Bruges, if they find that they are under his seal (*dicto signo in eisdem litteris inserto signato*)."[3]

An entry in 1356 indicates the manner in which English merchants were wont to trace their goods stolen abroad and

---

[1] *Cal. Close Rolls*, Edw. III, 1343–6, Feb. 24, 1343, p. 17.
[2] *Cal. Close Rolls*, Edw. III, 1346–9, pp. 10–11.
[3] *Cal. Close Rolls*, Edw. III, 1346–9, p. 13.

the extent to which they believed their seals had probative value in the courts of Flanders:

To the burgomaster, *échevins* and consuls of the town of Bruges in Flanders. Request to hear the complaint of Richard de Stanhope or of his attorney, and to cause speedy justice to be done to him in accordance with the markets and customs of their town, as they would wish the king to do for them in like case, writing to the king of what they do as quickly as possible, as the king has received Richard's complaint containing that he was plundered of 38 sarplars of wool under his merchant seal, whereof a part was laded in the River Twede in a ship of Flanders whereof Hugh Scuter, mariner of Lescluses, was master, and a part lodged in the town of Berwick upon Tweed and afterwards placed by the said thieves in the said ship, and the wool was then taken by those thieves to Flanders and was there arrested by the ministers of the burgomasters and others at the suit of Richard's servant or attorney, seeing his seal on the sarplars, and although the said servant has claimed the wool in Richard's name, praying that it may be delivered to him, yet the wool is still unjustly detained under arrest, whereupon Richard has petitioned the king to provide a remedy."[1]

In 27 Edward III (1353) there was passed an important statute[2] by which it was provided that foreign merchants who had been spoiled of their goods either at sea or on shore should have restitution of their goods, upon proof of their property therein without having to sue at the common law.[3] One of the three methods of proof of ownership enumerated by the statute affording this summary procedure for the restitution of goods was by evidence as to the ownership of the marks appearing on the goods:

[1] *Cal. Close Rolls*, Edw. III., 1354–60, pp. 305–6. For the functions and jurisdiction of the *échevins* and burgomaster of Bruges, see Malcolm Letts, "Law and Order in a Medieval Town," 39 *Law Quarterly Review*, p. 224. For additional instances of a similar probative use of merchants' marks see *Cal. Close Rolls*, Edw. III, 1343–6, *ibid.*, p. 71 (to the Sheriff of Southampton); *Cal. Close Rolls*, Edw. III, 1349–54, p. 3 (to the Mayor and Bailiffs of Sandwich); *ibid.*, p. 48 (to the Sheriffs of London); *ibid.*, p. 54 (to Thomas de Dagworth).

[2] Statute 2, c. 13, *Stat. of the Realm*, i, p. 338.

[3] "*Soit receu de prover les ditz biens estre les soens par ses marches ou par sa carte ou coket ou par bons et loialx marchantz privez ou estrangers et par tieles proeves soient meismes les biens deliveres au marchant saunz autre seute faire a la coë lei.*" See *Select Pleas in the Court of Admiralty*, Vol. I (Selden Society Pub. vol. 6), Introd. p. 1.

Item, We will and grant, That if any merchant, Privy or Stranger, be robbed of his goods upon the Sea, and the Goods so robbed come into any Parte within our Realm and Lands, and he will sue for to recover the said Goods, he shall be received to prove the said goods to be his own [by his marks, or by his Chart or Cocket (*per ses merches ou per sa carte ou coket*)], or by good and lawful Merchants, Privy or Strangers; and by such Proofs (*per tieles proeves*) the same goods shall be delivered to the Merchants, without making other suit at the Common Law: And in case that any Ships, going out of the said Realm and Lands, or coming to the same, by Tempest or other Misfortune, break upon the Sea Banks, and the Goods come to the Land, which may not be said Wreck, they shall be presently without Fraud or evil Device delivered to the Merchants to whom the Goods be, or to their Servants, by such proof as before is said. . .[1]

In an order "to the Mayor and Bailiffs and the true men of the town of Plummuth" in 1367 we see the practical working of the statute. The order requires those named to

take information by inquisition and otherwise, as they may best, concerning the goods and merchandise cast up from a ship of St. Antony . . . in consequence of the shipwreck thereof, and taken and carried off by the men of the said town and of the neighboring parts, and to cause all such as the merchants may, by marks, metes or other true evidence (*per signa metas vel alias evidencias veraces*) prove to be theirs which are withheld from them, to be without delay or difficulty delivered to . . . the shipmaster, . . . proctor of the said ship . . . or to . . . attorneys of the said merchants. . . .[2]

That considerable indignation existed at Westminster at the flagrant disregard of the provisions of the statute of 27 Edward III is shown from an entry in 1371, addressed to the Bailiffs of Shoreham, which was quite a center of thriving English piracy.[3] Piracy in this case had evidently been committed against merchants of London who, the order

---

[1] *Stat. of the Realm*, i, p. 338.
[2] *Cal. Close Rolls*, Edw. III, 1364–68, Feb. 7, 1367, p. 316.
[3] For piracy at Shoreham, see Henry Cheal, *The Story of Shoreham Piracy*, pp. 121 *et seq.*

shows, have not been given the protection afforded by the summary procedure of the statute of 27 Edward III, and "the King's will is that the statute be kept inviolate. . . ."[1] As late as 1771[2] the statute of 27 Edward III was invoked in Lord Mansfield's court by a plaintiff seeking to recover certain hogsheads of tallow which were cast ashore from a wreck, and which bore the same marks of plaintiff as appeared on the bill of lading. Defendant claimed these goods as "wreck," since no man, cat or dog escaped alive from the ship. Lord Mansfield indignantly brushed aside the plea of "wreck" and found for the plaintiff.

That the municipal authorities of the period regarded merchants' marks as evidence of ownership and the imposition of such marks as an act evidencing the assumption of ownership is well illustrated by a letter from the Mayor and Corporation of the City of London to the Mayor and Aldermen of Calais, reciting that one Henry Hangard and other Burgesses of Amiens had purchased in Gloucester from "John Pykenham, citizen of London," two hundred pieces of cloth for 1200 pounds sterling, "whereupon each piece of cloth had been sealed with the seal of the said Henry." The letter alleges the readiness of Pykenham to deliver the cloth in London to said Henry. "But neither the said Henry nor his goods . . . were to be found. Desire them, therefore, to assist the said John Pykenham in their country, that he might obtain payment . . . God Almighty have them ever in His keeping."[3]

In the sixteenth century the records of the Admiralty Courts, as well as of the Privy Council, are replete with reference to merchants' marks. These marks, in addition to being affixed to the goods themselves or the wrapping thereof,

[1] *Cal. Close Rolls*, Edw. III, 1369–74, August 22, 1371, p. 325.
[2] *Hamilton* v. *Davis*, 5 Burr. 2732. The case is confusedly referred to and inaccurately quoted in Campbell's *Lives of the Chief Justices* (N. Y. 1873) iii, p. 316.
[3] *Cal. of Letters from the Mayor and Aldermen of the City of London, 1350–70*, ed. R. R. Sharpe, p. 146, March 9, 1366. See also letter dated July 26, 1364, to the Admiral of France, etc. complaining of piracy by seamen from Normandy of 360 pieces of white tin, the marks on which are described for the information of those requested to obtain restitution of the goods. (*ibid.* p. 95.)

are found noted or reproduced in the bills of lading or in the ship's register.[1] For instance, a bill of lading dated November 28, 1541, and introduced in evidence in the Court of Admiralty, refers to "xlvj hogsheads of whales grece and on hogs hede of Cyvill oyle marked all with the mark in the margent and the by mark on the hogs hede of Cyvill oyle. . . ."[2] In the case of *Michell c. Wines in the Hands of Taylour,* certain goods spoiled from a ship in distress are ordered to be delivered to the plaintiff:

> Which 9 vessels or butts of Cretan wine were and are the proper goods of the said Vincent Michell, and, being marked and signed with his usual and customary mark or sign, remain and are in the hands and custody of the said Thomas Taylour . . . (*Que quiden novem vasa sive buttas vini Cretici fuerunt et sunt bona propria dicti Vincentii Michell et signo sive stigmate suo solito et consueto depicta et signata et in manibus et custodia dicti Thome Taylour remanent et existunt. . . .*)[3]

In a suit for freight in 1557 the bill of lading involved reads as follows:

> "I, Cornelys Denys, master under God of one hoye named the Job of the burthen of lv[th] tonnes or there abouts doo confesse to have receyved aboard at the kayes of Roane of Peter de Flo merchaunte there residente for and in the names of Mr. Thomas Walker and Richarde Saltonstall That is to saye xxxvj peces of prunes, sixe bales of canvas, thre demye bales of peper, two bales of threde, and one vessell of almandes togither with one barrel and a half of vergus (?) and drye peares, all well and duelie condicioned marked with the marke in the margent there resteth one demye bale of paper marked with this marke [the mark] . . . (*marcque de la marcque cy dehors reste ungue demye balle de pappier marcque de ceste marque . . .*[4]

The Acts of the Privy Council in the same period, dealing with matters of piracy and other questions of restitution of

[1] See W. P. Bennett, *History and Present Position of the Bill of Lading,* p. 2; Scrutton on *Charter Parties* (ed. 1923), Index *s.v.* "Marks on Goods."
[2] *Select Pleas in the Court of Admiralty,* vol. i (Selden Society Pub., vol. 6, p. 112.
[3] *Ibid.,* vol. ii (Selden Soc. Pub. vol. 11), p. 13 (1550).
[4] *Ibid.,* vol. ii, p. 62. For other illustrations see *ibid.,* pp. 2, 61, 63.

goods, lay equal stress upon the marks of the goods involved, and frequently reproduce these merchants' marks on the margin of the order in question.[1] For instance, there is a recognizance, dated June 24, 1545, for the release to a certain Spaniard of 241 "balettes of . . . canvas . . . marcked undre the marck in the margent hereof . . ."[2] There are no less than six cases reported in 1546[3] ordering restitution of goods, or rebuking the authorities for a failure to comply with prior orders to the same effect, in which these goods are described as "being marked with those marks in the margent." In 1570 the Council orders certain

merchaunt straingers to appere before the Lords of the Counsell, to thend they may upon their othes testifie upon sight of the markes of all such merchaundizes as in the said shippes are conteined, which of late were staied in certen portes, what part thereof do appertaine to Portingales and what do not.[4]

In 1585 the Lords of the Council, writing to the Lord Warden of the Cinq Ports concerning certain merchandise brought into Dover Haven and unlawfully sold "praie the Lord Warden"

to take order that of those merchandises and wares fourtene lastes and one barille of sope may be delivered unto Charles Talven, one hundred and twentie peeces of course Osteland cloth unto David Haeex, three bagges of woll, and six barrills of tallowe unto Jaques Gellee, beinge marked under their severall markes according to a note enclosed in the letter. . . .[5]

The case of the ship *Ugiera Salvagina* which runs through the Acts of the Privy Council from the year 1590 to the year 1593 and appears to have been quite a *cause célèbre* is the last one that will occupy our attention in this connection. The case arose by reason of the fact that twenty-five bags of pepper, part of the goods sequestered from the ship *Ugiera*

[1] See *Acts of the Privy Council* (New Ser.), vol. i, Preface, p. xvii.
[2] *Ibid.*, p. 201. See also p. 248.
[3] *Ibid.*, pp. 378, 382, 434, 435 (two entries), 537–8.
[4] *Ibid.*, vol. viii, p. 17.
[5] *Ibid.*, vol. xiv, pp. 10–11.

Salvagina, in the town of Dartmouth, "were uncased of the uppermoste bagges and contrary markes sett on the undermoste bagges."[1] The first entry (January 24, 1590)[2] refers to the complaint of the Venetian owners as to the alteration of their marks and other lawyers are joined by the Lords of the Council, with the Judge of the Admiralty Court, to determine the cause. The final disposition of this case occurred only after all proceedings in the Admiralty Court had been quashed and, on consent of all parties involved, the case had been sent by the Council to three members of the Council and to certain doctors learned in the civil law for arbitration.[3] Finally, in July 1593, upon the basis of the arbitrator's report, an order was made for the distribution of the cargo of the *Ugiera Salvagina* which incorporates the schedules from the "purser's book" and, opposite each entry of bags of pepper, elephants' teeth, camphire, etc., reproduces the merchant's mark of the owner of these goods.[4]

Summarizing briefly the evidence adduced in this chapter, medieval proprietary marks, while not, strictly speaking, trade-marks in the modern sense of the word, were an important factor in the development of modern trade-mark law. As appears from municipal documents and the records of the Admiralty Courts, and also from the statute of 27 Edward III, merchants' marks were regarded as establishing *prima facie* and often even conclusive evidence of the ownership of the goods to which they were affixed. This proprietary significance of merchants' marks still survives in and distinctly tinges the judicial concept of the function of a trade-mark.

[1] See *Acts of the Privy Council* (New Ser.), vol. xxiv, p. 386.
[2] *Ibid.*, vol. xx, p. 234.
[3] *Ibid.*, vol. xxiii, p. 92, August 2, 1592.
[4] *Ibid.*, vol. xxiv, pp. 385–93. An interesting Italian parallel is the case cited by Lastig (*op. cit.*, pp. 72–3) of the English merchants who registered their mark at the Customs House in Florence and shipped to Samuel Budriess, a Florentine merchant, certain goods to be sold by him on commission. Budriess sold some of these goods to Alessandro Pucci, who went bankrupt a few days thereafter. The English merchants were able to reclaim their goods from Pucci's creditors upon proof of their mark.

A Note on Swan Marks

One of the oldest English proprietary marks, which still serves its original function, is the swan mark. In the theory of English law the swan is regarded as "bird royal in which no subject can have property when at large in a public river or creek, except by grant from the crown. In according this privilege the crown grants a swan mark."[1]

A silver swan was the principal device on the badge of Henry IV and Henry V, likewise, before his accession to the throne, used the silver swan. By a statute of 1483 it was ordered that no person except the king's sons should have a swan mark, unless he possessed a freehold of the clear yearly value of five marks.[2] The swan mark itself, called by Sir Edward Coke "*cigninota*," was cut in the skin of the beak of the swan with a sharp knife or other instrument. The king's swanherd was bound to keep a book of swan marks and no new marks were permitted to interfere with the old ones. Owners of swans and their swanherds were registered in the king's swanherd's book. The marking of the cygnets was generally performed in the presence of all the swanherds on the stream in question and on a particular day or days of which all had notice. Cygnets received the marks found on the parent birds but, if the swans bore no mark, the whole were seized for the king and marked accordingly. No swanherd was permitted to affix a mark except in the presence of the king's swanherd or his deputy.[3]

How seriously the matter of swan marks was taken is evident from the records of those who were permitted to use them. For instance, the Records of the Borough of Reading contain the following entries:

[1] W. Yarrell, *History of British Birds*, (4th ed.) iv, p. 329.

[2] 22 Edw. IV, c. 6, *Stat. of the Realm*, ii, p. 474. The Statute recites that cygnets had been stolen from their lawful owners and that swans had found their way into the hands of yeomen and husbandmen who had marked them either with their own unauthorized marks or with the marks of those entitled to use them.

[3] *Ibid.*, p. 330. See also Browne on *Trademarks* (2nd ed.), p. 14; Edward Peacock, "Swan Marks," *Archæol. Journal*, vol. xli, p. 290; C. H. Mayo, "Swans on the Salisbury, Avon and Dorset Stour, *Somerset and Dorset Notes and Queries*, vol. xiii, p. 297.

(1507)   The vew of the Game of Swannys belonging to the Maire and Burges of the Gilde Hall of Redyng after the marke above drawyn, browght in by Thomas Randall of Sonnyng on our Lady evyn th'Assumpcion [Aug. 15], in the xxij^{ti} yere of Kyng Henry the VIIth.[1]

(1544)   At this day is graunted to Nicholas Niclas the game of Swannes, that is to witt, viij Swannes, to have to hym from the feast of Saynt Michaell th'Archaungell [Vacat, *in margin*] last past unto th'end and terme of xx yeres, if the seid Nicholas so long do lyve, yeldyng and paying therfor yerely to the seide Mayour and Burgeses viijs, sterling at ij° termys in the yere, that is to witt, at the feastes of th'Annunciacion of our Lady and Saynt Michaell th'Archaungell, by yeven procions; the seide Nicholas to maynteyn and kepe the stock, that is to witt, viij Swannes in the merke of the Hall contynowally, and in th'end of the seid terme, or after the disceasse of the seid Nicholas, shall delyver and yeld upp unto the seid Mayour and Burgeses or to their successours viij good white Swannes in the merke of the Hall.[2]

(1548)   At this day, that is to sey, the Fryday [Dec. 21] in the Imbryng weke before the feast of the Nativitie of our Lord . . . anno regni Regis E[dwardi] VI^{ti} secundo, John Bell beyng Mayour, hit was graunted to Thomas Benwell the game of Swannes, that is to sey, viij white Swannes, to have to hym from the feast of th'Annunciacion of our Lady next cummyng after the date herof, unto th'end and terme of xx yeres, then next followyng, if the seid Thomas shall fortune so long to lyve; yeldyng and paying therfor yerely to the seid Mayour and Burgeses vjs. viijd. sterling, and also to delyver yerely to the Mayour and Burgeses ther one good signet of a swanne.   The seid Thomas to maynteyn and kepe the stock, that is to sey, viij good white Swannes, in the Merke of the Hall, and in th'end of the seid terme, or after the disceasse of the seid Thomas, shall delyver and yeld upp to the seid Mayour and Burgeses, or to ther successours, viij good white Swannes in the seid Merke.[3]

---

[1] *Records of the Borough of Reading*, ed. J. M. Guilding, i, p. 104.
[2] *Ibid.*, p. 188.   [3] *Ibid.*, p. 212.

The records of the city of Oxford[1] for the year 1553 contain an entry of an allowance to the Chamberlain for "markyng of the swannys . . . iiijᵈ." In 25 Elizabeth a jury at Seaford, Sussex, presented John Comber "for markyng of thre duckes of Edw. Warwickes, and two ducks of Symon Brighte with his own marke, and cutting out theire markes."[2] A most minute description of the method of appointing swanherds and of the procedure for marking swans, registering the marks and protecting the swans on the River Witham in Lincolnshire is contained in "The Ordinances respecting Swans on the River Witham," dated 1570.[3] Accompanying these "Ordinances" is a "Roll of Swan Marks, Appertaining to the Proprietors on the Said Stream," the reproduction of which gives an excellent idea of the variations in such marks. In 1609 an entry in the Court Book of the Vintners Company of London requires that "the Swanherd of the Company, with His or Her Majesty's Swanherd and the Swanherd of the Dyers' Company assemble at Lambeth in August and proceed by the river to mark the swans."[4]

[1] Ed. W. H. Turner, p. 220.
[2] M. A. Lower, "Memories of Seaford," in *Sussex Archæol. Coll.* vol. vii, p. 99.
[3] J. Banks, "The Ordinances Respecting Swans on the River Witham" in *Archæologia*, vol. xvi, p. 155.
[4] W. H. Overall, "The Ward of Vintry," in *Trans. London and Middlesex Archæol. Soc.* vol. iii, p. 426.

CHAPTER III

PRODUCTION MARKS IN THE REGULATION OF TRADE BY THE GILDS AND COMPANIES

In the preceding chapter we have dealt with merchants' marks *as indicative of property* in the goods to which they were affixed or in relation to which they were used. These marks were very remote in their essential significance from the modern concept of a trade-mark. The trade-mark today is in itself an asset, often of far greater value than the physical property of the business in connection with which it is used. As Mr. Rogers has pointed out, the modern trade-mark is "good will symbolized."[1]

But if the merchant's mark considered in our last chapter did not approach the present notion of a trade-mark, the mark that we are now about to consider and that is often carelessly referred to in terms of modern trade-mark law, is even further distant in function and legal significance from our modern trade-mark. While the latter is, as has been pointed out above, an *asset*, the medieval mark indicating source or origin, or, as the Germans call it, the *Produktionsmark* or *Produktionszeichen*, is distinctly a *liability*. Except in a few instances, it is today entirely optional with a manufacturer whether he will use a trade-mark at all. The medieval craftsman would appear from a very early period in gild history to have had little choice as to the affixing of this "police mark" on his wares. In practically every trade, both in England and on the continent, these marks were compulsory.[2] Kohler describes the marks that the bakers of Verona, the fullers of Siena and other craftsmen of the Italian medieval towns were required

---

[1] E. S. Rogers, "Some Historical Matter Concerning Trade-marks," 9 *Michigan Law Review* 29, at p. 43.

[2] The most striking exception occurs in the printing and publishing industries, of which a special study appears at the end of this chapter.

to put upon their goods as *"häufig Pflichtzeichen."*[1] The French writers speak of such marks as *"marques de fabriques obligatoires."*[2] A Spanish authority on trade-marks points out the compulsory nature of the marks which the gilds of silversmiths, tinsmiths, candle-, taper-, or torchmakers of Barcelona required their craftsmen to affix to their wares in the 15th century.[3] In his study of painters' signatures, De Mély shows that, as early as 1426, an Ordinance of the Corporation of Painters of Bruges made the failure to register painters' marks a punishable offense.[4]

It has already been noted that, in a great many instances, the very same mark fulfilled the dual function of proprietary mark, as described above, and of production mark.[5] Hence, many of the marks that were compulsorily registered with municipal or gild authorities are identical in form with the merchants' marks we have described above. On the other hand, in some industries the production mark was often less complex or decorative. For instance, in the case of bakers' marks, some bakers stamped a regular merchants mark upon their bread,[6] others contented themselves with a certain number of pricks to indicate the origin of their bread.[7]

Before illustrating what we may term the liability nature of the craftsmen's marks of the Middle Ages, in contradistinction to the asset nature of the modern trade-mark, it will be necessary for us to consider briefly the machinery of

---

[1] *Das Recht des Markenschutzes*, p. 44.

[2] See M. de Gailhard-Bancel, *Les anciennes corporations de métiers et la lutte contre la fraude dans le commerce et la petite industrie*, p. 65.

[3] D. R. Pella, *Marcas de Fábrica y de Comercio en España*, (Madrid 1911), p. 20.

[4] Re-registration of such marks was required by an Ordinance of 1500. See F. de Mély, *Les primitifs et leurs signatures*, i, pp. 78–80. For counterfeiting of the marks of "old masters" by copyists, see M. Christ, *Dictionnaire des monogrammes* (tr. from German, Paris, 1672), pp. xvii, xix.

[5] See *supra*, p. 21.

[6] See J. H. Macadam, *The Baxter Books of St. Andrews*, p. 132.

[7] E.g. Three "prykkes" in the case of William Hobold, reported in *Cal. Letter Books, Letter Book K*, p. 247. I am informed by Mr. John C. Tingey, one of the editors of the Norwich records, that these prick marks were also used in Norwich. For other prick marks see E. Bain, *Merchant and Craft Guilds*, p. 213.

production and the economic theories under which this machinery operated during the Middle Ages.

The phases of medieval economic history that bear directly on our subject are threefold:

(1) In the first place, until the fifteenth century or even later, "so large a part of the manufacturing work of the country was arranged on the gild system, that that term may be fairly used to describe the whole organization of industry." [1] Even when industry became the subject of national, rather than local regulation, the gilds and companies were greatly relied upon by the Crown and Parliament to supervise manufacturing processes and trade.[2]

(2) Secondly, grants of monopoly "formed a regular and almost universal feature in gild charters,"[3] and the enforcement of the monopoly was accompanied by the preservation of high standards of production. "Work must be good and 'legal' . . ., an infraction of the regulations must be reported that the gild may not secure a bad reputation." [4] The supervision of industry by the gilds as well as the observation by the consuming public of the materials and methods of production employed were rendered easy by the physical conditions involved. "Wants were comparatively few and unchanging"; writes Ashley, — particularly of the earlier period of gild control, — "they were supplied by neighboring craftsmen; consumer and producer stood in direct relation with one another." [5]

The great majority of articles in the daily use of the mass of the people were bought by the consumer from the actual maker. If the making of an article was divided between several craftsmen as, for example, that of cloth between weavers, fullers and dyers, each of these groups of craftsmen

[1] W. J. Ashley, *English Economic History and Theory* (10th Impression, 1919), i, part i, p. 96.
[2] W. S. Holdsworth, *History of English Law* (3rd ed.), iv, p. 321. See also *infra*, pp. 81, 125.
[3] A. P. Evans, "The Problem of Control in Medieval Industry" in *Political Science Quarterly*, vol. xxxvi, pp. 610–11. See also W. S. Holdsworth, *op. cit.*, i, p. 568.
[4] A. P. Evans, *op. cit.*, pp. 615–16.
[5] W. J. Ashley, *op. cit.*, i, part i, p. 95.

lived within a narrow circuit and under the eyes of most of those who ultimately bought their manufactures.[1]

The members of each craft usually lived in the same street or neighborhood. Thus in London the saddlers lived round, and attended, the Church of S. Martin-le-Grand; the lorimers lived in Cripplegate, the weavers in Cannon Street, smiths in Smithfield, and bucklers in Bucklersbury. So in Bristol there were Tucker Street, the home of the tuckers or fullers, Corn Street, Knifesmith Street, Butcher Row, Cooks' Row, and the like. Such a grouping must have enormously strengthened the sense of corporate life in each craft, and must also have made the work of supervision comparatively easy.[2]

The difficulty of the "appropriation of trade values" in the face of the control of industry either by or through gilds under the physical conditions just described is apparent. From the consumer's standpoint, the greater his proximity to the producer, the better are his opportunities for personal inspection of the goods before purchase, and the less becomes his necessity for relying upon trade-marks or trade-names in the modern sense as a symbol or guarantee of excellence of material or workmanship. Furthermore, had the medieval craftsman been tempted to engage in unfair competition against his fellow-craftsman living in the same narrow street, his desire would seem to have been a very difficult thing to accomplish without detection.

(3) Unfair competition would, however, in all probability have been prevented by other and more fundamental considerations. The gilds sought to exercise and actually acquired a fairly rigid monopoly of the trade in their area,[3] and they strove by every means at their disposal to prevent "foreigners" — as the merchants coming from a town five miles away might be described — from competing with their

---

[1] *Ibid.*, p. 138.

[2] *Ibid.*, p. 96. For maps showing the localization of industries in medieval London, Paris and Bruges, see G. Unwin, *The Gilds and Companies of London*, pp. 32–4; *cf.* J. M. Lambert, "The Trade Gilds of Beverley," in *Trans. East Riding Antiquarian Soc.*, vol. xix, p. 91, at p. 99.

[3] See W. Cunningham, *The Growth of English Industry and Commerce*, i (5th ed.), p. 445.

gild. But within the gild itself — at any rate, according to the theory of their legislation — there was no such thing as competition, solely co-operation.[1]

As on the Continent,[2] so in England the gild records abound in oaths and ordinances that were calculated to prevent not only the enticing away of each others' apprentices [3] but all other forms of or tendencies towards intra-gild competition. The ordinances of the Plumbers of London, enacted in 1365, required "that no one of the said trade shall oust another from his work undertaken or begun, or shall take away his customers or his employees, to his damage. . . ." [4]

The ordinances of the Pewterers' Company of London of 1438 provide "that no persone of the said craft hire procure ne put othir persone of the same craft out of his hous shop or stonding place in the cite of London nor in faires markettes

---

[1] The ethical basis of the gild control of industry is an interesting problem in itself. Charles Gross, in his pioneer study of the *Gild Merchant* (vol. i, p. 36), warns against viewing the medieval gildsmen's motives through "the rose-hued glasses of sentimentality." The English "Guild Socialists," such as Penty in his *Guildsman's Interpretation of History* (London, 1920), in complete disregard of the evidence gathered by Gross and others, insist that "the guilds grew up around the idea of the Just Price" and picture "the whole hierarchy of the guild arising out of the primary necessity of maintaining the Just Price," (Penty, p. 40). However, as pointed out by Lipson (*Economic History*, i, p. 301) the "fair price" or "just price" was determined by the gild itself, and that such determination was not always in accord with the doctrines of Thomas Aquinas is easily discernible in the history of gilds and their relation to the state. One striking bit of evidence on the subject that seems to have escaped notice is the order of Edward III to his justices in 1372 to investigate the gild monopoly in marble for altars and gravestones at Bishop's Lynn, "to the oppression of the people setting a fixed price upon the sale thereof." (*Cal. Close Rolls*, Edw. III 1369–1374, p. 413.) For a recent discussion of the "Just Price" see A. P. Evans, *op. cit.*, pp. 610 *et seq.*

[2] *Cf.*: "Even the doctors at Florence might not undertake the cure of a patient who had already been attended by a colleague; but this rule was repealed, no doubt because it was dangerous to the patients. Again it was forbidden . . . to invite into your own shop the people who had stopped before a neighbor's display of goods, to call in the passers-by, or to send a piece of cloth on approbation to a customer's house. All individual advertisement was looked upon as tending to the detriment of others. The Florentine innkeeper who gave wine or food to a stranger with the object of attracting him to his hostelry was liable to a fine. Equally open to punishment was the merchant who obtained possession of another man's shop by offering the landlord a higher rent. Any bonus offered to a buyer was considered an unlawful and dishonest bait." — Georges Renard, *Guilds in the Middle Ages* (ed. Cole), pp. 41–2.

[3] W. Cunningham, *op. cit.*, i, pp. 338, 343, 350. *Cf.* A. H. Thomas, *Cal. of Early Mayor's Court Rolls*, p. 168, for action in trespass, 5 Feb. 1304–5, for enticement of plaintiff's apprentice by defendant.

[4] H. T. Riley, *Memorials of London*, p. 322.

nor in othir places out of this Citee. . . ."[1] Pursuant to their ordinances, 6 Edward IV, 1467–8, the tailors of Exeter took an oath upon entering the gild not "to stir, procure nor excite either by themselves or by any other men from a brother of the craft any of his customers" even if these customers were quite willing to be served by him.[2] According to the ordinances of the Brotherhood of St. Christopher of the Waterbearers of the City of London (1496):

> Also if ther be eny brother or syster that takeyth eny custemar owt of eny brothers handys without so be that the parties that he serveth wille no lengar have his service and that the said brother seith that he be content of his diewte that he shold have or ellis he to take no mannys custymer owt of hys hands under the payne of vj^{s}viij^d, be hit brother or syster.[3]

The "Barbers' Composition" at Shrewsbury (1483) provided that "no broder" might "induce or tyce any other Mastres Accostom" nor might he obtrude his wares before passers in the open street or erect booths "for to have better sale than eny of the combrethren."[4] Similar provisions against enticing away one another's customers are found in the ordinances of the Brewers of Oxford (1570),[5] and the Saddlers of London.[6]

---

[1] C. Welch, *History of the Worshipful Company of Pewterers of the City of London*, i, p. 10.

[2] Toulmin Smith, *English Gilds*, p. 317.

[3] H. C. Coote, "Ordinances of Some Secular Guilds of London," in *Trans. London and Middlesex Archaeol. Soc.*, vol. iv, p. 56.

[4] F. A. Hibbert, *Influence and Development of English Guilds*, p. 45.

[5] W. H. Turner, *Selections from the Records of the City of Oxford*, p. 334.

[6] J. W. Sherwell, *History of the Guild of Saddlers of the City of London*, p. 192.

In the Records of the Borough of Leicester appears the following entry, dated July 5, 1647: "It is ordered and agreed by all the Companie (name unspecified) that if any master of the said occupacion or any of his or theire servants, shall at any time call or entice any Chapman or Customer out of, or from, any other man's shopp, or stall in the markett, that then everie such master or servant shall forfeite for everie such offence 2s." (*Records of Borough of Leicester, 1603–1688*, ed. H. Stocks, p. 355.)

See also for a later application of the same principle Acts regulating methods of trade passed by the Merchant Adventurers of Newcastle-upon-Tyne, as most explicit and emphatic on this point: "[30 Sept. 1669] Whereas divers bretheren of this Fellowshipp have made complaint of severall disorders, and unbeseeming words and actions used by severall members of this Court and theire servants, not fitt for marchants to use, in selling theire marchandise,

To what extent the gilds and their successors, the companies, sought to repress the establishment of an individual good-will on the part of their members, as opposed to a collective or gild good-will, is evidenced by their reluctance to permit one gildsman to use a mark or sign of greater prominence than another, or to exploit the gild seal, which was always set upon goods conforming to gild standards, in conjunction with his own. This was so even in the seventeenth century when the influence of the gilds and companies and their control over their members had long been on the wane.

According to the Annals of the Barber-Surgeons of London:[1]

Here was Edward Park for yt he hath wretten upon his Surgeons signe the skoller of St. Thomas of Wallingforde and the said Edward Parke is comaunded by the aucthorytie of this worsshyphfull Courte That he the said Edward Parke shall with all expedicion put out of his said Signe the said wryting & to sett his signe as other Surgeons do without any superscryption yt upon and not else otherwyse as he wyll answere to the contrarye.

An example of the reluctance of the gilds to permit the association of their arms with the mark of one of their mem-

for redressing of which and the like that may followe, it is ordered, &c., That noe brother or sister shall, either by themselves, theire servants, or anie other person whatsoever, call too, or invite anie person, either by word or anie signe, to come to theire shopps or sellars, while such person is either speaking with another of this Fellowshipp or his servants, against theire owne shopps, sellar, or houses, or goeing with them to shew them anie commodity, or be present with them or anie of them; but shall dilligently attende their customers, comeing to theire owne shopps and sellars. And that in theire selling they shall not undervalue or disgrace theire neighbours goods, but leaveing every chapman to his owne discretion in buying the goods he is to buy, and hath presented to him. Upon paine that every brother or sister soe offending shall forfeite, for the first offence, twenty shillings, for the second forty shillings, and for the third five pounds. Neverthelesse it is and may be lawfull that, if anie chapeman have beene treating with anie brother or sister, or theire servants, for the price of anie sortes of goods, and doe not agree, the said parties may goe or sende after them to lett them know they may have the goods as they proffered, or the lowest price they will sell att; provided the said chapeman be not present with some brother or sister of this Fellowshipp, or theire servants, nor goeing into the shopp of anie brother or sister of this Companie. And it was further ordered, that such person or persons who should truely informe against anie brother or sister, for theire breach of the act afforesaid, or anie clause theirein specified, should be gratified as the Company shall thinke fitt." (*Surtees Society Pub.*, vol. xciii, pp. 76–77.)

[1] S. Young, *Annals of the Barber-Surgeons of London*, p. 316. Entry dated March 16, 1568.

bers is the ordinance of the Merchant Adventurers of New-castle-upon-Tyne (1651) that, at the burial of their members, upon their gravestones

the Companye's armes shall not be impaled in the same scucheon with their owne but severally. For every default herein it is ordered that every executor to the deceased brother or sister shall forfitt 5[li] to the use of this Fellow-shipp, and every brother, that is a carier, for every default shall forfitt 20[s], likewise for this Companye's use. The beadle at burialls is required to take care that the armes be thus ordered.[1]

Another trade in which individual initiative was strongly repressed was that of the Pewterers of London. In 1569 it was ordered "that Hugh Colyers rose and crowne shalbe made lesser . . ."[2], by which it was intended to prevent Colyer from appropriating to himself a mark awarded by the company for use upon goods of superior quality. A century later there was much discussion in the Court of the Pewterers' Company as to whether any member "of the Mistery may have liberty to strike his name at length. . . . It passed in the negative."[3] This question as to the desirability of making known to the consumers the name of the maker of pewter seems to have agitated the company for many years, and it was only as late as 1747 that it was finally settled in favor of this practice.[4] As has been remarked by a writer on pewter marks and old pewter,[5]

[1] *The Merchant Adventurers of Newcastle-upon-Tyne* (Surtees Society Pub. vol. xciii, p. 75. See T. P. Cooper, "The Armorial Bearings of Guilds and Livery Companies" in *The Antiquary*, vol. xlix (New Ser. vol. ix), p. 348. I am indebted to Mr. A. Hamilton Thompson of Leeds, the Honorary Secretary of the Surtees Society, for the following comment, 17 December 1923, with regard to this ordinance: "The reason for the enactment you mention was probably the undesirability of the practice from the point of view of the company. The impaling of the company's shield was in itself incorrect; but, if once impaled, the family of the man who did so, or any member of it, might claim the right to use it among his quarterings, irrespective of his own member-ship of the company. This seems to me the only possible reason, as the shield thereby would cease to have any distinctive meaning. . . . The measure was, I think, taken by the company to protect its own property from indiscriminate use."

[2] C. Welch, *op. cit.*, i, p. 264.   [3] *Ibid.*, ii, p. 164.
[4] *Ibid.*, ii, p. 193.
[5] C. A. Markham, *Pewter Marks and Old Pewter Ware*, p. 112.

Most of the regulations made by the Craft relating to makers' marks seem to have been made with the intention of preventing any form of self-advertisement. But while the Craft as a body were against the members advertising themselves, the members as individuals were very much in favor of doing so.

The sale of wares that were shoddy in material or imperfect in workmanship constituted, in the case of certain commodities, not only a violation of the criminal law or police regulations but also, from the civil standpoint, as intimated above, an injury to the collective good-will of the gilds.[1] In 1316 the Potters of London complained to the Mayor and Aldermen concerning the practices of those who

buy in divers places pots of bad metal and then put them on the fire so as to resemble pots that have been used, and are of old brass; and then expose them for sale . . . to the deception of all those who buy such pots: for the moment that they are put upon the fire and become exposed to great heat they come to nothing, and melt. By which roguery and falsehood the people are deceived and the trade aforesaid is badly put in slander.[2]

The Fourbours (or Furbishers) of London, in their petition for ordinances of the trade (1350) refer to "the perils which might befall the lords of the land and other folks of the people because of false workmanship and to the great scandal of the folks of the said trade (*en graunt esclaunder des gentz du dit mistier*)."[3] The Heaumers of London (makers of helmets) in their petition for ordinances (1347), protesting against the intrusion of strangers who, they allege, "have intermeddled, and still do intermeddle, in the making of helmetry, whereas they do not know their trade," state that "by reason whereof, many great men and others of the realm have been slain through their default, to the great scandal of the said trade. . . ."[4] Likewise, the Hatters of

[1] E. Lipson, *Introd. to Economic History of England*, i, p. 297 *et seq.*
[2] H. T. Riley, *Memorials of London and London Life*, p. 118.
[3] C. Welch, *History of the Cutlers' Company of London*, i, pp. 240–241.
[4] H. T. Riley, *op. cit.*, p. 237.

London in the same year pray for an ordinance prohibiting night work since "some workmen in the same trade have made hats that are not befitting, in deceit of the common people, from which great scandal, shame and loss have often arisen to the good folks of the said trade."[1] In the ordinance of the Skinners of Bristol (1408) certain trade practices "whereby the said craft may be defamed" are denounced.[2]

With the aforegoing anti-competitive and regulatory features of the gild system in mind, we now proceed to an examination of the marks with which the medieval craftsman stamped his wares. Every craft, of course, either had its own ordinances concerning such marks or administered statutory or municipal regulations of a similar nature. All of these regulations, whatever their source, made the use of the production mark compulsory. Their expressed purpose was to facilitate the tracing of "false" or defective wares and the punishment of the offending craftsman. The compulsory production mark likewise assisted the gild authorities in preventing those outside the gild from selling their products within the area of the gild monopoly. But what the whole theory of the legislation pertaining to production marks did *not* permit was, as we have already seen in the case of the pewterers, the exploitation of these marks to the direct individual advantage or for the personal advertisement of those who used them. In the course of time in certain trades these police marks or liability marks gradually became, as we shall see, asset marks, — that is to say, they became valuable symbols of individual good-will. This was so in the case of goods of durability and transportability for long distances, especially in the clothing[3] and cutlery[4] trades. But even in the case of these trades their trade-marks began as solely regulatory indicia or police marks of origin and only later developed as symbols of good-will.

---

[1] *Ibid.*, p. 239.

[2] *Little Red Book of Bristol*, ed. F. B. Bickley, ii, p. 97. See also letter to the Mayor of London concerning "false work" of the girdlers "to the damage and scandal of the men of the mistery" in *Cal. Close Rolls*, Edw. III, 1354–1360, p. 331; *MS. Archives of the Company of Grocers of the City of London*, ed. J. A. Kingdon, pt. i, p. 66.

[3] See *infra*, ch. iv.   [4] See *infra*, ch. v.

The function of such marks is made apparent not merely from the circumstances under which they were used, but in most cases from the laws and ordinances in which their use was prescribed.

The most typical regulatory mark of the Middle Ages and the one which, through the nature of the goods upon which it was imposed, always remained a regulatory or liability mark was that of the baker. The regulation of baking, the maintenance of standards of bread and the prevention of extortionate prices for bread have always constituted a source of anxiety to those who seek the welfare or the taxes of the people. "Those who supply the people with their necessary food or drink," observes Daines Barrington, an eighteenth century antiquarian, "(as bakers, millers and brewers) have not only always been suspected, more than other traders, of impositions, but have likewise been subject to regulations of peculiar severity."[1]

From the trade-mark law standpoint it should also be remembered that "bread could only be made in comparatively small quantities; it cannot be made for a distant or for a far-future market."[2] It is not surprising, therefore, that on the one hand there is much national as well as local legislation on the subject of bakers' marks, and that on the other hand, whatever references we find to these marks show their uses to have been solely regulatory. The latter fact is true in Scotland and on the continent as well as in England. Considerations of space will prevent any detailed reference to Scottish marks. A minute in the Council Registry of Aberdeen for 1457 gives a list of eleven bakers and reproduces their marks.[3] "Every neighbor of the calling was required to stamp his bread and numerous instances are recorded of the punishment of members of the craft for breach of this ordinance."[4] In the Baxter Books of St. Andrews[5] it is

---

[1] Quoted by Sidney and Beatrice Webb, "The Assize of Bread," *Economic Journal*, vol. xiv, 1904, p. 196, n. 1.
[2] W. J. Ashley, *op. cit.*, vol. i, pt. 2, p. 192.
[3] E. Bain, *Merchant and Craft Guilds*, pp. 212 *et seq.*
[4] *Ibid.*, p. 224.   [5] Ed. by J. H. Macadam, p. 131.

stated that Aberdeen bakers were required to adopt marks as early as 1398 and a St. Andrews ordinance is quoted that "ilk brother or brother relict Mark thair bread with thair name and surname."

As at Poitiers and St. Germain-des-Prés,[1] so also at Rheims,[2] the *Statutes des boulangers pâtissiers* (1561), Art. 17, provided that "*chaque boulanger aura marque diverse...*" In the statutes of the Gild of Bakers of Florence, each loaf had to bear the mark of the baker stamped upon it. Any bread offered for sale unstamped was at once confiscated by the "officers of abundance" and the offending baker was mulcted in heavy damages.[3] Kohler quotes a statute of the city of Novaria likewise severely penalizing the omission of the baker's mark or the counterfeiting of one baker's mark by another.[4]

National regulations as to the price, weight, quality, etc. of bread in England have been traced as far back as Anglo-Saxon times,[5] and Cunningham has cited ordinances of the eighth and twelfth centuries on this subject.[6] But the earliest statutory requirement as to baker's marks is found in the *Statutum de Pistoribus*, providing for the punishment of those who violated the more celebrated Assize of Bread (*Assisa Panis et Cervisiae*), usually ascribed to the 51st year of the reign of Henry III (1266). The *Statutum de Pistoribus* which, as just indicated, is a penal statute, provides that "every baker shall have a mark of his own for each sort of bread (*Quilibet Pistor habeat suum proprium signum super quodlibet genus panum suorum*)."[7] The regulatory feature of

---

[1] M. de Gailhard Bancel, *op. cit.*, p. 65.
[2] *Ibid.*, p. 68.
[3] E. Staley, *The Guilds of Florence* (2nd ed.), p. 440; G. Lastig, *op. cit.* p. 28.
[4] *Op. cit.*, p. 45.
[5] Sidney and Beatrice Webb, *op. cit.*, p. 196.
[6] W. Cunningham, *op. cit.*, i, pp. 567 *et seq.*
[7] *Stat. of the Realm*, i, p. 202. *Cf. Rotuli Parliamentorum*, v, 426a. That the crown officials, even prior to the *Statutum de Pistoribus*, recognized the efficacy of bakers' marks is evident from the royal confirmation of provisions made before Gilbert de Preston, who had been sent to Grimsby in 43 Henry III to adjust disputes there between "the rich men" and "the poor men." Among these provisions is one that "every baker shall have his own seal to mark the bread made by him." (*Cal. Charter Rolls*, ii, 1257–1300, p. 15.)

this provision was re-enacted by royal grant to the Mayor
and Bailiffs of Cambridge in the following year (52 Henry III)
for the keeping of the Assizes, in which is ordained that
"every baker shall have his seal and seal his bread (*Quilibet
pistor habeat sigillum suum et signet panem suum*), whereby
it may be know whose bread it is and if he did not do this
he shall be grievously amerced." [1]

The Assize of Bread and the *Statutum de Pistoribus*, or at
any rate, certain portions of these,[2] including a provision for
the registration of bakers' marks, appear to have been re-
enacted or incorporated in many of the local custumals or
municipal ordinances throughout the kingdom.   Section 38
of *The Usages of Winchester*, which probably antedate 1275,
requires every baker to put his recognized stamp ("*sun sel
cunu*") upon his bread.[3]   In the version of these *Usages*
in Toulmin Smith's *English Gilds* [4] it is pointed out that
this provision concerning bakers' marks was considered of
such importance that, in the margin of the Roll wherein it
appears, a special mark calls attention thereto.   In the
"Ancient Ordinary" of the Bakers of York a fine of 40^d was
provided for failure to mark bread.[5]   Another provision of
the Bakers of York, evidently designed to preserve the
monopoly of baking intact from encroachment by the inn-
keepers, and probably copied from a similar ordinance of
the Bakers of London, dated 1365,[6] ordained

that every loofe of bread be marked with the mark of the
baker of whom the sayd bread was bought, to thend and
intent that everye person may know that the bread is of
the right assize, of such value as it should be, whereby the

---

[1] *Cal. Pat. Rolls*, Hen. III, 1266–1272, p. 195.   The same grant provides
that "whosoever of the town of Cambridge shall brew for sale, shall hang out
his sign (*exponat signum suum*), otherwise he shall lose the ale."
[2] See L. Toulmin Smith, "The Bakers of York and their Ancient Ordinary,"
in *Archæol. Review*, vol. i, p. 125.
[3] J. S. Furley, *City Government of Winchester from the Records of the XIVth
and XVth Centuries*, p. 82.
[4] P. 355.
[5] L. Toulmin Smith, *op. cit.*, p. 131.
[6] H. T. Riley, *op. cit.*, p. 323.

inkepers, harborers and osteiers may advouch the sale of their bread by the mark of the baker.

A fine in the extraordinarily large amount of 20^s to the "common Chambre" and 20^s to the "Presenter" was prescribed for bread sold not so marked, to be paid by the innkeeper, harborer or hostler in question.[1] A similar provision that horsebread shall not be made by hostlers but only by bakers and that each loaf was to be stamped with the mark of the baker from whom it had been purchased by the hostler is contained in the Hull Compositions.[2] The proclamations of the town of Bristol in the fourteenth century also required bakers to put their marks on the loaves they make ("*quod ponant signa sua in panibus quos faciunt*") under a penalty of forfeiture.[3]

The prevention or punishment of the infraction of such bread-marking ordinances was in some cases part of the function of the local Leet Courts and, in others, came within the jurisdiction of the gild organizations themselves. As we shall see in the case of London, where the bakers' organization was strong and the enforcement of their monopoly the main concern, the bread-marking provisions were often and rigorously enforced. On the other hand, when such matters were left to the local Leet Court and where only the public interest was involved, violations of the ordinances do not appear to have been regarded in a very serious light by the Court. In John Wilkinson's noted *Treatise . . . Concerning the Office . . . of Coroners and Sherifes, together with an Easie and Plaine Method for the Keeping of a Court Leet . . .* (London 1638) is contained the instruction that "also a Baker must set his owne proper marke upon euery loafe of bread that hee maketh and selleth, to the end that if any bread be faultie in weight, it may bee then knowne in whom the fault is."[4] But the Leet Courts do not appear to have

[1] L. Toulmin Smith, *op. cit.*, p. 218.
[2] J. M. Lambert, *Two Thousand Years of Guild Life*, p. 305.
[3] *The Little Red Book of Bristol*, (ed. F. B. Bickley) ii, p. 224.
[4] Quoted by J. P. Earwaker, *Court Leet Records of the Manor of Manchester*, i, Introd., p. xiv, n. 1.

been greatly troubled by infractions of the Assize. An entry in the Manchester Leet Court records [1] recites: "*et Dicunt* that all the Bakers and Brewers within this manerr hathe offended and broken the Assize," and indicates that a fine of one penny was the penalty. In the same way, in Southampton, although bakers were required to have the impress of their seal clearly appearing on every loaf "that they might the more readily be detected if they broke the assize" and although bakers' marks seem to have been registered with the municipal authorities, [2] nevertheless, "time after time, the same bakers were guilty of breaking the assize and yet they escaped with paltry fines of 3^d, 4^d or 6^d." [3]

The history of the baking industry in London is even richer in this connection than that of the provinces. The bakers appear to have been among the earliest organized industries of London with, at first, a practically autonomous hallmoot of their own.[4] According to the *Liber Albus*,[5] a compilation in the latter half of the fifteenth century of ordinances of a very much earlier date:

(1) Each baker shall have his own seal, (*soun seal*) as well for brown bread as for white bread; that so it may be the better known whose bread it is (*issaint que mieutz soit conus a qi le payn soit*).

(2) Each Alderman shall view (*veit*) the seals of the bakers in his ward (*en sa Garde*)[6].

(3) The bread of the bakers shall be taken (that is, for

---

[1] April 18, 1560.

[2] P. Studer, *The Oak Book of Southampton* (in Southampton Record Society, vol. II) ii, Introd. pp. xxvi–xxvii.

[3] *Ibid.*, p. xxviii. Not without justification J. W. Jeudwine, *Tort Crime and Police*, p. 220, remarks that "the assize was broken so wholly and with such regularity that the fines look like excise licenses."

[4] G. Unwin, *The Gilds and Companies of London*, p. 31.

[5] *Liber Albus* in *Munimenta Gildhallae Londoniensis* (Rolls Series) i, pp. 264–5.

[6] At the end of the *Liber Albus* (i, p. 702), where references are given to matters found in the Letter Books, the wording is "*Quod quilibet Aldermannus habeat signum in custodia.*" The wording in *Letter Book A* reads "that each Alderman shall view (*videat*) the seals in his ward (*custodia*)." (R. R. Sharpe, *Cal. Letter Books of the City of London, Letter Book A*, p. 216). It would therefore appear that possibly the earlier practice may have been for the baker to leave his seal in the custody of the alderman who, at the proper time, either sealed the bread himself or delivered the seal to the baker for the particular occasion.

examination as to weight and quality) every month, once at the very least, or more times if it might be necessary.

(4) Each baker shall show his seal at each Wardmote, so that it may be known (*si qil soit conuz*).[1]

The antiquity as well as the importance of bakers' marks in London is strikingly indicated by two entries in the Rolls of the Mayor's Court for the year 1303. The first of these entries reads as follows:

A jury of the venue of St. Clement's Lane, consisting of Thomas de Wynton and others, said on oath that Stephen de Wynton did not make the brown bread (*panem bissum*) which was seized in the bakehouse of Thomas de Wrotham in St. Clement's Lane, for which he was arrested on the ground that bread weighed 20s 8d less than it ought to do, but that a certain Thomas de Bedeford, oven-man (*furnator*) of Thomas de Wrotham, made it and *sealed it with the seal belonging to the house of his master*, to his master's profit. Judgment that Stephen go quit, and that Thomas de Wrotham be distrained to answer concerning what may be charged against him.[2]

Four days later it is recorded that

A jury was summoned from the venue of St. Clement's Lane by Candelwykstrete to say whether Thomas de Wrotham made a certain brown loaf &c. . . . Finally a jury consisting of Stephen le Potter and others said on oath that the above Thomas had no profit from bread made in his bakehouse, except 4d the quarter, which was the rent for the use of the bakehouse and utensils, and that a certain Thomas de Bedeford made the bread and sustained judgment for the same. Judgment that the defendant be acquitted.[3]

The system of registration of bakers' marks, especially when considered in connection with the ordinance of 1365 for the stamping of all bread sold by hostlers,[4] affords an excellent illustration of the monopolistic aspect of gild activity and

---

[1] *Munimenta Gildhallae Londoniensis* (Rolls Ser.) iii, p. 264.
[2] A. H. Thomas, *Cal. of Early Mayor's Court Rolls of the City of London*, p. 152. (Italics, the writer's.)
[3] *Ibid.*, p. 153.
[4] See *supra*, p. 50.

purposes.[1] This phase is again strikingly manifested in an incident that occurred in 1440 when, according to *Letter Book K* of the City of London [2]

came William Hobold, baker, before Robert Large, the Mayor, and the Aldermen, and complained of John Halle, a foreign baker of Southwerk, marking the bread with his (*i.e.*, the said William's) mark, viz., with three "prikkys," a mark that from time immemorial had belonged to his house in Clement Lane, whereas every baker ought to have his own mark. Thereupon the Mayor and Aldermen forbade the said John Halle to use the said mark, except (*sic*) [3] for bread exposed for sale in the City, and so to be weighed like all other bread made in the same borough.

This passage at first blush reads much like a modern case of trade-mark infringement. But the explanation of it is to be found in the antipathy of the London bakers for the bakers of Southwark. The importation of "foreign bread," that is, of bread made outside the walls of the city of London was often prohibited,

and against that made in Southwark, as against most other things connected with that locality, there seems to have been an extraordinary degree of prejudice, the bread of that place being more than once excluded by name, "because the bakers of Southwark are not amenable to the justice of the city."[4]

I am indebted to Mr. A. H. Thomas, the courteous and learned Clerk of the Records of the Guildhall, London, for the explanation that the case of William Hobold was simply

the case of a foreigner either intentionally or unintentionally adopting the trade-mark of a citizen . . . It appears that the trade-mark went with the bake-house which will explain why Hobold asserted that the "*signum*" belonged to

---

[1] See *supra*, pp. 40, 42, n. 1.
[2] *Cal.*, p. 247.
[3] The word *except* renders this passage meaningless and should be omitted. I am advised by Mr. Thomas who writes in a letter dated Oct. 31, 1923, containing much valuable information concerning this case, that Dr. Sharpe "clearly made an error in his abstract of the passage."
[4] *Munimenta Gildhallae Londoniensis*, Introd. to *Liber Albus*, i, p. lxvi.

his bake-house in Clement Lane from a time whereof the memory of man runneth not to the contrary.[1]

Mr. Thomas concludes that "Hobold was afraid of being called to account if Halle's bread was found unsatisfactory. . . ."

The cases of Thomas de Wrotham in the fourteenth, and of William Hobold in the fifteenth century, are therefore merely incidental to the general plan of attempting the restriction of local trade to local bakers and, from the trade-mark standpoint, merely indicative of one baker's fear of being held responsible for the defective goods of another. The anxiety of a baker not to be held liable for his fellow-baker's sins of commission and omission in the baking of bread is quite intelligible when we consider that the penalty for selling "false bread" was the hurdle, or later, the pillory.[2]

That, at any rate in the sixteenth century, the bakers of London regarded the sale of "false bread" and the failure to

[1] For a similar but later association of a mark with a certain business or premises in which the business was conducted, rather than with the individual owner or occupant, see R. Fitch, "Notices of Norwich Brewers' Marks" in *Norfolk Archæology: Norfolk & Norwich Archæol. Soc.*, vol. v, page 313, with plates of forty marks. E.g., the mark (no. 1) "borne by Henry Woodes in 1606, and after him, by five successive brewers, ending . . . in 1725."

[2] According to the *Liber Albus* (compiled 1419), the law was that, for the first penalty, the baker of defective bread was to "be drawn upon a hurdle from the Guildhall to his own house, through the great streets where there may be most people assembled, and through the midst of the great streets that are most dirty, with the faulty loaf hanging from his neck. If a second time he shall be found in the same transgression, let him be drawn from the Guildhall through the great street of Chepe, in form aforesaid, to the pillory; and let him be put upon the pillory, and remain there at least one hour in the day. And the third [time that such] default shall be found, he shall be drawn, and the oven shall be pulled, down and the baker [made to] forswear the trade within the City for ever. . . ." (*Munimenta Gildhallæ Londoniensis* (Rolls Ser.) i, p. 265; iii, pp. 83–4). The punishment of the hurdle was instituted in 10 Edw. I, 1281–2 (*Cal. Letter Books, B*, p. 244, n. 1; *French Chronicle of London*, tr. H. T. Riley, p. 240), and in *Letter Book A* (*Cal.*, pp. 120–1) appears a list of bakers "condemned to the hurdle" in 1282. According to *Letter-Book B* (*Cal.*, pp. 243–44), in 1297 it was ordained that the pillory be substituted for the hurdle. However, the following colorful entry in the *Early Mayor's Court Rolls* would indicate that use of the hurdle continued for some years subsequent to 1297:

"[19 March, 1299–1300] Richard Davy, baker, was attached to answer the Mayor and Aldermen on a charge that, whereas on Friday the Feast of the Translation of St. Edward, he was dragged on the hurdle because his bread was false, when he arrived home and descended from the hurdle and entered his house, he took a bone and threw it at the tabor-player [*i.e.*, the musician customarily marching ahead of such offenders in their procession through the streets], and broke the tabor through the middle . . ." (A. H. Thomas, *op. cit.*, p. 67).

impress a mark upon the bread as injurious to the whole craft is evident from the records of the Bakers' Company. An entry for January 16, 1536, states that

every baker that doth not seall or marke apparantly on almaner lofe brede, white and wheten and houshold, that it may be knowen of whoes bakyng it is, shall forfaytt and pay without any redempcion as often as it shall be founden defectyff, vjs. viijd. to th'use of the Company.[1]

The following month "Davyd Johns is commaunded to bryng in vjs. viijd. at the next Great Day for noon-sealyng of his halff-peny manchettes."[2]

In how heinous a light the mis-use of seals on bread was regarded is evident from an entry in the year 1554 which recites that "at this Co\(^r\)te . . . John Davys was charged in all his offence, that is to say, as-well for lack of weight, as for having a wrong seall, and for beating his wife, for the which he hath not onely deserved shame but also banyshment."[3]

If bread was essential for the sustenance of the king's people, drink of good quality and in good measure was likewise necessary for their cheer and contentment. Consequently, not only were the ale-sellers required, as indicated above,[4] to display their signs (*signa*) for their proper control under the Assize of Ale, but barrels and bottles were to be carefully marked to insure full measure, and both the manufacturer of a short-measure container as well as the actual seller of the liquids in such containers were to be punished. As early as 1373 an ordinance of the Bottle-Makers of London prescribes that "every bottle-maker shall place his mark on bottles and other vessels, made of leather, in order that his work may be identified.[5]

Likewise, all "turnours," *i.e.*, makers of wooden measures for wine and ale, were in 1347 summoned before the Mayor and Aldermen of London and ordered,

[1] J. G. Nichols, " Bakers Hall and the Muniments of the Company ", in *Trans. London and Middlesex Archaeol. Soc.*, vol. iii, pp. 59–60. See also entry April 16, 1537, on same page.
[2] *Ibid.*, p. 60.   [3] *Ibid.*, p. 62.   [4] E.g., *supra*, p. 50, n. 1.
[5] *Cal. Letter Books, City of London*, Letter Book G, p. 317.

that each of these makers shall have a mark of his own, and should place such mark upon his measures at the bottom thereof, without, when by the standard they should have been examined; that so, when any measure made by one of the makers aforesaid shall in any tavern or brewhouse be found to be false or defective, then as well the person by whom such measure shall have been made, as he who shall have sold by such measure, shall incur the punishment at the discretion of the Mayor and Aldermen to be ordained for the same . . . and the said makers of the city aforesaid were ordered to bring here samples of their marks . . . and deliver the same to . . . the Chamberlain, there in the Chamber of the Guild Hall to remain. Which marks at the end of this book [Letter Book F] are set forth.[1]

For the same purpose an ordinance of the "Bere Breurs" (1453) required that beer brewers make their vessels according to the Assize and "and have them stamped with their own iron marks, which marks are to be recorded in the Chamber. . . ."[2]

In the reign of Henry VIII the subject of coopers' marks was considered of such importance that a statute was passed, requiring that "every couper marke his vessell with his own marke upon the payne of iij[s] and iiij[d]."[3]   However, long before the enactment of this statute, coopers' marks were the subject of local regulations. In 1420 it was ordained by the Coopers' Company of London that every cooper should have his own mark or sign of iron (*soun propre une merche ou signe de ferre*), which he was to record in the Coopers' Court.[4] A lengthy petition of the Coopers' Company to the Lord Mayor and Aldermen of London in 1440 indicates how important the coopers believed it to be to prevent the misappropriation of their marks. The petition, after reciting prior efforts to protect coopers' marks, states:

Also, the seid Coupers besechyn to be graunted that when

[1] H. T. Riley, *Memorials*, p. 235.
[2] *Cal. Letter Books, Letter Book K*, p. 354.   See *supra*, p. 55, n. 1.
[3] *Stat. of the Realm*, vol. iii, p. 368, 23 Hen. VIII, c. 4, clause XI.   See W. S. Holdsworth, *op. cit.*, vol. iv, p. 560 for extract from Lambard's *Eirenarcha* (1581) concerning enforcement of this Act by Justices of the Peace.
[4] J. F. Firth, *Coopers' Company, London*, p. 10.

ony Couper of the citee aforseid dieth or passeth away, that his executours or assignes brynge in or do bryng, to the chamb'layn of this citee for the tyme beyng, the same iren marke the which he hath vsed in his life in his warde, to be keped for dowte of alienynge of the seyde marke in to the handes of evyldoers or counterfetors, be the which the common people mught be dyscevyd and the craft reproued to grete hurt and damage, on the peyn to pay at euery tyme in whome suche defaute is found x^s, to be departed betwene the chambre and the crafte in fourme aforsayde.

Also, the seide Coupers besechen that ordenñce might be made that no man, fre nor foreyne, ymagyne nor falsly con-trefete the markes of Coupers, the which thei haue in grete charge, and ar entrid in the Yeldhalle, nor vnder the colour of theym bere no by marke be the which the common people might be disceuyd and the craft gretely hurt; but that euery Couper wel and pesabily his marke jeioyse and occupie vnto the same entent that the seid markes wer ordeigned. . . .[1]

These marks were entered in the *Letter Books of London*. For instance in *Letter Book I* (1419–20) the ordinance of January 27, 1419–20 (7 Henry V), requiring all coopers to have their own mark or sign for making barrels or kilderkins, recites the very heavy penalty of £10 for not recording these marks and 40^s for selling unmarked vessels. The entry in the *Letter Book* records that, pursuant to the above ordinance, 'coupers' residing within the franchise of the city were to present to the court within fourteen days their marks, made of iron, to be recorded. The names of such 'coupers' and their respective marks are subsequently entered in the *Letter Book*.[2] Some of the marks in question are reproduced in the frontispiece to this volume.

Despite much legislation on the subject,[3] the enforcement

[1] *Ibid.*, pp. 12–13. The ordinance prayed for was granted 6 May, 1440 (*ibid.*, p. 14).
[2] *Cal. Letter Books, Letter Book I*, pp. 237–8. From the standpoint of any early traces of a succession of marks it is interesting to note that in this list of coupers' marks there is a reference to a transfer of a mark after death of the holder to another cooper. Again in *Letter Book K* (see *Cal.*, p. 134) the marks of a number of coopers are entered, and at the end of *Letter Book L* (see *Cal.*, p. 322) are entered the marks of twenty-four coopers.
[3] For Aberdeen regulation, 1507, see E. Bain, *Merchant and Craft Guilds*, p. 237.

of the regulations concerning coopers' marks would in many instances appear to have been even less successful than in the case of marks on bread. In London a member of the Coopers' Company was amerced in 1444 "for defective marking,"[1] and the Southampton Court Leet records contain a constant succession of fines for failures of the coopers there to "sett there marks upon there caske by reason whereof we cannot come to the true knowledge of the offenders."[2]

But it was not only in the matter of eating and drinking that the craft and the consumer were enabled to trace defective wares through the use of regulatory marks. From the standpoint of coinage, the crown had a .vital interest in maintaining the standards and regulating the assay of gold and silver plate.[3] Furthermore, from considerations already indicated with regard to other crafts, it was to the interest of the goldsmiths themselves to maintain such standards. A statute of 37 Edward III (1363) provided that

every Master Goldsmith shall have a Mark by himself (*un merche a per lui*) and the same Mark shall be known by them which shall be assigned by the king to survey their work and Allay . . . and after the assay is made the surveyors shall set the King's Mark [i.e., the leopard's head] and after the Goldsmith his Mark for which he will answer (*& puis lorfeure son merche per quel il veot respondre. . . .*)[4]

The ancient customs and liberties of the town of Beverly indicate that the local point of view coincided with that of the national authorities as to the regulatory nature of the goldsmiths' marks.

[1] J. F. Firth, *op. cit.*, p. 41.
[2] *Southampton Court Leet Records*, vol. ii, (Southampton Record Soc. Pub., Vol. IV) p. 446, entry No. 64. Cf. *ibid.*, p. 447, entry No. 67, also Vol. i, p. 105, entries No. 63, 64, 65, 66.
[3] W. Cunningham, *op. cit.*, pp. 326 *et seq.*
[4] C. 8. *Stat. of the Realm*, i, p. 380. For further provisions requiring the imposition and registration of goldsmiths' marks, see 2 Hen. VI (1423) c. 17 (*Statutes of the Realm*, ii, p. 224); 17 Edw. IV (1477-8) c. i (*ibid.* ii, pp. 456-7). For legislation concerning goldsmiths see C. J. Jackson, *English Goldsmiths and Their Marks* (2nd ed. 1921) ch. 2. This monumental work completely justifies its sub-title: "History of the Goldsmiths and Plate-Workers of England, Scotland and Ireland."

Also Tuesday next before St. Martin's Day in winter A.D.
1365, Simon of Corby, Walter of Swine . . . goldsmiths,
took oath before the twelve keepers of the town of Beverly
. . . that they would not let any vessels or other works
wrought or to be wrought by them pass out of their hands
unless they have been marked with their usual marks (*nisi
signis suis consuetis fuerint signata*).

Again in 1409 an order was made that "gold and silver
wrought in the town of Beverly should be pure and fine and
of true alloy, without fraud or defects that should be prevented, and that everyone's mark should be known in the
Guild Hall." [1]

The regulatory nature of the goldsmith's mark is well stated
in a valuable seventeenth century treatise for goldsmiths,
entitled *The Touchstone for Gold and Silver Wares*, printed in
London in 1677:

Our law (as I conceive) did think the thus setting up the
marks on the work to be the securest way to prevent
fraud . . .; for if it would not deter from the working and
selling coarse gold and silver wares, yet would it be a sure way
to find out the offenders and to have the injured righted. But
if the mark might be omitted and the works should pass but
into a third owner's hand, for the most part it would be impossible to discern one man's work from another, by reason
that divers workers made all sorts of work in shapes so near
alike.[2]

There is hardly a phase of medieval industry in which similar
ordinances do not occur and in which the basis of these ordinances is not recited in the law itself. Every court hand-
writer or scrivener of the city of London was required (1373)
to "put his name to the deeds which he makes; that it may
be known who has made the same." [3] Every master bladesmith of London (1408) "shall put his own mark upon his
work, such as heads of lances, knives and axes . . . that it
may be known who made the same, if default be found

[1] *Beverly Town Documents*, ed. A. F. Leach (Selden Soc. Pubs. vol. 14),
p. 40.
[2] Quoted by C. J. Jackson, *op. cit.*, p. 56.
[3] H. T. Riley, *op. cit.*, p. 373.

therein." [1] The Northampton Waxchandlers' Ordinances (1466) required that, "after the seal of the wardens had been affixed to torches and torchettes", "the Owner of the Torches or Torchettes shall have Anothere seall of his owne, that he may sett upon Torches or Torchettes . . . in witnessyng of his owne deede." [2] The Worcester Tilers' Ordinances (1467) provide that

every tyller makynge and sillynge it into the cite, sett his propre marke vppon his tyle, to that ende, yf it be defectif or smalle, that men may have remedy of the seid partie a[s] lawe and resonne requirith. And he that refusith to marke his tyle as it is aforn reherced, shalle lese to the comyn tresor xx.s, as ofte tyme as it ápperith to be areryd. [3]

A complaint in the Norwich Assembly (1512) was made that weavers "leue out . . . their woven markys" to conceal the origin of worsted "defectiff in stuff and workmanship." [4]

But a further recital of these ordinances would be supererogatory. The joiners of London (1309), [5] the heaumers of London (1347), [6] the weavers of Bristol (1355), [7] the cutlers and bladesmiths of London (1365), [8] the fullers and walkers of Coventry (1468 and 1472), [9] the pewterers of London (1501-2), [10]

---

[1] *Ibid.*, p. 570.

[2] W. L. D. Adkins, *Records of the Borough of Northampton*, i, p. 306.

[3] Toulmin Smith, *English Gilds*, p. 399.

[4] *Records of the City of Norwich*, ed. W. Hudson and J. C. Tingey, i, p. 108. Under date November 17, 1923, Mr. Tingey has been good enough to refer me to the "usual formula: 'We find a piece of cloth marked thus (indicating mark) to be defective in . . .' The weaver's mark was forced upon him and its appropriation by another was a matter for the officers of his craft, for it could not be tolerated by the Company."

[5] *Liber Custumarum* in *Munimenta Gildhallae Londoniensis*, ii, p. 538.

[6] *Cal. Letter Books of the City of London, Letter Book F.*, p. 169; H. T. Riley, *Memorials*, p. 238. *Cf. Cal. Letter Books, K*, p. 334. See *infra*, ch. v, for further references to helmet-makers' and other armorers' marks.

[7] *The Little Red Book of Bristol*, ed. F. B. Bickley, ii, pp. 5-6.

[8] C. Welch, *History of the Cutlers of London*, i, p. 249. *Cal. Close Rolls*, Edw. III, 1364-8, p. 182. See *infra*, ch. v, on cutlers' marks.

[9] *Coventry Leet Book*, ed. M. D. Harris, i, pp. 338, 375.

[10] See C. Welch, *History of the Pewterers' Company*, vol. i, pp. 94-6. *Cf.* statute 19 Hen. VIII, c. 6, clause III (1503-4) requiring pewterers and braziers to mark all hollow wares of pewter ley mettal "with severall markes of their own." (*Stat. of the Realm*, ii, 651-2). Further reference to pewterers' marks will be found in the chapter on cutlers' marks.

the hatmakers of Norwich (1543),[1] the cordwainers and shoemakers of Hull (1564),[2] the cutlers of Sheffield (1564),[3] the
founders of London (1614),[4] — all insisted, or were compelled
by local or royal authority to insist that the products of their
members should be marked not only with the seal of their
organization but with the individual mark or seal of the
producer in question. A single illustration of the practical
application of this system will suffice. In 1428 proceedings
were held before the Mayor of York concerning the sale
of adulterated metal products, one John Fysshe being accused
of selling "gyrdels of mengeld metaill agayn ye ordenaunce
of hys crafte." Fysshe defended himself by setting up the
claim that he had bought the metal from John Lyllyng. In
the subsequent proceedings against Lyllyng, which ended
in his being adjudged guilty, the record states:

> And, after this, come William Kyam of York merchaunt, and
> sayd to ye sayd Mayr and other that he was late at Hull,
> and come to John Bower stathe, and thar John Bower pro-
> fered to sell hym a laste of osmundes [a certain quantity of
> iron], and yar this William Kyam saw ij barells of osmundes
> market with ye marke of John Lyllyng. . . .[5]

To summarize briefly, neither the physical circumstances
surrounding gild life nor the economic theories underlying the
functions actually exercised by the gilds encouraged the development of an individual gildsman's good-will, nor the exploitation of the symbol of such goodwill, i.e., his trade-mark.
The profuse legislation of the gilds concerning marks was designed solely to maintain standards of workmanship for the
protection of the collective good-will of the gild and to permit
the tracing of the sale of "foreign goods" for the enforcement of the gild monopoly. The marks used by the medieval

[1] Records of the City of Norwich, ed. W. Hudson and J. C. Tingey, ii, Introd.
pp. lxiii to lxiv.
[2] J. M. Lambert, op. cit., pp. 316–17.
[3] R. Leader, History of the Cutlers of Hallamshire, i, p. 7.
[4] W. M. Williams, Annals of the Founders Company, pp. 26, 30, 71, 91, 98,
114, 118, 130.
[5] "English Miscellanies," in Surtees Soc. Pub. vol. lxxxv (1888, vol. ii),
p. 2.

gildsman, *quâ* gildsman, were in their origin purely regulatory or police marks, and, as such, liabilities, not assets. The same mark might ultimately acquire a secondary significance as a symbol of the excellence of its user's workmanship and wares, but this secondary development is found only in certain industries dealing in commodities capable of transportation for a long distance, such as cloth, cutlery and to a lesser degree pewterware, and not in perishable foodstuffs. The same was true of those marks which craftsmen were required by statute to affix to their wares. The gildsman might, or might not, as he saw fit, and often did use his compulsory production mark or some other mark to establish the ownership of his goods, but this proprietary mark or merchant's mark, as it was called, has no inherently necessary historical or legal relation to the production mark.

A NOTE ON EARLY PRINTERS' AND PUBLISHERS' DEVICES [1]

Writers on the history of trade-mark law have always attached much significance to the oft-quoted warnings concerning infringement of devices by three famous printers and publishers of the Renaissance.[2] They cite Aldus Manutius, (*fl.* 1494–1515) who, in his preface to his edition of Livy of 1518, said,

. . . to Aldus' *Institutiones Grammaticae*, printed in their offices, they [that is, the Florentine competitors of Aldus] have affixed our well-known sign of the dolphin wound around the anchor. But they have so managed, that any person who is in the least acquainted with the books of our production cannot fail to observe that this is an impudent

---

[1] Although the printers' and stationers' organizations much resemble in form and purpose other gilds and companies, it has been deemed advisable to separate all references to printers' devices and marks in a note at the end of this chapter. The primary function and origin of printers' devices and marks would, upon careful investigation, appear to have been decorative rather than regulatory.

[2] J. Kohler, *Das Recht des Markenschutzes*, p. 41; W. H. Browne, *Treatise on the Law of Trademarks* (2 ed. Boston 1898) pp. 12–14; E. S. Rogers, "Some Historical Matter Concerning Trademarks, in 9 *Michigan Law Review*, p. 29, at pp. 35–6. Mr. Rogers states, at p. 36: "The use of trademarks by printers was the inevitable consequence of the conditions which resulted from the absence of any notion of property in literary work."

fraud; for the head of the dolphin is turned to the left, whereas that of ours is well known to be turned to the right.

Josse Badius Ascensius who flourished at Paris from 1502 to 1532 wrote: "We beg the reader to notice the sign, for there are men who have adopted the same title and the name of Badius, and so filch our labor."[1] Benedictus Hector of Bologna (*fl.* 1487–91) in his edition of *Justinus et Florus* inserted the following notice: "Look at my sign which is represented on the title page and you can never be mistaken."

However, these warnings uttered by early printers must be regarded as the exclamations of outraged victims of unfair competition rather than as a threat to invoke the protection of the law for a definite legal right in a device. No inference can properly be drawn therefrom that the original employment of printers' devices was "merely an attempt to prevent the inevitable pirate from reaping where he had not sown,"[2] that is to say, in some way or other, to protect the copyright of the books in which they appeared.[3] Bibliographical researches into the history of printers' devices have established that at any rate in their origin and primary *raison d'être* they bear no resemblance to the industrial marks which we have described above, but that on the contrary: (1) their use was optional, — never compulsory; (2) that they were variable or replaceable at the will of the user; (3) that there was no limitation upon the number of devices used; (4) that their use was that of a symbol of self-expression — a mark of personality; and that their functional development was decorative rather than regulatory.

---

[1] For the counterfeiting of Badius' devices and imitation of his publications, see P. Renouard, *Bibliographie des impressions et des œuvres de Josse Badius Ascensius*, i, pp. 24, 46.

[2] W. Roberts, *Printers' Marks*, p. 1. An interesting recent application of the view that printers' devices were in origin essentially trade-marks is to be found in H. R. Plomer's study of *English Printers' Ornaments* (London 1924). Explaining his exclusion of printers' devices from that work, Mr. Plomer writes (Preface, p. vii): "Printers' devices, being in the nature of trade marks, have no place in this volume, as, although decorative in themselves, they were not used simply for the sake of embellishing the page."

[3] See A. W. Pollard, "Printers' Marks of the Fifteenth and Sixteenth Centuries," in *The Connoisseur*, vol. ii, p. 262, at p. 264.

Gutenburg appears to have seen no necessity for the use of any device,[1] and it was not until 1457, three years after the earliest dated piece of printing (1454),[2] that the first known printer's device — the twin-shields — was used by Fust and Schoeffer of Mainz in their colophon to the Mainz Psalter. The original function of printers' devices and their relation to colophons has been dealt with at some length by Pollard in his *Essay on Colophons*.[3] He there points out that in 1472 Schoeffer concludes his colophon to the *Decretum Gratiani cum glossis* with the phrase, "*suis consignando scutis feliciter consumavit.*" ". . . Here," says Pollard, "on the authority of the printer who has used one, we have a clear indication of the reason which made him put his mark in a book — the simple reason that he was proud of his craftsmanship and wished it to be recognized as his: 'By signing it with his shields Peter Schoeffer has brought the book to happy completion.' "[4] "As between printers in different cities, there was certainly no copyright in colophons"[5] and both Schoeffer's colophons and his device of the twin-shields were used, without recorded complaint on his part, by printers at Nuremburg and Basel in their reprints of his edition.[6] The relation of device to colophon is thus elsewhere explained by Pollard:

Sometimes it was placed so as to separate the colophon from the text, sometimes it followed the colophon and sometimes superseded it. . . . In any position the device was sure to be decorative and effective and long after the introduction of the title page it maintained its position as an appropriate ornament to the end of a book.[7]

[1] K. A. Barack, Introd. to *Elsässische Büchermarken* (ed. Heitz, Strassburg 1892), p. xii.

[2] A. W. Pollard, *Fine Books*, p. 47.

[3] A. W. Pollard, *An Essay on Colophons* (The Caxton Club, Chicago 1915), p. 21. In 1473 a similar colophon and device of twin-shields was used by Schoeffer and the device and phrase, "*suis consignando scutis feliciter consumavit,*" occur again in colophons of 1475 and in those to several of his books of the three following years. In 1479 the phrase is varied to "*cuius armis signantur*" (*ibid.*, p. 22).

[4] *Ibid.*, p. 22. For further evidence adduced by Pollard see *ibid.*, p. 23.

[5] *Ibid.*, p. 17.

[6] *Ibid.*, p. 18. See also A. W. Pollard, *Fine Books*, pp. 60–61.

[7] A. W. Pollard, *Last Words on the History of the Title-Page*, pp. 12–13.

In the third decade of the sixteenth century, when the label title-page became more common, printers' devices, especially in Italy and Germany, were often used to decorate the blank space beneath the title.[1]

If the evidence of the colophons wherein printers' devices were first used as to the reason for the use of these devices is insufficient, the remarkable series of studies of printers' devices in various European cities, *Die Büchermarken oder Buchdrucker, — und Verlegerzeichen*, edited by Heitz of Strassburg, may be said to have adequately established their original function and nature. Barack in his introduction to the volume on Alsatian marks has pointed out how devices began as a simple monogram or merchant's mark or *Hausmark* in a shield, — often accompanied by a cross for the protection of the sale or goodwill of its user, — and how later these devices became highly decorative and ornamental.[2] Heitz's great series of studies, supplemented by later researches, has likewise established the use of printers' devices to have been entirely optional and without legal significance, — at any rate until toward the end of the sixteenth century.

For instance, Ulrich Zell, who printed at Cologne from about 1463 to nearly the end of the fifteenth century, did not commence to use a device until practically the end of his career and then did so but seldom. Among the early printers of Basel many omitted their devices as they did their names.[3] The early Strassburg printers likewise used no mark.[4] Kristeller, the historian of Italian printers' devices and of Italian woodcuts, has shown the close relation of the two and points out that devices occur more commonly in early illustrated and popular books than in un-illustrated and in later works.[5] It has been estimated that the 351 marks reproduced by Kristeller belonged to 184 printers or publishers, "perhaps a

[1] A. W. Pollard, *Early Illustrated Books* (2nd ed. London 1917), pp. 33–34.
[2] See K. A. Barack, Introd. to *Elsässische Büchermarken*, p. xii; *cf.* H. G. Aldis, *The Printed Book*, p. 25.
[3] C. Bernouilli, Introd. to *Basler Büchermarken*, p. x.
[4] K. A. Barack, *op. cit.*, Introd. p. xii.
[5] Paul Kristeller, *Die Italienischen Buchdrucker, — und Verlegerzeichen bis 1525*, p. xi.

third of the whole number at work in Italy up to 1525 so that plainly many Italian firms never used them at all."[1] Haebler, the historian of the early printers of Spain and Portugal, has shown that many famous early Spanish printers such as Johan Kronberger,[2] of Lisbon and Seville, Juan de Burgos[3] and Luschner[4] of Monteserrat and Barcelona, used such devices indifferently and inconsistently if at all.

Printers who adopted devices often used several at the same time or in succession.[5] According to Roberts, "a full description of the various marks used by Christophe Plantin alone would fill a small volume."[6] While some Italian firms used no devices, on the other hand, "Lucantonio Giunta at Venice had ten different variations of the Florentine Lily, and Filippo Giunta at Florence employed five more."[7] The Elzevirs used four major as well as several minor devices.[8] Johann Rosenbach, the second printer in Barcelona (1492), used two quite different marks at different times, the first with the initial of his native town Heidelberg as the principal feature, the second, late in the sixteenth century, featuring the arms of Burgundy supported by two stags.[9] Jan Van Doesborgh, who flourished in Antwerp in the first quarter of the sixteenth century and specialized in the English book trade, used during his career three variations of one device and two variations of another.[10]

Furthermore, as has been pointed out by Mr. Falconer Madan in the case of the three devices showing the printing press, first used by Badius[11], the same devices with slight varia-

[1] *Bibliographica* pt. 1, p. 124. *Cf.* A. Freimann's article "Printers' Marks" in *Jewish Encyclopedia*, x, p.200.
[2] Konrad Haebler, *The Early Printers of Spain and Portugal* (Bibliographical Soc. Illustrated Monographs, No. IV, 1897), pp. 63–4, 77.
[3] *Ibid.*, p. 67.
[4] *Ibid.*, p. 75.
[5] M. P. Delalain, *Inventaire des Marques d'Imprimeurs et de Libraires*, Introd. p. xiv.
[6] W. Roberts, *op. cit.*, p. 203.
[7] *Bibliographica*, pt. i, p. 124.
[8] W. Roberts, *op. cit.*, pp. 205 *et seq.*
[9] K. Haebler, *op. cit.*, p. 70.
[10] See R. Proctor, *Jan Van Doesborgh* (Bibliographical Soc. Illustrated Monographs, No. II (1894)), pp. 9–10.
[11] Reproduced by P. Renouard, *op. cit.*, i, pp. 43–45.

tions might be in use at approximately the same time by a dozen different printers or publishers scattered throughout the continental printing centers.[1]   Thus, the oldest Cologne device resembles that of Peter Schoeffer, — the small shield.[2] Again Friedrich (or, as he was called in Castilian, Fadrique) of Basel, once a partner of Michael Wensler, who settled in Burgos about 1485, for one of his two marks practically reproduced that of two well-known printers of Basel.[3]

The French printers appeared to have shared their continental fellow-craftsmen's indifference towards the consistent use of devices.[4]   However, comparatively early in the history of French printing, printers' devices appear to have been regarded as industrial property worthy of some protection. In 1539 François I issued an ordinance requiring every printer and bookseller to have his own mark so that the purchasers of books might easily know where the books were printed and sold.[5]   This statute, which was re-enacted in identical form for the printers of Lyon in 1541,[6] may have been intended to aid in the suppression of heresy [7] as well as of trade piracy.

[1] See Falconer Madan, "Early Representations of the Printing Press," in *Bibliotheca*, pt. ii, p. 223 *et seq.* For additional illustrations of the contemporaneous use of the same mark in various printing centres, see W. Roberts, *op. cit.*, Introduction; A. Freimann, *op. cit.*, x, p. 200.

[2] *Die Kölner Büchermarken*, ed. Paul Heitz, Introd. by Otto Zaretzky, p. vii.

[3] See K. Haebler, *op. cit.*, p. 34.

[4] When Josse Badius, whose complaint of piracy we have referred to above (p. 64), printed books for publishers having their own mark, or when he shared the printing of a book with another printer, he did not use his own mark, but theirs. (See P. Renouard, *op. cit.*, i, pp. 46–47.) In the case of one of the early Paris printers, Antoine Verard, he appears to have been a publisher as well as a printer and to have given some of his work out to other printers. One of these latter, named Pierre LeCaron, shortly after 1486, cut out Verard's monogram from the heart in the center of the device and his name from the lower edge and printed his own name in the place thus left blank. See J. Macfarlane, *Antoine Verard* (Bibliographical Soc. Illustrated Monographs, No. VII, 1900), Introd. pp. xxv–xxvi.

[5] Art. 16: "Ne pourront prendre, les Maîtres Imprimeurs & Libraires, les marques les uns des autres, ains chacun en aura une à part soi, & différente les unes des autres; en maniére que les acheteurs des Livres puissent facilement connoître en quelles Officines les livres auront été imprimés & lesquels se vendront aux dites Officines, & non ailleurs." (C. M. Saugraine, *Code de la librairie et imprimerie de Paris*, Paris 1744, pp. 93–4.)

[6] F. A. Isambert, *Anciennes lois Françaises* (Paris 1828), xii, p. 763.

[7] The first *Index Expurgatorius* was not issued till 1544, but was preceded by partial edicts on the subject of heresy addressed to provincial Parliaments on December 16, 1538 and June 24, 1539. See *Cambridge Modern History*, ii, p. 288; G. H. Putnam, *The Censorship of the Church of Rome*, i, pp. 96 *et seq.*; H. Reusch, *Die Indices Librorum Prohibitorum des XVIten Jahrhunderts*, p. 2.

Subsequent legislation and also punitive proceedings before various French tribunals indicate a considerable amount of infringement in the sixteenth and seventeenth centuries.[1]

That the repression of the counterfeiting of devices had become a matter of decided importance to French printers and bibliographers, — at any rate by the seventeenth century, is strongly suggested in a quaint work of Adrian Baillet, entitled *Jugemens des savans sur les principaux ouvrages des auteurs*, first published in Paris in 1685. The author, after discussing the infringement of devices, finds that it may be *"peut-être pas mauvais"* to include a table of the marks and devices of the principal printers and booksellers which have appeared until the middle of his century.[2]

In England, the early history of printers' devices runs parellel to that on the continent. Their use was optional and occasional and until the end of the seventeenth century their infringement was not the subject of litigation, — and even then, as we shall see, quite incidentally. Indeed McKerrow, in his introduction to his invaluable compilation of English devices, finds English printers to have been even less consistent in the use of devices than their continental fellow-craftsmen.[3] "The fashions change," he writes, "no doubt, in these as in other things, and what in one period was a necessity to every reputable printing house and to every well printed book, in others was a thing of no moment at all.[4]

To the lack of originality in English devices and to the extent to which English printers adopted continental devices, Pollard has attributed much of the trouble in the history of English bibliography. "Thus," he points out,

the earliest device used by Pynson [*fl.* 1492–1530] seems to be adapted from that of de Talleur, that of Richard Faques [*fl.* 1500–1530] is an altered copy of Thielmann Kerver's, the "wild men" of Peter Treveris [*fl.* 1522–32] are taken from

---

[1] See C. M. Saugraine, *op. cit.*, pp. 94–5.

[2] See Adrian Baillet, *Jugemens des Savans* (2nd ed. 1722), i, pp. 400–404. In 1730 Friederich Roth-Scholtz published at Nuremburg a *Thesaurus Symbolorum et Emblematum*, reproducing 508 printers' and publishers' devices.

[3] R. B. McKerrow, *Printers and Publishers Devices*, Introd., p. xli.

[4] *Ibid.*, p. xliii.

those of Pigouchet, and John Bydell's figure of Virtue (a very ungainly and not too decent lady) is copied from a device used by Jacques Sacon, a Lyons printer of the beginning of this century. The list might easily be lengthened, and though printers borrowed each other's devices in other countries, the imitativeness of English firms is certainly exceptional.[1]

Although the first English book was printed by William Caxton in 1477,[2] he used no device until 1487,[3] and McKerrow estimates that only eleven such devices in all were used in England between 1485, when the first one was imprinted by the St. Albans press, and 1500.[4] Caxton's chief workman, Wynkyn de Worde, adopted Caxton's most famous device consisting of his initials W. C. and certain hieroglyphics said to stand for the figures 74, and in addition had no less than fifteen other devices in use at one time or another.[5]

Both legal and bibliographical writers on English devices have based their overestimation of the importance of these devices as a form of industrial property upon their misreading of the will of a famous sixteenth century printer, Reynold Wolfe, whose sign was a brazen serpent. Upon Wolfe's death his trade was continued by his wife, Johanne, who made her will on July 1, 1574,[6] bequeathing to her son, Robert Wolfe, the sign of the Brazen Serpent. Dibdin, in his *Typographical Antiquities*,[7] merely refers to this bequest of the sign of the Brazen Serpent in conjunction with the bequest of another piece of real estate known as the Chapel House. But Larwood and Hotten, in their interesting *History of Signboards*,[8]

---

[1] A. W. Pollard, "Some Notes on English Illustrated Books," in *Trans. Bibliographical Soc.*, vol. vi, p. 29 at p. 35. See also R. B. McKerrow, *op. cit.*, Introd., p. xxv.

[2] H. R. Plomer, *Short History of English Printing*, 2nd ed., p. 6.

[3] *Ibid.*, p. 14.

[4] R. B. McKerrow, *op. cit.*, Introd. pp. xi, xli.

[5] H. Plomer, *op. cit.*, pp. 30–31. For an interesting combination of several marks on one title-page, see 1609 Edition of Spenser's *Faerie Queene* reproduced on the opposite page and described by Silvanus Thompson, "Peter Short and His Marks," in *Trans. Bibliographical Soc.*, vol. iv, p. 124; R. B. McKerrow, *op. cit.*, Device No. 335, described p. 130.

[6] Printed in full abstract in H. R. Plomer, *Abstracts from the Wills of English Printers and Stationers from 1492 to 1630*, pp. 19–22.

[7] Vol. iv, p. 6.

[8] 3rd ed. 1908, p. 7.

THE
SECOND
PART OF THE
FAERIE QVEENE:

Containing

The $\begin{cases} \text{FOVRTH,} \\ \text{FIFT, \&} \\ \text{SIXT BOOKE.} \end{cases}$

By Ed. Spenser.

Imprinted at London for *Mathew Lownes.*
1609.

TITLE PAGE OF 1609 EDITION OF SPENSER'S *FAERIE QUEENE* SHOWING A PRINTER'S DEVICE COMBINING THE BRAZEN SERPENT (IN CENTRAL OVAL), TWO PRINTER'S DEVICES OF PETER SHORT (RIGHT AND LEFT CENTER), HIS MONOGRAM (LOWER RIGHT), AND THE ARMS OF STATIONERS' COMPANY (LOWER LEFT).

quoting the passage in question from Dibdin, state: "No wonder then, that a sign was considered an heirloom and descended from father to son . . ., which was the case with the Brazen Serpent, the sign of Reynold Wolfe." The same reference by Dibdin to the bequest of the Brazen Serpent has also been quoted by Mr. E. S. Rogers, in his article entitled "Some Historical Matter Concerning Trademarks",[1] as evidence that "these symbols were regarded as valuable property." Roberts, in his work on *Printers' Marks*, likewise states that the "possession" of the Brazen Serpent "was considered of sufficient importance to merit special mention among the goods bequeathed by his [*i.e.* Wolfe's] widow to her son Robert."[2]

All these references to the bequest of the Brazen Serpent are evidently produced by a confusion in the minds of their authors between the signs that were used by printers,[3] in common with other tradesmen, over their shops and to denominate their places of business, with the devices used by printers or publishers in their books.[4] It is true that certain printers both in England and on the continent used their signs as the bases of their devices,[5] but the most perfunctory study of English as well as continental devices will show that such a coincidence of sign and device had no legal significance and was furthermore by no means the general rule. The distinction between a printer's sign and his device is clearly

---

[1] 9 *Michigan Law Review*, p. 36. This statement is repeated by Mr. Rogers in *Good Will, Trade-marks and Unfair Trading* (1919) pp. 42–3.

[2] W. Roberts, *op. cit.*, p. 20.

[3] See H. R. Plomer, *Abstract from the Wills of English Printers and Stationers, 1492–1630*, p. 23, where various premises are referred to by names such as "The Sign of the Green Dragon," "The Sign of the Parott and Angell."

[4] See R. R. Sharpe, *Calendar of Wills*, ii, p. 711, bequest of a dwelling house called "The Sign of the Lute and Maydenheads"; also, p. 723, bequest of the "Grene Dragon." As has been pointed out by Mr. E. G. Duff: "There does not seem to have been any kind of copyright in the signs themselves." (E. G. Duff, *A Century of the English Book Trade*, Introd. p. xviii.) See *ibid.*, Appendix III for index of London printers' and stationers' signs before 1558.

[5] E.g., Thos. Berthelet, who succeeded Pynson as the King's Printer, used the latter's sign, *Lucretia Romana*, in 1535 and 1554 as his devices. (See R. B. McKerrow, *op. cit.*, Device No. 80, p. 27.) John Bydell used a device consisting of a sign where he traded from 1533 to 1535, — "Our Lady of Pity" — together with his merchandise marks. (See R. B. McKerrow, *op. cit.*, Device No. 82, p. 27.) For similar examples on the continent see W. Roberts, *op. cit.*, pp. 8–9.

illustrated in the case of Julian Notary, who from about 1498 to 1518 printed at various establishments in London, known as "At the Sign of the Three Kings."[1] He never used the "Three Kings" in any of his devices.[2]

A full abstract of the will of Johanne Wolfe has been published by Mr. Plomer and in several places it specifically refers to "that tenement . . . called or known by the sign of the Brazen Sarpent",[3] again to "my saide dwelling house called the Brazen Sarpente,"[4] and to "the saide Tenement called the brason Sarpent."[5] The will specifically bequeathes to Robert Wolfe "the presses, letters, furniture, Coppies and other necessarie tooles being within my prynting house or belonging vnto the same for concerning or belonging to the arte of prynting,"[6] but contains no reference whatsoever to the *device* of the Brazen Serpent. The subsequent history of the device of the Brazen Serpent which, it may be remarked, had originally been borrowed by Reynold Wolfe from foreign printers[7] shows that Robert Wolfe never used the mark of the Brazen Serpent, but that this mark was used from time to time by Henry Binnerman and another apprentice of Reynold Wolfe as well as by successors of Henry Binnerman.[8]

There is, therefore, no evidence at all in the will of Johanne Wolf, — nor indeed in any of the published wills in connection with the printing trade[9] — of the actual bequest of a printer's device. McKerrow in his "Notes on the Transfer of Marks from One Printing-House to Another"[10] gives no indication of any legal machinery by which transfers of printers'

[1] See E. G. Duff, *op. cit.*, Introd. p. xviii; Roberts, *op. cit.*, p. 61.
[2] See R. B. McKerrow, *op. cit.*, Devices, Nos. 8, 13, 26, 28.
[3] H. R. Plomer, *op. cit.*, p. 20.
[4] *Ibid.*, p. 20.
[5] *Ibid.*, p. 20.
[6] *Ibid.*, p. 20.
[7] See Dibdin's *Typographical Antiquities*, iv, p. 2 and 3rd note thereto.
[8] For the history of the *caduceus* device and its use in England and on the continent see Silvanus B. Thompson, *op. cit.*, p. 163; H. R. Plomer, "The Eliot's Court Printing House," in *The Library*, 4th Ser., vol ii, pp. 177, 179; also R. B. McKerrow, *op. cit.*, No. 293, p. 114. As to the subsequent history of the shop called "The Brazen Serpent," see H. R. Plomer, *Wills*, p. 23, n. (4).
[9] See wills in H. R. Plomer, *Wills;* Gray and Palmer, *Wills of Cambridgeshire Printers;* S. Gibson, *Abstracts from the Wills of Oxford Printers.*
[10] R. B. McKerrow, *op. cit.*, pp. 164 *et seq.*

devices might have been effected; that is to say, by will or descent, by deed, by bill of sale or otherwise. Indeed, the carelessness with which the blocks from which these devices were printed were sometimes handled would lead one to believe that the wood or metal block itself, the tangible property, rather than the device itself, or the intangible property, was alone of importance. As McKerrow has pointed out,

> The owner of a device would send it to a printer to be used in a particular book which was being printed for him. . . . When, however, the publisher died or went out of business there was a considerable chance that the device would not be reclaimed, and I suppose after a certain time the printer would feel quite justified in considering it as his own.[1]

Furthermore, those printers or stationers who did care to use devices, were not under any compulsion to register them when recording their publications with the Stationers' Company. In fact, in striking contradistinction to the records of the Cutlers' and Goldsmiths' Companies or to the municipal registries for coopers' marks, the registers of the stationers contained no entries concerning the registration or transfer of printers' or stationers' marks.

Edward Arber, in his introduction to the *Transcript of Registers* of the Stationers' Company, thus describes the function of these Registers: " . . . the primary object of these book entries was to account for the fees received in connection therewith . . . the *Registers* — most precious as they are to posterity — are practically in their original intention the subsidiary cash books of a London guild. . . ."[2]

As further evidence of the little regard in which these devices were held as species of property or as legal symbols of im-

---

[1] *Ibid.*, pp. xlvi–xlvii.

[2] E. Arber, *Transcript of Registers, 1554–1640*, vol. iii, Introd. p. 18; see also Eyre and Rivington, *Transcript of the Registers of the Company of Stationers, 1640–1708*, vol. i, Preface, p. v: "At no time was the Register complete, for in its inception it was simply a record of the property of members of the Stationers' Company established by the Governing Body with the object of avoiding disputes as to ownership, and it does not include publications issued under Letters Patent and other Royal grants. . . ."

portance, it should be noted that, while in other trades royal charters or licenses contained a specific grant of a mark or of the right to use a mark [1] for distinguishing products made under the royal authority, such was not the case with patents or licenses for printing. Reynold Wolfe's license as printer to the king, granted in 1547,[2] Thomas Vautrollier's patent of 1574 to print the Bible, Ovid, Cicero and other books for ten years,[3] John Day's three privileges for the printing of various books including the *A. B. C. with a little cathechisme* and for the printing of music,[4] and similar privileges and patents for the printing of music [5] contained no reference to marks.[6]

In connection with the enforcement of these printing monopolies and also with the suppression of heresy — the main considerations of governmental control of the book industry,[7] — it is evident that if a printer's device was no asset, neither was it a liability. As to the tracing of heretical publications through such devices, McKerrow writes:

No doubt in cases where it was very important to conceal the origin of a book, the printer would attempt to eliminate all traces whatever of his work, but a comparatively large number of books are to be found in which the printer seems not to have wished to advertise his share, and yet not particularly anxious to conceal it. Thus the printer of the three "Pasquil" tracts against the Martinists in 1589–90 refrained from putting his name on them, using such fantastic imprints as "printed between the sky and the ground within a mile of an oak", . . . and "printed where I was," but nevertheless placed on these tracts a device which must surely have revealed to those in the trade from whose press they came.[8]

[1] See *infra*, p. 94, n. 4.
[2] Dibdin, *op. cit.*, iv, pp. 4–5.
[3] E. Arber, *op. cit.*, ii, p. 745.
[4] Reprinted by R. Steele in *Earliest English Music Printing* (Bibliographical Soc. Illustrated Monographs, No. XI), pp. 21 *et seq.* I am indebted to Mr. H. R. Plomer for this reference.
[5] *Ibid.*, pp. 26–29.
[6] Nor did the privilege given to Aldus by the Senate of Venice in 1502 contain any such reference. (See A. Firmin-Didot, *Alde Manuce*, Paris 1875, p. 479.)
[7] A. Birrell, *The Law and History of Copyrighting Books*, pp. 49 *et seq.*
[8] R. B. McKerrow, *op. cit.*, pp. xlii–xliii. For an ingenious but fantastic and thrilling rather than convincing theory that printers' devices themselves

At the end of the sixteenth century printers' devices came for the first time under the scrutiny of English law. The first case involving the misuse of a printers' device occurs in 1581 in connection with a patent for the printing of the *A.B.C. with a little cathechisme* which had been granted to John Day and to which we have referred above. Day, who achieved remarkable typographical skill,[1] had three devices.[2] In 1580 Day became Master of the Stationers' Company[3] and two years later he became engaged in a series of lawsuits for the enforcement of the monopoly granted by his patent in the *A. B. C. with a little cathechisme*.[4] In the Bill of Complaint to the Privy Council in this case of *Day* v. *Ward* no allegation is made as to the misuse of Day's mark but solely as to the unauthorized setting of Day's name to the fraudulent edition of the *A. B. C. with a little cathechisme*. Among the evidence adduced by Day was the imitation of the particular type used by him in printing the *A. B. C. with a little cathechisme*, and also the use of one of his marks. The interrogatories to the defendant in this case which was heard in the Star Chamber inquired "whi . . . was the marke of the sayd John Day sett therunto and who made you the same marke."[5] The reply to this question is:

To the iiij he saith he doth not knowe what the cause was whie the name of the said John Day was sett thervnto . . . but the cause whie the marke of the said John Day was put therunto was to th[e] ende to haue the same artificiall as those were which passyd from the said John Daye and it was a Frencheman Dwelling within the blackefriers whose name he knoweth not that made the same marke for this defendant.[6]

were used, with water-marks, for secret symbolic communication by various heretical sects, see Harold Bayley, *A New Light on the Renaissance* (London 1909) ch. ix, mentioned to me by Dr. S. L. Wolff of Columbia University. *Cf.* criticisms in C. M. Briquet, *Les Filigranes*, vol. i, Introd. pp. 8–10, also in *The Bookman*, vol. xxix, p. 531; The *Athenæum*, vol. ii, p. 327.
[1] D. B. Updike, *Printing Types, their History, Form and Use*, ii, p. 90.
[2] H. R. Plomer, *Short History of English Printing*, p. 80.
[3] *Ibid.*, p. 77.
[4] For the history of this case see *ibid.*, pp. 77 *et seq.*; G. Unwin, *Gilds and Companies of London*, p. 259.
[5] E. Arber, *op. cit.*, ii, p. 758.
[6] *Ibid.*, ii, p. 760.

Of course this answer may have been sheer fraud but it is
unlikely that the suggestion would have been made that
Day's mark had been used to make the infringing work
"artificiall," that is to say, to display special art or skill,[1]
unless it possessed at least some degree of plausibility. In
other words it is possible that even as late as the case of *Day*
v. *Ward* printers' devices were regarded as essentially of a
decorative nature. In any event, it is quite evident from a
study of the interrogatories in this case that the question of
the infringement of Day's mark was quite incidental to that
of the infringement of Day's patent.[2] Despite the evident
interest in the case of *Day* v. *Ward*, the first Star Chamber
decree regulating printing, promulgated June 23, 1586,[3]
makes no mention of marks. The second Star Chamber
decree regulating printing, 1637, provides as follows:

. . . That no person or persons whatsoeuer, shall hereafter
print, or cause to be printed, or shall forge, put, or counterfeit
in, or vpon any book or books, the name, title, marke or
vinnet of the Company or Society of Stationers, or of any
particular person or persons, which hath or shall haue lawful
priuiledge, authoritie, or allowance to print the same, without
the consent of the said Company or party or parties that are
or shall be so priuiledged, authorized, or allowed to print the
same booke or books, thing or things, first had and obtained,
vpon paine that euery person or persons so offending, shall
not onely loose all such books and other things, but shall also
have and suffer such punishment, by imprisonment of his
body, fine, or otherwise, as by this Honourable Court, or high
Commission Court respectiuely, as the seuerall causes shall.
require, it shall be to him or them limited or adiudged.[4]

It was not until 1662 that for the first time the printing
trade became the subject of parliamentary, instead of royal
regulation. The Statute of 14 Charles II, the objects of which

[1] Murray's *New English Dictionary*, i, p. 473.
[2] T. B. Reed, *History of Old English Letter Foundries*, pp. 125–6, suggests
that this was a case of the infringement of type rather than infringement of
a mark. *Cf.* H. F. Brown, *The Venetian Printing Press*, pp. 48 *et seq.* concerning
the forgeries of the Aldean Italic.
[3] E. Arber, *op. cit.*, ii, p. 607.
[4] E. Arber, *op. cit.*, iv, p. 531.

were declared therein to be the prevention of the dissemination of "heretical schismatical blasphemous seditious and treasonable Bookes Pamphlets and Papers" and the general control of the printing trade,[1] reproduces substantially [2] the provision concerning the counterfeiting of devices from the second Star Chamber decree quoted above. It will be noted that in neither the Star Chamber decree of 1637 nor the statute of 1662 is there any suggestion, much less compulsion, of the registration of devices.

Recapitulating the results of the foregoing investigation, we find that printers' and publishers' devices, as such, appeared to have originated as simple marks of personality which gradually acquired a decorative function rather than any particular legal significance. They were used optionally and occasionally,[3] not compulsorily or consistently. From the legal standpoint they constitute neither asset (except perhaps in France in the middle of the sixteenth century) nor liability. While the blocks with which they have been printed may have been transmissible by will, gift, or other legal machinery, there is no evidence that the devices themselves were so transferable.

[1] See *Stat. of the Realm*, v, 428 *et seq.* (14 Car. II, c. 33, Preamble and cl. VI) also A. W. Pollard, "Some Notes on the History of Copyright in England, 1662–1674," in *The Library*, 4th Ser., vol. iii, p. 97. This Act lapsed toward the end of 1679; in 1685 it was renewed for seven years and then for one year more, and was then finally dropped.

[2] "VI. No person or persons shall hereafter print or cause to bee imprinted nor shall forge, put or counterfeit in or upon any Books or Pamphlet the Name, Title, Marke or Vinnet of any other person or persons which hath or shall have lawfull Priviledge, Authority or Allowance of sole printing the same, without the free consent of the person or persons so priviledged first had and obtained."

[3] In this respect printers' and publishers' devices resembled paper marks, the first appearance of which in Europe antedated the twin-shields of Fust and Schoeffer by almost two hundred years. C. M. Briquet in his introduction to his great work on paper marks, *Les filigranes* (Paris 1907), states (vol. i, p. 10) that for a long time prior to the appearance of the first paper mark in Europe — a cross — about 1282, papers had been manufactured both by the Arabs and by European paper makers without any mark at all; further (p. 17) that after the introduction of paper marks the same mark was used simultaneously by many paper makers and that despite many complaints as to the counterfeiting of paper marks the practice seems to have been fairly common.

CHAPTER IV

TRADE–MARKS AND THE NATIONAL REGULATION OF
INDUSTRY — THE CLOTH TRADE

IN the previous chapter we have seen that the characteristics of the typical craftsman's mark of the Middle Ages were: (1) that it was compulsory, not optional; (2) that its purpose was the preservation of gild standards of production and the enforcement of gild or other local monopolies rather than the impressing on the mind of the purchaser the excellence of the product in question and thereby the creation of a psychological need for that product; (3) that, consequently, while the modern trade-mark is distinctly an asset to its owner, the medieval craftsman's mark was essentially a liability. These characteristics of the medieval mark we have ascribed to a great extent to the proximity of the producer to the consumer and of one producer to another, and also to the theory and practice of gild control of industries in each locality.

When, however, we come to industries such as the cloth and cutlery trades, the situation is quite different. In these trades is clearly noticeable the evolution of the trade-mark from a mark of origin to a mark of quality and hence from a liability to an asset, of distinct value to the owner of the mark. In a later chapter we shall trace the systems of trade-mark law developed by the cutlers of London and Sheffield, and we shall find that, while the rivalry between the cutlers of London and Sheffield was very great, the rivalry between the members themselves in each of these centers of industry appears to have been no less keen, with a consequent emphasis upon the importance of individual cutlers' marks. On the other hand, in the cloth trade, the trade-marks which became of importance and the subject of protection were not only those of individual clothiers but, to a more considerable degree, the collective marks of the centers of the cloth industry. Furthermore, while the cutlers developed their own law mainly within their own organizations, the development of trade-mark law in the cloth industry was, as we shall see, largely the creation of administrative law concerned with the national expansion of that industry. While we shall refer first to the protection of collective or geographical marks and shall perforce devote considerably more space to these marks than to individual marks, we shall find the development of the latter to be of at least as great significance as that of the former.

The idea of a collective good-will enjoyed by a given locality or organization and of the protection of a mark or seal as the symbol of that collective good-will is very common in the history of medieval as well as of modern commerce.[1] We have seen in the preceding chapter that practically every gild, in the exercise of its right of search or supervision, affixed its seal or mark to the products of its members.[2] In many instances, these seals or marks or the symbols of the municipal authorities became assets of great value to the corporation or *universitas* from which they emanated, and goods to which they were affixed were sold merely upon the strength of these marks without the formality of opening or carefully scrutinising the bales or bolts to which they were affixed. The Parisian weavers, for instance, sought to prevent the use of the phrase *façon de Paris* upon foreign-made goods;[3] at Ypres, towards the end of the thirteenth century the pieces of cloth stamped with the name of the town numbered eight thousand a year.[4] The mark of the town of Osnabrück, the center of the Westphalian linen industry, was held in so great respect and esteem abroad that, in England, in the

---

[1] Recent examples of the protection of "regional good-will" are to be found in Sheffield steel, Rochester clothing, Durham tobacco, Minnesota flour, Swedish matches, champagne, cognac, Madeira, Rhine and Moselle wines, Pilsen beer. See Hopkins on *Trade-marks*, 4th ed., pp. 67 *et seq.*; G. C. Henderson, *The Federal Trade Commission*, pp. 189–90; W. Notz, "New Phases of Unfair Competition and Measures for Its Suppression" in 30 *Yale Law Journal* 384, at pp. 392 *et seq.*; also *infra*, p. 105, n. 2, at p. 106.

[2] See *supra*, p. 44.

[3] M. de Gailhard-Bancel, *Les anciennes corporations de métiers*, p. 101.

[4] G. Renard, *Guilds in the Middle Ages*, (ed. Cole), p. 34.

middle of the fifteenth century, linen bearing this mark commanded a price twenty per cent higher than other West-phalian linens.[1] A similar development of collective good-will and of corporate and regional marks is to be found in the case of the weavers of Barcelona and Torroella,[2] in the gilds of Florence [3] and in the famous cutlery and armor manufac-turing centers at Toledo, Ferrara, Passau and Solingen.[4]

In England the development of corporate or collective marks is particularly conspicuous in the cloth industry and is, in its origins, to a considerable degree associated with the royal interest in and regulation of the trade. In the later Middle Ages wool was the main article of export from Eng-land.[5] "But England was not content," writes Ashley, "thus to furnish Europe with the raw material: its government made continuous and strenuous efforts to gain for it the manufacture also; and its measures succeeded. Cloth be-came 'the basis of our wealth' and at the end of the seven-teenth century, woolen goods were 'two-thirds of England's exports.' " [6] In these constant efforts of the crown to capture and maintain supremacy in the European cloth markets and also in its efforts to derive as much custom as possible from the trade, (and incidentally to insure for the subjects of the realm the maintenance of certain standards in the manufac-ture of clothing) the government began to foster and protect the reputation of the trade-marks of the various centers of industry in England. Of course, just as in the case of the individual craftsman whose trade-mark began as a purely regulatory or liability mark, so in the case of the corpora-tions or localities engaged in the cloth industry the affixing of seals was a compulsory part of the scheme of national regulation.

In discussing the relation of national regulation of the cloth

---

[1] H. Potthoff, *Die Leinenleggen in der Grafschaft Ravensburg*, pp. 38–9.
[2] D. R. Pela, *Marcas de Fábrica*, p. 18.
[3] E. Staley, *The Guilds of Florence*, 2nd ed., p. 148 (woolen cloth); p. 262. (mercers, veilmakers, perfumers and stationers).
[4] See C. Ffoulkes, *The Armourer and His Craft*, p. 70.
[5] W. J. Ashley, *Economic History*, i, pt. ii, p. 191.
[6] *Loc. cit.*

industry to the development of trade-mark law, it will not be necessary to consider at any length the causes of the decay of the gilds or the effect of this decay upon the supervision of industry by the gilds. From very early times the crown undertook the regulation of the cloth industry.[1] This Royal supervision was effected partly through officials of the crown and partly through the gild officials acting practically in the same capacity.[2] "It was in the nature of things inevitable," says Lipson,

that the dealers, who traded in cloth, should organize the different branches of the woolen industry under their own control. The gild system broke down earlier in the weaving industry than in any other direction. The rapid growth of the cloth trade was incompatible with the old restrictions, and the manufacture overflowed from the towns into the suburbs and country districts, where it ran its course free from any impediment or restraint.[3]

In the fifteenth century, outside the towns, to quote Ashley again, "a new class of men called *clothiers* or *clothmakers* to arose, commanding an amount of capital great relatively previous conditions and bringing into dependence upon them selves large numbers of work-people."[4] However, the replacement of the gilds by the domestic system, or the transformation of the gilds "to be at once the organs of and subject to national regulation"[5] does not, as we shall see, retard, but rather accelerates and broadens the development of trade-mark law. With the capitalists who engaged extensively in the manufacture of cloth, the government entered into direct relationship,[6] and the crown came to concern itself more and more with the various individual weavers' and clothiers' marks, as well as with both gild and town seals.

Without attempting to trace the evolution of the cloth

[1] See E. Lipson, *op. cit.*, ch. ix.
[2] W. Cunningham, *op. cit.*, p. 226.
[3] E. Lipson, *op. cit.*, pp. 415–16.
[4] W. J. Ashley, *op. cit.*, pt. ii, p. 222.
[5] W. Cunningham, *op. cit.*, p. 447; see also *ibid.*, pp. 509 *et seq.*
[6] See Stat. 4 Edw. IV, c. 1, *Stat. of the Realm*, ii, p. 404.

industry, it should be observed that, by the end of the fifteenth century, a large number of important local varieties of cloth, such as Bristol, Norwich, Guildford, Colchester, Kendal, Coventry and Taunton had acquired individual reputations, which naturally enhanced the value of cloths made not only in the particular towns in question, but in cloth-making settlements in proximity to these towns. For instance, a statute of 15 Richard II, enacted in 1391 and containing "the first definite notice we have of the cloth-making industry of Surrey",[1] recites that "of old times divers cloths were made in the town of Guildford and other places within the counties of Surrey, Sussex and Southampton, called Cloths of Guildford, *which were of good making and of good value, and did bear a great name. . . ."*[2]

That these local reputations were most jealously guarded by the local authorities, quite irrespective of their protection by the crown, is well illustrated in the cases of Salisbury and Coventry. In a Convocation at Salisbury held in 1417 before the Mayor and Council proceedings were taken against a counterfeiter of the City cloth seal, Salisbury being then noted for its "motley cloths and whites."[3]

As early as 1398 trade in the "frieze of Coventry" had become international. "In that year £200 worth, the export of one merchant, lay in the port of distant Stralsund on the Baltic Coast."[4] *Frise de Coventre* is also mentioned in a statute of the following year, together with Cogware, Kendal Cloth and Cloth of Kersey.[5] "In London and other places the cloth was in great request during the fifteenth and early sixteenth centuries. But about 1518 there was a great depression in the local industry."[6] In that year the Leet Court, which was largely in the hands of the great cloth merchants

---

[1] *History of the County of Surrey*, (Victoria History of the Counties of England, ii, p. 342).
[2] C. 10, *Stat. of the Realm*, ii, p. 81. (Italics the writer's.)
[3] *Modern History of Wiltshire*, iii (Ed. by R. Benson and H. Hatcher), pp. 113–114.
[4] M. D. Harris, *Life in an Old English Town*, p. 253.
[5] 1 Hen. IV, c. 19 (1399) *Stat. of the Realm*, ii, p. 119.
[6] M. D. Harris, *op. cit.*, p. 253.

of Coventry,[1] in an evident desire to retrieve the lost trade in frieze, enacted "an order for the True Makinge of Clothe" which clearly indicates the importance to the trade and the town of attaching the noted town seal — the elephant — to cloth of very high standard:

Hit is to be had in mynde that for a trueth of Clothmakyng to be had in this Cite as foloeth, if it myght be folowed & the execucion of the same to be don schortly, Or else the Cite wol-be so fer past that it wol-be past remedie to be recouered to eny welth or prosperite– hit is thought hit were good to haue ij weuers & ij walkers [fullers] sworn to make true serche of the weuers doyng & also fo the walkers & to present the trueth: and also to be chosen vj Drapers to be Maisters & Ouerseers of the doyng of the serchers, That if some of them cannot a-lesour to be at the serchyng at the dayes of the serchers yet some of these vj Maisters schall euer be ther; and by-cause it were to great a besynes for the serchers to go to euery mannes howse, hit is enacted (etc.) to haue a howse of the gilde or of some other mannes nyghe the Drapery doore to be ordeyned Well with perches to drawe ouer the Clothes when they be thykked, and also weightes & ballaunce to wey the Cloth. And when it cometh frome the walkers, The walkers to bryng it to the serchyng house, & to serche it & to se it ouer a perche; and if it be good Cloth, as it owght to be, in brede & lengh, that the Cite may haue a preise by hit & no sklaunder, then to sett vpon hit the Olyvaunt [the elephant and castle are the city arms] in lede, and of the Bak of the seall the lengh of the Cloth, by the which men schall perceyve & see it is true Couentre Cloth; ffor of suertie ther is in London & other places that sell false & vntrewe made Cloth, & name hit Couentre Cloth, the which is a gret [er] slaunder to the Cite than hit deserueth by a gret partie. And if ther be eny man that hath eny Cloth brought to the serchyng house, what degre so euer he be of, if it be not able for the worship of the Cite to be let passe, let hym pay for the serche & lett hym do his best with hit, but set not the Olyvaunt vpon it.[2]

[1] *Ibid.*, pp. 258–9.

[2] *Coventry Leet Book*, (Early English Text Society), ed. M. D. Harris, pp. 656–7. The official recognition or even authorization of the surreptitious disposal of sub-standard goods in such a way as not to injure the town or gild from which they emanated is not unusual; Renard (*Guilds in the Middle Ages*, ed. Cole, p. 34) mentions the deliberations of the medieval goldsmiths of Paris concerning a plated bowl which might have been mistaken for solid

The necessity or desirability of regulating the sealing of cloth by the towns is evident from the statute of 1 Richard III (1483–4), c. 8, which provided that:

afore the seid fest [of St. Michael the Archangel] by the Treasurer of England be provided and ordeigned Seales to be impressed in lede havyng [the Royal] Armes of Englond on the oon side and on the other syde the Armes signe or tokyn of every Citee Burgh or Towne within this Realme when the Cloth is made, havyng any such armes signe or tokyn, for a merke and evident tokyn and knowlege of the Cloth made within every suche Citee Burgh and Town of this Realme; and over that Seales for every Shire of this Reame for the sealyng of all maner Cloth made within every Shire. . . .[1]

So detailed did the legislation concerning marks in the cloth industry become that even individual weavers' marks in some localities were the subject of regulation.[2]

During the reign of Elizabeth, in which came the strong centralization of the control of industry, with the Council as the "pivot" of the system,[3] the seals on cloth appear to have

metal: "It was decided after deliberation, to sell it secretly, and he was cautioned never to make another." The wardens of the Grocers of London likewise, upon examining John Palmer for selling ginger not up to standard, fined him 5 marks, and "they ordered the corrupt ginger to be sealed up and sent oversea, there to be sold. . . ." (J. A. Rees, *The Worshipful Company of Grocers*, p. 99.)

[1] 1 Ric. III (1483–4) c. 8. *Stat. of the Realm*, ii, 486. Other legislation referring to individual towns or counties prescribed the use of *individual* weavers' marks within these areas. As early as 1467 an act regulating deceits practised in the making of worsteds in Norfolk and Norwich required "that no Man of the said Craft make any Worsted unless he put *his proper Mark fixed or woven* (*son propre signe tistez ou entexez*) upon the same, by the Ordinance of the said Warders." (7 Edw. IV, 1467, c. 1, *Stat. of the Realm*, ii, 420.)

[2] For local requirements as to registration of weavers' marks in Norwich, see Acts of Assembly (1460) in *Records of the City of Norwich* (ed. Hudson and Tingey), ii, No. CLXII, p. 94, also Act of Assembly, 19 July 1580, No. CCXLVI, p. 145. An Act of 14 and 15 Henry VIII, c. 3 (1523), regulating the weaving industries of Yarmouth and Lynn, requires the Wardens of those towns to "lymytte distyncte and severall markes to every of the said Worstede Weavers of the same Towne and the same markes by the said Warden to be registred in a book." (*Stat. of the Realm*, iii, 210.) In 1534 "an Acte for makinge of Worstedes in the citie of Norwiche and yn the towns of Lynne and Yermouth," it was likewise enacted that ". . . everie Warden of the said Towne shulde lymytte distincte and severall markes to everie of the said Worsted weavers of the same Towne of greate Yermouthe and the same Markes by the said Warden to be regestrid in a boke." (26 Hen. VIII, c. 16, *Stat. of the Realm*, iii, 511.)

[3] W. Cunningham, *op. cit.*, ii, p. 53, The Privy Council delved into such minute industrial questions as the recovery of broadcloth stolen from a Dublin

been the subject of much popular interest and comment. The famous preacher, Clement Armstrong, writing (circa 1535) on "How to reforme the Realme in Settyng them to work and to restore Tillage", exhorts the king

to make a staple of all wollen clothes in London and that all clothe makers . . . dwell to gethers in market townes like as in old tyme, and that every market towne of clothe making have a common seale . . . to recourde the trew making of wollen clothes so sealed with the sealles of the towns, wherein they be made. . . [1]

England, says Armstrong, "shall cause the more nombre of common people to drape clothes and to worke theym so substancially and truly by the recorde of every towne seale. . . ."[2]

On the other hand, in *A Discourse of the Common Weal of this Realm of England*, an imaginary dialogue written about 1549, not only the credit given to the various town seals of cloth but also their subsequent debasement by their use upon inferior goods is indicated. In the second dialogue (between the doctor and the knight) the former compares the debasement of the currency and of the attempt to "marke a halfe pound with the marke of the pound, and the halfe ounce with the marke of the ounce" with the loss of credit by the towns for their seals on cloth:

. . . and they consequently lost theire credit, much like as I haue knowen certain townes in england to haue donne; which weare wount to make theire clothes of a certaine breadth and length, and to sett theire sealles to the same; while they kept theire Rate truly, strangers did but looke vppon theire seall, and received theire wares, whearby those townes had greate vent of theire cloth, and consequently prospered very well. Afterward some in the townes, not content with reasonable gaynes, continually desiringe more

merchant (*Acts*, N. S., xxv, 1595, p. 49), abuses in the leather trade in Devon (*ibid.*, xxvii, 1597, p. 260), and the right to make and sell gingerbread in Norwich (*ibid.*, xxviii, 1597, p. 417). See also W. S. Holdsworth, *Hist. of English Law*, iv, p. 360.

[1] Reinhold Pauli, *Drei Volkswirthschaftliche Denkschriften aus der Zeit Heinrichs VIII von England* (Göttingen 1878), p. 65.

[2] *Ibid.*, p. 70.

and more, devised clothes of lesse lengthe, breadthe, and goodnes then they weare wounte to be, and yet, by [the commendacion] of the seall, to haue as muche monie for the same as they had before for good clothes; and for a time they gat much, and so abased the credit of theire prodescessors to theire singuler luker, which was recompensed with the losse of theire posteritie; for after these clothes weare founde faultie, for all theire sealles they weare not only never the better trusted, but much lesse for theire seall, yea, thoughe theire clothes weare well made; for whan theire falsehod and vntrewth was espied, then no man would bie theire clothes till they weare searched and vnfolded, Regardinge nothinge the seall. And yet, because they found theim vntrew in sume part, they mistrusted theim in other; and so would give lesse for theire clothes then they would for anie other like, havinge no sealles to the same; whearby the credit of the same townes was lost, and the townes vtterly decayd.[1]

In the third dialogue the doctor again mentions the importance of the town seals or trade-marks: "Also an other thinge I recken woulde healpe muche to releve oure townes decayed, yf they could take order that all the wares made theire should haue a speciall marke, and that marke to be set to none but to suche as be truly wrought." [2]

In view of the popular desire to be able to continue the purchase of cloth upon the basis of their seals and in view also of the great losses to the clothing trade and consequently to the royal revenues occurring through the debasement of these seals, it is not surprising that the whole subject of trade-marks upon clothing, both individual and collective, soon came under the observation and regulation of the Privy Council. In 1591 an Act of the Privy Council, referring to the "ambiguous abridgement" by the clothiers of Wiltshire, Gloucestershire, Somerset and Oxon of the seals required by the statutes of 27 Edward III[3] and 27 Henry VIII[4] to indicate the true amount

[1] *A Discourse of the Common Weal of this Realm of England* (ed. E. Lamond) pp. 77–8). Miss Mary Dormer Harris, the editor of the Coventry Leet Book and the historian of Coventry, quoted above, to whom I am indebted for this reference, writes, November 12, 1923, that in her opinion this quotation clearly refers to the seal upon Coventry cloth.
[2] *Ibid.*, p. 130.   [3] *i.e.*, 27 Edw. III, stat. i, c. 4 (*Stat. of the Realm*, i, 330–1).
[4] *I.e.*, 27 Hen. VIII, c. 12 (*ibid.*, iii, 544).

of yardage, "by which abuse Her Majestie in her custome may be much deceaved," also refers to the weavers' private marks in the following language:

> . . . it is therefore this daye ordered by their Lordships for avoiding of these inconveniences that the said cloathes (*sic*) shal from henceforth weave into every of their said white broad cloathes hereafter to be made their proper markes or tokens according to the statute of 27 Henry 8. How-beit whereas some clothiers have used in some few cloathes of greater price to work in with a needle with threed of gold or copper guilt their said markes for the beautifieng of their said fine cloaths, their Lordships thinke yt not inconvenient that the clothiers of Wiltes, Glocester, Somerset and Oxon should continue their use in that behalfe yf they shal thinke yt good, so that they do not omyt also to weave their markes or tokens into the said cloathes according to the said statute. . . .[1]

In the following year the Council intervened to protect the individual marks of a Taunton clothier [2] with the following order:

> A letter to Hugh Portman, John Coles, Gabriell Hawley and William Hall, or to anie 3 or 2 of them. Whereas a peticion hathe ben exhibited unto us by John Godsall of Tanton in the countie of Somerset, clothier, wherein he complaineth as well of a greate abuse commytted by one John Cole and other badd persons in makinge of cloth in those partes with flockes and thrummes and dyinge of them in false cullours, as in counterfaictinge to the same false clothes the usuall markes (long tyme used by the suppliant, and other clothiers which make clothe of good and perfect stuff). If therefore the informacion be true, yt ys fraud and deceipt that deserveth to be severelie punished, and a greate abuse besides unto this suppliant and the rest that are true makers of cloth, in so moche as theire clothes which heretofore have ben well sold and esteemed of beyond the seas (by the deceipt of these badd persons) are now greatlie dyscredyted. Wee have therefore thought good to praie and require you by

---

[1] *Acts of the Privy Council of England*, New Ser., xxi, 1591, pp. 98–9.
[2] For Taunton cloth, which was known merely as "Tauntons," see *History of the County of Somerset* (Victoria County Histories), ii, pp. 411 *et seq.*; J. Toulmin, *History of Taunton* (ed. Savage, 1822), p. 372.

vertue hereof to call before you as well the said Godsall as John Cole and anie others of the clothiers or false makers of clothe that are chardged with this deceiptfull makinge of clothes, and to examyne by all good waies and meanes this manner of abuse, and also to viewe and conferr together the mark of this suppliant and others that are alledged to be true makers of clothe with the marke of the said Cole and others that use that fraude. The which yf you shall find to be counterfaited, wee then doe require you not onlie to certyfie us thereof and of all soche abuses which you shall perceave to have ben commytted by them and others, but also to take good and sufficient bondes to her Majesty's use of Cole and the other parties faultie by a certaine daie lymitted to appeere at the Court before us, to the ende that wee maie tak soche order for reformacion of these abuses as to us shall seeme expedyent.[1]

The strongest evidence of the interest of the national government in the protection of collective or geographical trade-marks occurs in the case of the Colchester baize industry. As early as the fourteenth century Colchester became an important center of the cloth industry.[2] But it was only upon the settlement there in 1570–1571[3] of the Flemish refugees, driven from the Low Countries by the persecution of the Duke of Alva, that Colchester acquired a particularly enviable reputation for cloth-making.[4] The so-called "Dutch congregation" was practically a semi-autonomous community under the direct supervision of the crown, and officers of the "Dutch Bay Hall" spared no effort to maintain the high standards of workmanship for which their organization soon acquired a national and later an international reputation. John

[1] *Acts of the Privy Council of England*, New Ser., xxii, 1591–2, pp. 406–7. This interest of the Privy Council in the protection of the mark of an individual clothier of Taunton is important, not merely as a recognition of the existence of individual trade-marks, but also because the particular trade-mark in question was not that of the weaver but of a *clothier*. For further discussion on this point see *infra*, pp. 94–95, in connection with the proclamation of Charles I in 1633.

[2] *History of the County of Essex* (Victoria County Histories) ii, pp. 382–3.

[3] *Ibid.*, ii, p. 387.

[4] "As early as 1568 there were not less than 1132 Flemish-speaking and 339 Walloon-speaking strangers within Norwich; and similar settlements were made in Colchester, Sandwich, Canterbury, Southampton, London, Southwark and elsewhere." (W. Ashley, *Economic History*, i, pt. ii, p. 240.)

Evelyn, in his diary, refers to Colchester as "the only place in England where these stuffs are made unsophisticated," [1] and Samuel Pepys reports a conversation with a former ambassador to Spain, who "talked much of the plain habit of the Spaniards; how the King and Lords themselves wore but a cloak of Colchester bayze." [2]

Philip Morant, in his *History and Antiquities of Colchester*,[3] thus describes the method and reasons for sealing the baize:

Among other regulations to keep up the goodness and reputation of their manufactures they had this standing rule: that all Bays should be searched and surveyed at the Dutch Bay Hall by sworn searchers maintained by their Company, and, according to the contents and the goodness of the said Bays, they were sealed, whereby the buyer or merchant might know the length and goodness of every Bay. There were Four several Sorts of Bays made in Colchester which were allowed to be sealed, viz. Rents, Cuts, Crowns, and Crosses: and different leaden Seals were affixed to each, to show what sort they were of. A Rent (so called because both the Selvages were rent off) had two leaden seals: A Cut (so called because one end was cut sloping) had three seals. A Crown-bay, being the most common sort, had four seals. A Cross-Bay, which was the last sort, had five broad leaden seals, whereof one was the same that was affixed to all sorts, the other four only to Cross-Bays.[4]

It is not to be expected that so valuable a trade-mark as that of Colchester should have gone uninfringed for any length of time. "The Bays being sold upon the credit and bare inspection of their seals," writes Morant,

without opening the bags and examining the length and goodness of them, the exactest care possible was taken to prevent all undue practices, and when discovered, to punish them . . . but these seals were, as early as the year 1588,

---

[1] *Diary of John Evelyn* (ed. Austin Dobson 1906), ii, p. 113, July 8, 1656.
[2] *Diary and Correspondence of Samuel Pepys* (ed. Bright, New York 1884), vii, p. 34, Feb. 24, 1666.
[3] (London 1748), pp. 74–5.
[4] Morant explains that there was about 30s difference in the values of a Cross, Crown, Cut or Rent. For reproductions of leaden "Bay" and "Say" seals used at Colchester, see *History of County of Essex* (Victoria County Histories), ii, Fig. 7, facing p. 388.

counterfeited by the Bay-makers at Halstead and afterwards
in London; and even falsified in this very town . . . to the
scandal of the whole nation and great prejudice of this
town. . . .[1]

The action of the Privy Council with regard to the infringement of the Colchester mark by the weavers of Halstead is
significant. These infringers were also Flemish refugees;
their settlement in Halstead was indeed an offshoot from
the Dutch Bay Hall, at Colchester.[2] Nevertheless the
Council took great care to differentiate the marks of the two
towns in the following letter to Sir Thomas Lucas and Edmund
Huddlestone (28 July 1592):

We have considered of your reporte [3] in the cause betweene
the towne of Collchester and Hallstedd concernynge the
markes they·do use to sett in theire bayes, wherein they of Collchester do find fault that Hallstedd men use the same marke
and stampe which first was used by them of Collchester, being
parte of the armes of that towne, wherein we do lyke very
well the order that ys by you devysed for more apparaunt
dyfference, that the bayes makers of Hallsted shall have a

[1] Morant, *op. cit.*, p. 75.
[2] W. J. Hardy, "Foreign Settlers at Colchester and Halstead," in *Proceedings of the Huguenot Society of London*, vol. ii, p. 182. Also *Acts of the
Privy Council*, New Ser., xix, pp. 127–8, — Letter to the Bailiffs of Colchester.
[3] Submitted in response to a request dated May 12, 1592, reading as follows:
"By a supplicacion lately exhibited unto us on the behalf of such as make baies
in the town of Colchester in the county of Essex we are geven to understand
that other of the same trade that do inhabit in the town of Halsted apperteining
to Sir William Walgrave, knight, should of late have taken upon them to sett
the same markes unto the baies by them made that they of Colchester have of
longe tyme used, notwithstanding that it [is] avouched that the said baiemakers
(*sic*) of Halsted heretofore used other marke different from that of Colchester,
that is with a crowne and six fethers. Forasmuch as for divers good considera-
cions we think it verie convenient that every corporacion and towneshipp
should reteine their owne particuler and accustomed markes for the wares
by them made, and that other straungers should not use the same, wherebie
many abuses maie be committed and by such a confuzion it cannot be knowne
where the fault is committed and maie be amended, we praie you uppon receipt
hereof to consither (*sic*) of this matter, and finding the informacion·trew, to
take order that from hence forthe they of Halstid maie be inhibeted to use
anie seale or seales comonlie heretofore used to be sett by those of Colchester
uppon the baies there made, but either to use their former markes or some
other, so as there maie be a distinction betwene th'one and th'other. Otherwise we praie you to informe us what you shall have understood tuching the
premises, and what lawfull cause maie be pretended to the contrarie, so as
there upon we maie take such other order as shalbe thought convenient. And
so praing you to use all expedicion you maie therein, we bid you, &c." (*Acts
of the Privy Council*, New Ser., xxii, 1591–2, p. 444.)

rose underneath the crowne full stamped, the second sorte two crownes one above an other with a rose full stamped at the foote of the lowest crowne, the third sorte, three crownes sett two and one with a rose full stamped at the foote of the lowest crowne, the fourth and best sort of bayes, three crownes with a plaine crosse and roase full stamped at the foote of the crosse and lowest crowne. Which performed, seeing they both doe use two seales, and the other hath in letters expressed the name of the towne, and therefore wee doe hereby require you to take order that the said towne of Halstedd maie hereafter, observe in the marking of theire bayes the said difference, and that no other towne hereafter that maie use the lyke trade shall use markes lyke to these, wherein in one respect those of Halstedd doe deserve to be favored because they sett a woork theire owne contry people in this trade. So fare you hartilie well. From, &c.[1]

The attitude of the Privy Council towards the infringement of the Colchester mark in London indicates to an even greater degree the amount of protection which they desired to give this mark and strongly supports Cunningham's statement that, in the period of the Stuarts, "the system of trade-marks seems to have established itself, at all events in the cloth trade, before very many years had elapsed."[2]

In 1632 one Thomas Jupp of London, cloth-worker, was punished for affixing counterfeit Colchester seals "to other bays of meaner condition, namely, to bays manufactured at Bocking." Under examination at the Star Chamber by the Attorney-General, Jupp admitted his fraud, disclosing an elaborate scheme for smuggling inferior cloth with Colchester seals out of the country. Jupp was fined £1000 and condemned to stand in the pillory in Cheapside, in Cornhill, at Bocking and at Colchester

upon several market days with a Paper on his head, wherein shall be inscribed words declaring the nature of his offense. At which time it is also thought fit and ordered that this Decree shall be publikely read, and severall Copies be thereof Printed, and set up upon Postes and other eminent places

---

[1] *Acts of the Privy Council*, New Ser., xxiii, 1592, pp. 76-7, July 28, 1592.
[2] W. Cunningham, *Growth of English Industry and Commerce*, iii, p. 311.

about and neere the said Pillary, to remaine there, so as the cause of his punishment may be generally knowne, and other like lewd persons deterred from committing the like offences.

And it is also further Ordered and Decreed, that the said Jupp shall in like manner be set upon the Pillary in Cornehill over against the Exchange, at Blackwell Hall, Bocking and Colchester, upon severall Market dayes, with the like Paper on his head, inscribed as is aforesaid. At all which said severall times and places it is Ordered, that this Decree bee publikely read, and that severall Printed Copies of this Decree shall also be set up on severall eminent places, on, and about, and neere the said places and Pillaries, to remaine there for the purposes aforesaid; and specially at Blackwell Hall the officers there shall continue the said Printed Copies upon Postes and open places, in, and about the said Hall so long that the Clothiers of all parts of the Kingdome comming thither may have notice thereof.[1]

The examination of Thomas Jupp reads very much like the evidence on the question of user in a modern trade-mark case:

He saith also that Colchester Bayes are commonly somewhat dearer than the Bayes of Bocking. He taketh it that Colchester Bayes sell better beyond the Sea than other Bayes, and hath long beene of that opinion. He saith, that he having long beene a Worke-man, is able to discerne a Colchester or Sandwich or Bocking Bay one from another, but other men that are not Worke-men discerne them by their Seales.[2]

The findings of the Council also have a very modern ring about them:

That the people of this Towne of Colchester and of the parts adioyning, receive a great part of their sustenance by the making of Bayes: That for many yeeres past, by occasion of the carefull Search there made, they have beene truely and

---

[1] The proceedings in this case are digested in Rushworth's *Historical Collections*, ii, pp. 148–9, and are published in full in the appendix to vol. iii, pp. 102–5. However, in view of the importance of the case and also of certain discrepancies between Rushworth's version and that of the original imprint of these proceedings by Robert Barker, the King's Printer, dated London 1632, the latter's imprint of the decree has been reproduced in full in an appendix to this chapter (*infra*, pp. 96–100.)

The decree also offered informers in similar cases in the future one-half of any fines that might be imposed by the Council. For comment upon the "*turbidum genus*" of informers created by such provisions, see W. S. Holdsworth *op. cit.*, iv, p. 356.   [2] *Infra*, pp. 96–97.

not deceitfully made, and of a knowne goodnesse: That such of them as are fully wrought are sealed with a Seale attesting their goodnesse: If upon Search any proove not so good, they are marked for such; so as the buyers both within the Realme and abroad, may bee ascertaind of the goodnesse of the Merchandize by view of the Seale, wherein (the Law requiring it) such great care hath beene had from time to time, that upon the credit of the Seale alone they were plentifully and readily vented in all places.[1]

The Restoration brought with it a confirmation of the ancient privileges of the Dutch Community of Colchester by an Act of Parliament,[2] which gave temporary relief and protection to the industry. The preamble to this statute recites that "slight and naughty Bays have been and daily are, by the secret and crafty practices of some men made in the said Towne," and, being inferior, are secretly carried out of the town unsealed and "transported beyond the Seas under the name and oftentimes with the Seal of Colchester Bayes whereby the Bayes there made are not of that credit and esteem as formerly." [3]   Clause IV of the Act provides that, for counterfeiting any of the seals used by the Corporation or Congregation of the Dutch Bay Hall in Colchester, "the summe of 20 poundes to be recovered in any of His Majesty's Courts of Record or in the Towne Court of Colchester." Despite the drastic powers of search and the severe penalties of the pillory, confiscation and imprisonment for reported counterfeiting of the seals of Colchester, the decay of the trade was so rapid that in 1728 the Dutch Congregation was dissolved and by 1826 the trade was "at so low an ebb in Colchester that only a single establishment for the manufacture of the article now commonly called baize exists in the town or out-parishes."[4]   The seal is thus, at present, solely of archæological interest.[5]

[1] *Infra*, pp. 98–99.   [2] 12 Car. II (1660), c. 22, *Stat. of the Realm*, v, p. 253.
[3] *Ibid.*, ii, 254.

[4] Thomas Cromwell, *History and Description of the Ancient Town and Borough of Colchester*, 1826, ii, pp. 288–9.

[5] For information regarding the trade and seals of Colchester I am indebted to Mr. George Rickword, Librarian and Secretary of the Public Library at Colchester.

We have seen how, under the protection of the national government, the local or collective trademarks of such places as Colchester, Coventry, Guildford, Norwich, etc., were developed and protected, and the notion of a trade-mark as an asset, rather than a liability, was fostered. But, before leaving this phase of our subject, we must refer to a proclamation of Charles I "against frauds and deceits used in Draperie." [1] It refers to and evidently was designed to clarify much preceding legislation, reciting that the "frauds and deceits used in Drapery . . . in time, if prevention be not made, may bring dis-esteeme upon the Clothes of this Realme, and decay on Draperie, by which a great number of His Maiesties people haue their livelihood." [2]

Promulgated forty years after the action of the Privy Council in protecting the mark of John Godsall of Taunton referred to above,[3] this proclamation indicates, to even a greater degree than in *Godsall's* Case, an arrival of the notion among lawyers — though not yet among judges, of a trade-mark as a symbol of good-will, as an asset of value, instead of merely as a regulatory mark of origin, and consequently a liability.[4] These two functions of a mark upon goods are very clearly differentiated in the proclamation. "Every weauer

---

[1] Cited by W. Cunningham, *Growth of English Industry and Commerce*, ii, p. 311, n. 4. Through the courtesy of the British Museum the writer has obtained a photostat copy of the five pages of this proclamation.

[2] The discredit of English cloth in foreign parts or, as we should say today, the destruction of the national good-will abroad, and consequent loss to English subjects caused by the manufacture of defective cloth, is a constant theme of English legislation and official correspondence. See *Acts of the Privy Council*, New Ser., xxii, 1591–2, pp. 89–90 (concerning the weaving of Devonshire kersies); *ibid.*, xxx, 1599–60, pp. 481–2, 490–2, 602–4, 606–7; *ibid.*, xxxi, 1601–2, pp. 387–9; *ibid.*, xxxii, 1601–4, pp. 162–5 (concerning French embargo upon British goods alleged by the French to be defective). See also Petition of the Silk men, Silk dyers, Silk weavers and Silk dealers of London "for some remedy to the great abuse in dyeing silk, whereby English silk manufactures in foreign parts are greatly injured. . . ." (*Cal. State Papers*, Dom., Charles II, 1661–2, p. 395.)

[3] *Supra*, pp. 87–88.

[4] Royal patents and grants also indicate an appreciation of the value of a symbol of good-will. The patent granted in 13 Elizabeth (1371) to Richard Matthewe of London, "our cutler", for the manufacture "of haftes . . . for knyfes" states that "for his marke to have upon the blade . . . a half Moone." (Edmunds on *Patents* (2nd ed.), Appendix, p. 885) The patent to Jones and Palmer, for hard and soft soap, in 1623 (W. H. Price, *English Patents of Monopoly*, p. 210, and the charters of 2 James II to the White Paper Makers

shall to euery Cloth that hee shall weaue, set the first two letters of his name of Baptisme and Surname, or at the least the first letter of his Surname, and no other marke. . . ." [1] This requirement is evidently merely a police regulation such as in the case of the weavers of Norwich and Yarmouth prescribed by the statute of Henry VIII.[2] But the proclamation makes a clear distinction between these marks, which the modern manufacturer would call factory marks, and the marks of the clothier, which the same modern manufacturer would call trade-marks. In other words, the proclamation not merely conceives of a trade-mark as an asset, but also regards it as symbolizing the good-will, not of the actual maker or craftsman of the goods, but of the capitalist who furnishes the material or tools for the production of the article. "And whereas," states the proclamation,

there is great abuse found to bee practised in the Markes of the Clothiers, some that make worse Cloth using the Markes of others that make best, or making of so slight a difference from it, as the buyer cannot easily discerne it: His Highness willeth and commandeth, that every Clothier shall have one seuerall marke for his Cloth, and shall use that one marke onelie for all the time of his Clothing, without altering or changing the same, and *no man shall give the same marke which another useth, though with addition or difference or change of the colour:* And where at present seuerall men use the same marke, such of them as haue longest used the same shall continue the use thereof, and the others shall betake themselues to the use of new markes not used by others . . . .[3]

The foregoing represents the contribution of the English cloth trade to the history of British trade-mark law up to the eighteenth century. This contribution still leaves us far from

and of 3 William and Mary to the Hollow Sword Blades Company (*Select Charters of Trading Companies*, Selden Soc. Pub., vol. 28, pp. 206 and 221 respectively) grant the right to use a distinguishing mark for products made under the royal authority.

[1] *Proclamation*, Charles I, April 13, 1633 (Brit. Mus. 506. h. 12 [19]), p. 2.

[2] *Supra*, p. 84, n. 2.

[3] *Proclamation*, Charles I, April 13, 1633, p. 3, (Italics, the writer's.)

the notion of "property in trademarks . . . as a legal possession, which may be bought and sold and transmitted." But
at any rate it brings us to the point where trade-marks are
regarded as identifying not merely the defects but also the
good qualities of the source of production from which they
emanate. In this light trade-marks are already being regarded by administrative courts, such as the King's Council
and the Court of the Star Chamber, even though as yet not by
the common law courts, as assets of value that are worthy of
protection.

APPENDIX

DECREE OF THE STAR CHAMBER, OCTOBER 12TH, 1632, CON-
CERNING THE COUNTERFEITING OF SEALS TO
COLCHESTER BAIZE BY THOMAS JUPP.

In Cam. Stell. coram Conc. ibid. xij° die Octobr.

Anno Octauo Caroli Regis.

This day one Thomas Iupp a Cloth-worker of the City of London,
being at the Barre of this Court, His Maiesties Atturney Generall informed this Court, that hee had taken the Examinations of the said
Thomas Iupp, concerning the counterfeiting of Seales usually affixed to
the Bayes of Colchester, and fixing of them to other Bayes of meaner
condition, and shewed foorth certaine Iron Stampes, and pieces of
Bayes, sealed some with the true Seales of that Towne, attesting that
some of them were truly wrought, and that others of them were deficient,
and others of them sealed with counterfeit Seales, put to Bayes not of
the making of Colchester, but of lesse estimation; which being shewne
to the said Thomas Iupp, hee acknowledged his Confession made upon
that Examination to be true, and that those Stampes and pieces of
Bayes came from his hands to His Maiesties Atturney; which Confession
followeth in these words:

The Examination of Thomas Iupp of Abbchurch Lane in the Citie
of London Cloth-worker, taken before William Noy His Maiesties
Atturney Generall, the fift day of September, in the eighth yeere of
His Maiesties Reigne:

Hee saith that in July last he bought in Leaden hall Bay Market of
John Bryant of Bocking, one hundred and ten Flemish ells of Munikin
Bayes of Bocking making, at xxjᵈ ob. the ell, and three other pieces of
about fiftie like ells, the piece at xxxiijᵈ ob. the ell.

He saith also that Colchester Bayes are commonly somewhat dearer
than the Bayes of Bocking.

THE LAW RELATING TO TRADE-MARKS

He taketh it that Colchester Bayes sell better beyond the Sea than other Bayes, and hath long beene of that opinion.

He saith, that he having long beene a Worke-man, is able to discerne a Colchester or Sandwich or Bocking Bay one from another, bot other men that are not Worke-men discerne them by their Seales.

He saith that he bought these Bayes for one   Goddard a Sea-faring man then abiding about Deptford, but what his Christian name is he knoweth not, but thinketh it is either George or William, and that he was allowed no more for those Bayes but as he paid for them, save for his labour in buying and Baling of them, and Canvase, hee had about xxv^d and for some other labour.

He confesseth that when the Bayes had been bought Goddard asked the Examinate how he should doe for Seales, and the Examinate told him he would doe his indeavour or the best he could to grace his commodity.

And further acknowledgeth, that when the Bayes were brought to the Examinates house he put Seales to them like the Colchester Seales used for Bayes, and saith that the Seales shewne to him by the Atturney Generall, in one side whereof is depicted a Griffin or a Dragon, and the other side three Crownes, which he takes to be the Armes of Colchester, and on another is written D.W.C. COLSEST. BAY. 1571. were stamped on by himselfe, but it is bungerly and not well done: And those Seales that hee put to one of those Bayes, is closed up in a paper sealed by the Atturney and the Examinate.

He saith that those depictures are graven in Iron, and that the Irons are in the Examinates keeping. And hee saith that he will deliver the Stampes to the Atturney Generall.

Being demanded who did grave those Irons, which he used for Seales, hee saith that hee knoweth not who did grave them, but sieth that some of them were graved in Foster Lane about halfe a yeere sithence, and the Examinate paid for the graving of them, for some of them more and for some lesse. Thomas Iupp. William Noye.

Upon Friday the seventh day of the same September, the said Thomas Iupp being againe examined, delivered to the Atturney Generall seven Iron Stampes, in one a Griffin, in another Three Crownes, another D.W.S. Colsest. Bay 1571. in the other foure severall numbers are graven. And then being told, that it appeareth by two of the Stampes that they had often been stamped, and demanded how long he hath had them, saith at one time, that he hath had them about halfe a yeere; at another time, about a yeere; he saith that one Thomas Downes who is in Ireland, as he hath heard, did deliver them unto him at his last being in England, but remembreth not the time.

Being demanded for whom hee hath stamped any Seales, besides Goddard, he refuseth to declare.

Hee saith that the buyers doe commonly buy Bayes for Colchester Bayes, without further enquiring then view of the Seales.

Hee saith that those Stampes doe differ from the Seale of Colchester.

Hee saith that the Seales of Lead shewne unto him sealed up in paper

by him and the Atturney Generall, were made of the Stampes now produced by him, by himselfe, without the helpe of any other, and fixed
to one of the Bayes which the Examinate bought and delivered to
Goddard, as he formerly declared.

Hee saith that the ordinary price of Baling of five Bayes in Canvase
Ropes and labour, comes to about viij⁸. and if in three Bales, it comes
to about a Marke, and these Bayes were made up in three Bales.

The Iron Stampes are bound up in a piece of Canvase which hee
hath sealed, and remaineth with the Atturney Generall.   Thomas Iupp.
William Noy.

Upon Friday the fourteenth of the same September, in presence of
the Examinate and of the Atturney Generall and others, one piece of
the Bayes which he sealed with the counterfeit Seales, was brought and
shewne to the Examinate, which he confesseth to be the same which he
sealed for Goddard, and saith that it is no Colchester Bay, and hee
knoweth it by the Worke. At the same time two other pieces of Bayes
were brought and shewne to him, which hee knew by the Worke (himselfe
being a Workeman) to be Colchester Bayes, whereof one hath the whole
Seale, and is not faulty, the other is marked as faultie, by cutting off a
piece and fixing the Seale at the Angle; and he saith that the Bay marked
as faultie, is better then the Bocking Bay which he sealed with the
whole Seale.

The Examinate also saith that he hath often made the faultie Bayes
have the whole Seale, by cutting off the Puckle of the Bay at the Angle,
and drawing it, and fixing that Seale in another place, so as in view it
is sealed with the whole Seale, which he did shew the manner in the
presence of the Atturney and others; and saith that he hath so done
above a hundred and a hundred times for Merchants, and many of
them he hath done within this moneth. 1 Piece of each Bay remaineth
with the Atturney marked by the Examinate. Thomas Iupp. William
Noye.

Which being read, and view taken by their Lordships of those pieces
of Bayes, and the Stampes and Seales, His Maiesties Atturney Generall
humbly prayed their Lordships that some exemplary punishment
might bee inflicted upon the said Thomas Iupp: Whereupon their Lordships taking into consideration the many Lawes that have provided
for the true Draping of the Wooll of this Realme, by ordaining the
Searching, Measuring, Marking, affixing Seales of Divers Places where
they are Draped, and the publike Seale of the Aulnager unto the Clothes:
That the people of this Towne of Colchester and of the parts adioyning,
receive a great part of their sustenance by the making of Bayes: That
for many yeeres past, by occasion of the carefull Search there made,
they have beene truely and not deceitfully made, and of a knowne goodnesse: That such of them as are fully wrought are sealed with a Seale
attesting their goodnesse: If upon Search any proove not so good, they
are marked for such: so as the buyers both within the Realme and abroad,
may bee ascertained of the goodnesse of the Merchandize by view of
the Seale, wherein (the Law requiring it) such great care hath beene had

from time to time, that upon the credit of the Seale alone they were plentifully and readily vented in all places. And albeit there had not beene hitherto any discovery made of Delinquents in this kinde, yet their Lordships taking into their serious consideration, that the offense of the said Thomas is a false cousenage, by which the buyers being deceived, will not bee so ready to buy any other Clothes upon the credit or attestation of the Seales, so as the good and true Workers of Cloth will not receive the encouragement to make true Workemanship as they were wont, but be enforced for vent, to make their Clothes like unto those whereunto such counterfeit Seales shall be affixed, and in time produce a disaffiance to the attestations of the Seales, whereof will insue many inconveniences; And they can foresee that if this new falsitie should be unpunished, it will grow further abroad. And therefore their Lordships have thought fit, Ordered, Adiudged, and Decreed, that the said Delinquent, Thomas Iupp, shall stand and be committed to the Prison of the Fleete during his Maiesties pleasure, and not be then enlarged until he shall discover and make knowne the names of such Merchants for whom hee hath used and practised the said deceit: And if at any time His Maiestie shall be pleased to inlarge the said Iupp; It is then Ordered, that before his inlargement, hee shall finde good Sureties for his good behaviour.

And it is also Ordered and Decreed, that the said Delinquent shall pay a fine of one thousand pounds to His Maiesties use.

And the Court doth further declare, that if in case the said Iupp shall continue stubborne, and shall refuse to discover the names of such Merchants or other Tradesmen for whom he hath used and practised the aforesaid fraud and deceit, their Lordships doe reserve a power of inflicting some further compulsory meanes to cause him to confesse their names. And to the end the world may take notice how much this Court doth dislike and condemne such notorious cousenages and deceits, their Lordships have further Ordered, Adiudged, and Decreed, that the said Thomas Iupp shall on some market day be set upon the Pillarie in Cheapeside, with a Paper on his head, wherein shall be inscribed words declaring the nature of his offence. At which time it is also thought fit and ordered that this Decree shall be publikely read, and severall Copies be thereof Printed, and set up upon Postes and other eminent places about and neere the said Pillary, to remaine there, so as the cause of his punishment may be generally knowne, and other like lewd persons deterred from committing the like offences.

And it is also further Ordered and Decreed, that the said Iupp shall in like manner be set upon the Pillary in Cornehill over against the Exchange, at Blackwell Hall, Bocking and Colchester, upon severall Market dayes, with the like Paper on his head, inscribed as is aforesaid. At all which said severall times and places it is Ordered, that this Decree bee publikely read, and that severall Printed Copies of this Decree shall also be set up on severall eminent places, on, and about, and neere the said places and Pillaries, to remaine there for the purposes aforesaid; and specially at Blackwell Hall the officers there shall continue the said Printed Copies upon Postes and open places, in, and about the said Hall so long that the Clothiers of all parts of the Kingdome comming thither may have notice thereof, whereby it may bee divulged to all the Clothing Townes and Countreys of the Kingdome, how unlawfull and how dangerous it is to use any falsities and deceits tending to the discredit of the Clothing of the Realme, and how carefull His Maiestie, and the State, and all his Courts of Justice will be to see the same severely punished.

And lastly, to the end such Merchants and other Tradesmen as have set this Delinquent or any other Cloth-worker at worke, to practise this deceitfull Sealing of Bayes, may bee knowne and discovered, The Court doth hereby publish and declare, that such person or persons as shall make such discovery, and bring the Delinquents to receive the Sentence of this Court, shall for their reward have halfe the Fine or Fines which shall by this Court be imposed upon them. And any Cloth-worker who have used and practised such deceit shall discover their Procurers and Encouragers, such persons so confessing, shall receive the mercy and favour of this Court.

CHAPTER V

THE DEVELOPMENT OF TRADE–MARK LAW IN
THE CUTLERY TRADES

THE upshot of our investigation of the history of trade-marks in the cloth trades was our arrival at a point where, in the fifteenth and sixteenth centuries, and more especially in the seventeenth century, the modern concept of a trade-mark as an asset of value begins to appear. But, as indicated above,[1] we have so far seen no evidence of "property in trade-marks . . . as a legal possession, which may be bought and sold and transmitted." Furthermore, aside from sporadic administrative action, there are no indications of any sort of protection being afforded to these marks. For the link between the typical regulatory and liability mark of the Middle Ages and the modern asset mark, and for the immediate foundations of the systematic legal protection of trade-marks as property, we must go to the cutlery trades. As will presently appear, the trade-marks in these industries, just as in all other industries, were in their origin essentially compulsory police marks, but in no other phase in the history of British trade can we so clearly discern the evolution of marks from liability to asset marks as in the case of the cutlers' marks. We shall see in the records of the cutlers of London and, later, of Sheffield of what great value these marks became to those who used them and how there developed, within the tribunals having jurisdiction over these craftsmen, the doctrine of at least a qualified legal ownership in marks, with certain corollaries, such as the individual's right to the protection of his mark and damages for its infringement, his right to sell or lease his mark and, notably, his widow's right to a life estate in his mark and his son's claim to a reversion in his mark. These

[1] *Supra*, p 96.

concepts are practically exclusive to the cutlery trades although, occasionally and at a much later date, the records in some other phase of industry may possibly give evidence of the germination of similar principles of trade-mark law.[1]

The cutlers' trades were among the most ancient and widely dispersed in the history of British industry.[2] Not only London but Sheffield, Birmingham, York,[3] Salisbury, Thaxted[4] and Derby contained powerful cutlers' gilds or other organizations before the end of the Middle Ages. As in all other phases of medieval industry,[5] so in the cutlers' trades there was

[1] In all the writer's investigation of the various trades in London and the provinces he has come across only one instance containing any such suggestion, namely, in the case of the pewterers of London. Pewterers' marks were in their origin compulsory. The Act of 19 Hen. VII, c. 6, recited the stealing of pewter vessels and the sale of defective goods and required the marking of such wares "to the entent that the [markers] of such wares shall avowe the same Wares,. . ." (Welch, *Pewterers*, i, 94 *et seq.*) The first ordinance of the Pewterers Company, dated 1522, making marking compulsory, enacted "pursuant to yᵉ Statute of 19 H. 7" (*ibid.*, i, 106), prescribed "that the said vessell and stuff shall be marked with the mark of the workman therof to thentente it may be knowen of whoos makynge the seide vessell or stuff is . . ." (*ibid.*, i, 107). See also similar provision of 8 June, 1552–3 (*ibid.*, i, 174–5), of 13 December, 1574–5 (*ibid.*, i, 280), of 20 March, 1592–3, concerning re-registration of "tuches" (*ibid.*, ii, 11), of 19 July, 1637–8 (*ibid.*, ii, 98). For reproductions of "touchplates" see *ibid.*, ii, Appendix III.
    However, there are certain indications in the records of the Pewterers' Company that these compulsory marks gradually acquired a secondary significance as symbols of their user's good-will. See entry for 21 July, 1566–7, concerning the "privilege of Assistants to have their 'marks' set up in the Hall (*ibid.*, i, 255), also the following entries:
    [3 July, 1622] "Thomas Hall maketh request to the Court that hee may vse or strike Mr. Sheppards touch which was graunted." "The same touch was at the next court (24th July) granted to John Netherwood 'in regard that Thomas Hall hath le oft it f.'" (*ibid.*, ii, 81).
    Reference has already been made (ch. iii, p. 45) to the efforts of the Pewterers' Company in the sixteenth and following centuries to repress the development of an individual good-will among its members. While there was actually such a development, it cannot be said that there was a corresponding development to any marked degree of any system of protection of the individual's mark.
    [2] See G. I. H. Lloyd, *The Cutlery Trades*, ch. iv, "The Rise and Localization of the Industry."
    [3] See *York Memorandum Book* i, (Surtees Soc. Pub., vol. cxx), p. 136. The Ordinances of the Cutlers and Bladesmiths of York (1479–80) provide "that every bladesmith of this city shall cut and use his own marks on his knives that he will make, different to the mark of every other man of the same trade, under pain of 40ᵈ to the Chamber and the bladesmiths in equal portions." See also *ibid.*, ii (Surtees Soc. Pub., vol. cxxv), Introd. p. xli.
    [4] R. W. Dixon, "Thaxted," in *The Antiquary*, vol. xvii, pp. 10 *et seq.*, 57 *et seq.*, G. E. Symonds, "Thaxted and its Cutlers' Guild," in *Trans. Essex Archæol. Soc.*, N. S., vol. iii, p. 254.
    [5] W. J. Ashley, *Economic History*, i, pt. i, p. 95.

at first a separate organization of different branches of the same industry.[1] "Every knife," recites the Ordinance between the Cutlers and Sheathers of London in 1408,

is prepared separately by three different crafts, viz.: first, the blade by the smiths called "Bladsmythes," the handle and the other fitting work by the cutlers, and the sheath by the sheathers; and that if the articles are good, commendation is the result, but if bad, then blame and scandal falls and is charged upon the said trade of the Cutlers.[2]

Under this system of minute sectional organization the cutlery trades of London before their amalgamation into the Cutlers' Company in the middle of the fifteenth century consisted of independent gilds of sheathers, bladesmiths and cutlers.[3] A similar differentiation and ultimate amalgamation occurred in York and other English communities of cutlers and also on the continent, as, for instance, in Paris, Solingen and Ruhla (Thüringen).[4]

At the present time the most,—if not the only,—famous center of British cutlery manufacture is Sheffield. Its reputation has existed since the days of Chaucer who, in "the Reve's Tale," wrote

A Shefeld thwytel[5] bare he in his hose,
Ronde was his face and camysed was his nose.[6]

Similarly, until recently, Sheffield cutlery marks were considered to be the most important marks in the kingdom from the standpoint of their contribution to the history of comparative trade-mark law. Writing forty years ago concerning the Sheffield registry of trade-marks, Joseph Kohler said:

So bietet uns das Recht der Sheffielder Messerschmiedmarken das interessante Beispiel einer Markenentwickelung,

---

[1] G. I. H. Lloyd, *op. cit.*, pp. 81 *et seq.*
[2] C. Welch, *History of the Cutlers' Company of London*, i, p. 283.
[3] *Ibid.*, i, p. 24.
[4] G. I. H. Lloyd, *op. cit.*, p. 81.
[5] A knife carried by those not entitled to wear a sword.
[6] Joseph Hunter, *History and Topography of the Parish of Sheffield* (ed. A. Gatty), p. 59. For a collection of literary allusions to Sheffield cutlery in the reign of Elizabeth see G. I. H. Lloyd, *op. cit.*, p. 95.

welche von den mittelalterlichen Zunftwesen bis in die heuti-
gen Verkehrsverhältnisse hineinreicht, und es wäre vielleicht
zweckmässig gewesen, wenn das deutsche Gesetz der rhein-
ischen Eisenindustrie in gleicher Weise ihre altbewährte
Einrichtung neben dem allgemeinen Rechte belassen hätte.[1]

It must, however, be remembered that the history of the
London cutlers is almost two centuries older than that of
Sheffield. The first regulations concerning London cutlers'
marks occurred as early as 1365,[2] while "the first known
holder of a Sheffield trade-mark" occurs in 1565.[3] Very
recently there has been published an admirable history of the
Cutlers' Company of London,[4] the records of which have not
only thrown an entirely new light upon the relation of cutlers'
marks to the whole history of trade-marks but have also, as
far as English cutlers are concerned, antedated the prior records, namely, those of Sheffield, by almost two centuries. Our
study of cutlers' marks will therefore largely be drawn from
London rather than from Sheffield sources, despite the fact
that, at any rate since the eighteenth century, Sheffield has
predominated the British cutlery trade and that, since that
time, the manufacture of cutlery in London has been steadily
dwindling away.[5]

The origins of the London cutlery trade somewhere in the
thirteenth century [6] are obscure, but the regulations concerning their marks in 1365 above referred to indicate that by
that time they were sufficiently powerful to seek and obtain
protection for their monopoly and for their marks. This was,
of course, especially so in the case of those engaged in making
weapons, armor and other war *materiel*, regarded as essential

---

[1] *Das Recht des Markenschutzes*, p. 66.
[2] *Cal. Close Rolls*, Edw. III, 1364–8, p. 182. Robert Leader, in his *History of the Company of Cutlers in Hallamshire* (Sheffield 1905), which will often be referred to in this chapter, is incorrect in his supposition (i, p. 12, asterisk note) that the Ordinance of 1408 may be "the earliest reference to the impression of distinctive marks on cutlery."
[3] R. E. Leader, *op. cit.*, i, p. 7.
[4] Charles Welch, *History of the Cutlers' Company of London*, vol. i, 1916, vol. ii, 1923, cited hereafter merely as "Welch, *Cutlers*."
[5] G. I. H. Lloyd, *op. cit.*, pp. 98–9.
[6] Welch, *Cutlers*, i, p. 2.

for the national defense and common weal.[1] The order of 1365 reads as follows:

To the Mayor and Sheriffs of London. Order to cause proclamation to be made that smiths who make swords, knives and other weapons in the city of London shall put particular marks upon their handiwork (*certa signa sua super omnibus operacionibus suis ponant*), that the same being so marked (*dictis signis signate*) shall be shown before the Mayor, sheriffs and aldermen of London in the Gildehall of the city so that every man's work may be known by his mark (*per ejus signum*), and that they shall forfeit any works sold without such mark (*dictis signis suis non consignatas*) or the price thereof, causing the premises to be observed and any works found to have been sold or exposed for sale in the City and suburbs of London without marks (*dictis signis suis non consignatas*) to be seized as forfeit into the king's hand and answer to be made to him for them.[2]

[1] In the "Articles of the Heaumers" (Makers of Helmets) dated 1347, already cited above (p. 61), it was provided that "each one of the makers aforesaid shall have his own sign and mark, and that no one of them shall counterfeit the sign or mark of another; on pain of losing his freedom, until he shall have bought the same back again, and made satisfaction to him whose sign he shall have so counterfeited; and further, he shall pay to the Chamber 40 shillings." (H. T. Riley, *Memorials of London*, p. 238.) *Cf.* statute of 7 Hen. IV, c. 7, concerning Arrow-Heads: "Because the Arrow-smiths do make many faulty Heads for Arrows and Quarels, defective, not well, nor lawful, nor defensible, to the great Jeopardy and Deceit of the People, and of the whole Realm; It is ordained and established, That all the Heads for Arrows and Quarels after this Time to be made shall be well boiled . . .; And that every Arrowhead and Quarel be marked with the Mark of him that made the same; and that the Justices of Peace in every County of England . . . shall have the power to enquire of all such deceitful Makers of Heads and Quarels, and to punish them as afore is said." (*Stat. of the Realm*, ii, p. 153.)

In Lambard's *Eirenarcha*, published 1581, a treatise on the duties of Justices of the Peace, among "Articles of the Charge Given by Justices of the Peace" are "If any Arrowhead Smith have not wel boiled, brased and hardened at the appoint with steel, and marked with his mark, such heads of Arrowes and quarels, as he hath made. 7 Hen. IV, cap. 7." (See W. S. Holdsworth, *op. cit.*, iv, p. 561.)

[2] *Cal. Close Rolls*, Edw. III, 1364–8, p. 182, 39 Edw. III, June 26, 1365. This order was enrolled in *Letter Book G* of the City of London and is reprinted in the Latin original from that source in Welch, *Cutlers*, i, pp. 248–9. *Cf.* the statute of Parma, 1262, prohibiting the counterfeiting of marks upon knives and swords and further providing: ". . . if any person in such guild has continuously used a mark upon knives, swords or other steel or iron articles for ten years, and any other person is found to have used, within one or two years, the same mark or an imitation thereof, whether stamped or formed in any other way, the latter shall not in the future be allowed to use such marks upon knives, swords or other steel or iron articles, under penalty of ten pounds of Parma for each and every offense, and that regardless of any compromise or award of arbitrators which may have been made." (Quoted by E. S. Rogers,

In 1408 complaint was made by the bladesmiths and cutlers that

"foreign" cutlers from various parts of England brought for sale to London knives and blades bearing forged marks of London bladesmiths, and that the sale of such "faulty and defective" goods tended to the discredit of the two Misteries and to the public loss. They therefore prayed that London

9 *Michigan Law Review* at p. 37, from J. Kohler, *Das Recht des Markenschutzes*, p. 46). Mr. Rogers (*op. cit.*, p. 37) calls attention to the resemblance between the ten-year user feature of the Parma statute and the "old mark" section of the English Trade-Mark Act of 1875 and also Sec. 5 of the U. S. Trade-Mark Act of 1905 (since amended by the Act of March 19, 1920), pointing out that both in England and America the protection of "old marks" was regarded as "a dangerous innovation." For elaborate Florentine legislation concerning armorers' marks, 1355, see G. Lastig, *Markenrecht und Zeichenregister*, pp. 26–8. G. F. Laking, in his monumental *European Arms and Armor* (vol. i, p. lix) discusses the statutes of the *Universitas* of armorers of Milan enacted in 1587, providing for the compulsory registration of marks, and forbidding the changing of a mark, once it had been registered. See also "Statutes des Armuriers Fourbisseurs d'Angers" and other provisions in Appendices to C. Ffoulkes, *The Armourer and His Craft*.

However, despite the abundance of continental legislation prohibiting the counterfeiting of armorers' marks, the appropriation of such marks, both collective or geographical as well as individual, appears to have been almost as frequent and as lightly regarded as was the imitation of the early printers' and publishers' devices discussed at length in a previous chapter (*supra*, pp. 67–70, 72). There was very much less counterfeiting of the marks on defensive armor than of those on sword-blades, "and where it exists it is obviously done for ulterior reasons." (C. Ffoulkes, *The Armourer and His Craft*, pp. 70–71). Sword-blade makers often used not only the marks of competitors, but the names of competitors' localities or the marks of their gilds. "Toledo, Passau, Ferara, Solingen are . . . very often stamped upon the blades of an entirely different nationality." (*ibid.*, p. 70). For counterfeiting of Spanish cutlers' marks in England, see *infra*, p. 107, n. 1. The effect of such legislation as that above quoted would appear to have been to prevent *intra-gild* competition only.

But in the study of armorers' marks it should be remembered that famous armorers and bladesmiths, like the early printers, wandered all over Europe from the original centers of their art, — often at the summons of some particular prince or noble. According to Froissart, armorers were sent over with armor made for the Earl of Derby in Milan when the Earl-Marshal proposed a duel against him in 1398 (C. Ffoulkes, *The Connoisseur*, vol. xxv, p. 29); English armorers were not good enough for Henry VIII, who imported not only German armor, but also "Almayne" armorers to teach the English armorers their craft (C. Ffoulkes, *ibid.*, vol. xxiv, pp. 99, 101). "Italian armourers worked in Germany, France and Spain, and German and French armourers were also liable to roam abroad in large numbers" (G. F. Laking, *op. cit.*, i, 204). As among the early printers and publishers, there appears to have been considerable indifference to any consistent use of marks upon the part of continental armorers, both itinerant and stationary. Laking speaks of Milanese armorers of the fifteenth and sixteenth centuries, borrowed from the Duke of Milan by the King of France, working at Tours, Lyons and Bordeaux and using their Italian stamps (*ibid.*, i, pp. 201, 204–5). Boeheim also points out that an armorer in adopting another's mark, might do so in conjunction with his own name, — sometimes also with the actual place of production (*Handbuch der Waffenkunde*, p. 643).

cutlers should be forbidden to purchase knives and blades bearing such forged marks.[1]

The language of the joint petitions of the cutlers and blade-smiths of 1408 resembles the complaints as to the injury of the collective good-will of the gild, to which we have referred above,[2] and also indicates the monopolistic usage of crafts-men's marks during the Middle Ages.

Unto the honourable Lords, the Mayor and Aldermen of the City of London, shew all the good folks of the misteries of the Cutlers and Bladesmythes, free of the said City, how that foreign folks, from divers parts of England, do sell unto the cutlers and others of the said City as well knives as blades, marked with marks resembling the marks of the bladesmythes free of the said City; the which knives and blades are faulty and defective, to the very great scandal of the said misteries

Ffoulkes mentions a suit in the Royal Armoury at Turin ascribed to Antonio Missaglia but bearing *no* mark (*The Connoisseur*, vol. xxv, p. 31).

For reproductions of marks on armor, see C. Ffoulkes, *The Armourer and His Craft*, pp. 147–52; W. Boeheim, *op. cit.*, pp. 648–80; B. Dean, *The Collection of Arms and Armor of Rutherford Stuyvesant*, pp. 11, 17, 21, 63, 95; C. J. Ffoulkes, *Inventories and Survey of the Armouries of the Tower of London*, ii, pp. 221, 406 *et seq.*; H. I. Gilchrist, *Catalogue of Arms and Armor Presented to the Cleveland Museum of Art . . .*, pp. 265 *et seq.*; also articles cited *supra* p. 24, n. 3.

[1] Welch, *Cutlers*, i, p. 110. Leader points out (*op. cit.*, i, p. 6) that "it is simply guess work to conjecture that it may have been the Hallamshire competition" which provoked this petition. However, reference will not be made in the text of this chapter to the constant charges and countercharges by London and provincial — and later continental cutlers — as to the infringement of trade-marks, which make interesting though unedifying reading for the student of the so-called "evolution of trade morality." The London cutlers were loud in their outcry against the Sheffield and Birmingham rivals who put the London mark, — the mark of the dagger — upon their wares, and in 1610 "It is agreed that the M^r & his Wardeins by advice of counsell shall prefer a bill into the Star Chamber against such obstinat persons. . . ." (Welch, *Cutlers*, ii, p. 339.) On the other hand, shortly thereafter the London cutlers were in their turn accused of stamping Spanish and other marks on their goods (Petition of Benjamin Stone in *Cal. State Papers*, Dom., Charles I, 1638–9, p. 237, No. 62), and in the nineteenth century were "convicted of making up provincial blades and forging London marks on them" (Lloyd, *op. cit.*, p. 98), while the Sheffield manufacturers, bitterly complaining of the misuse of their marks by German rivals, were forced to admit that they themselves were appropriating each other's marks. (See *Report from the Committee on Trade-Marks Bill* in *Reports of Committees, 1862*, Session Papers xii, Question No. 661.) And, to complete the unsavory record, twice within the last five years, the Federal Trade Commission of the United States has been compelled to issue orders requiring respondents to desist from using labels containing the word "Sheffield" upon inferior American-made cutlery (See *Federal Trade Commission v. Bernstein*, 4 F. T. C. D. 114; *Federal Trade Commission v. Sheffield Razor Co., ibid.*, 373.)

[2] *Supra*, pp. 46–47.

of the Cutlers and Bladesmythes, and to the common hurt. May it therefore please your very wise discreetness to ordain, that no one of the said mistery of Cutlers shall buy of any other person from henceforth any such knives or blades made in the country with marks forged in resemblance [of such], as well for the honour of the said misteries, as for the common profit of the City.[1]

Among the Articles of the Mistery of Bladesmiths in the same year occurs the following:

Also, that every master of the said mistery shall put his own mark upon his work, such as heads of lances, knives and axes, and other large work, that it may be known who made the same, if default be found therein; on the pain aforesaid. Also, that no one of the said mistery shall counterfeit the mark of another maker upon his own work; but let him use and put his own mark upon his own work, on the pain aforesaid.[2]

So far we have found nothing in the London cutlers' records to differentiate their marks from the ordinary regulatory marks of the Middle Ages. But in 1452 a case arising before the Mayor and Aldermen of London, who at that time appear to have had jurisdiction over such matters,[3] puts an entirely different aspect on these marks. The issue in that case was the right to use the mark of the Double Crescent which, until his death in 1450 had been used by Robert Hynkeley, citizen and bladesmith of London.[4]

On that day it was granted and agreed by the Mayor and Aldermen abovesaid that John Leylond, citizen and skinner of London and Agnes his wife who was the wife of Robert Hynkeley late citizen and bladesmith of London should be restored and have again their old mark of the double crescent notwithstanding the petition to the contrary presented by the Mistery of Bladesmiths. And that John Morth bladesmith shall not further use that mark but shall be altogether forbidden under the penalty attaching, etc.[5]

[1] Welch, *Cutlers*, i, p. 284. The petition was granted (*ibid.*, i, p. 285.)
[2] *Ibid.*, i, p. 287.
[3] See Unwin, *Gilds and Companies of London*, pp. 235 *et seq.*
[4] *Ibid.*, i, p. 201.
[5] *Ibid.*, i, p. 329. Cf. Kohler, *op. cit.*, pp. 51–2, citing an interesting case of the sale in 1515 by a German widow of a cutler's mark inherited with her husband's business in 1485, "*weil sie Alters halber vom Handwerk abstehen müsse.*"

The importance of the case of the mark of the Double Crescent is twofold in that it shows (1) that by 1452 the cutler's mark had become of sufficient value to be the subject of litigation for its restoration and (2) that the notion of property in a mark had developed so far that the widow of the owner of a mark, as long as she remained in business, was entitled to retain the use of the mark (*marquam suam pristinam*), even subsequent to her remarriage.[1]

---

[1] Reference should be made to the subsequent ordinances concerning cutlers' marks throughout the 15th and 16th centuries. Most of this legislation emphasizes the regulatory and monopolistic aspects of these marks and does not contribute much to the development of a law of property in trade-marks. The Ordinances of the Bladesmiths in 1463 prescribed: "And ouer that forasmoche as diuers fforeyns dwellyng in ferre contrees of this Reaume conterfeten the markes of Bladesmythes of this Citee and sellen theire blades to diuers persones of this Citee and by the same persones aren solde ayen for london blades to grete disclaunder of the seide Craft and disceyte of the kyngs people." (Welch, *Cutlers*, i, pp. 334–5.) "Noo personne of the seide Crafte shall not bere nor sende his marke to eny foreyn to be sette vpon eny werke by the foreyn to be made without that there be noo man enfraunchesed of the seide Crafte of sufficient konnyng to make the same . . ." (*Ibid.*, i, p. 336.) The Bladesmiths' Ordinances of 1501 provided for registration of bladesmiths' marks as follows: "And that they nor any of theym shalle haue nor stryke any marke vpon any bladys or tolys by them or any of theym hereafter to be made but such marke or markes as shalbe yeven to theym by the Wardeyns of the same Crafte of Bladesmythes for the tyme beyng and the same marke or markes firste to be enrolled in the yeldhalle afore it be sette or stryken vpon any suche blade or tole. . . ." (*Ibid.*, i, p. 344.) The "Ordinance Concerning the Bladesmiths and Armourers," giving the bladesmiths the right to enroll the armourers' marks, *does* contain an intimation as to the value of marks to their owners: "Also yt is agreed bytwene the seyd Wardens that all persones of the seyd Craft of Armurers occupying the seid Craft of Bladsmythes shall haue a marke by the seyd Wardens of Bladsmythes to theym assigned as euery ffreman of the seyd Craft of Bladsmythes haven. And the seyd marke to be enrolled in theldhall as all other vsing the occupacion of Bladsmythes don according to an acte made in the seyd Craft of Bladsmythes so that all suche ware by theym made may be knowen for good able and profitable for the kings liege people. . . . (*Ibid.*, i, p. 346.) The Petition of the Bladesmiths for Union with the Armourers in 1515 is followed by a set of Ordinances for the government of the Armourers' Company containing the following provisions concerning the Bladesmiths' Marks: "And that euery maister of the seid Craft sette his owne proper marke vpon his owne worke as vpon heeds of speres knyves & axes & vpon other groose workes that it may be knowen whoo made the same bicause of defawts that perhaps may be found in the makyng of theym. . . . And that if any foreyn counterfeite the marke of eny ffreeman & sell enymaner blades so marked w^t a ffreemans marke to eny ffreeman w^{t}yn this Citie of eny other Craft, that than it shalbe liefull to the seid wardeyns w^t other certyn honest persones of the seid Craft accompanyed w^t an officer of the Chambre of london for the tyme, to make due serche in all places of the Citie where eny such wares be to be sold, or if that eny such seid wares be wrought deceivably either by ffreeman or fforeyn, the same wares by theym w^{t}yn the Citie so founden in whose hands so euer they be, to be brought to the Guyhall & vtterly to be forfeited. . . . And that no persone enfraunchised of the seid Craft shall goo oute of his hous to pray desyre nor fetche eny ware or

It is perhaps surprising that there are no further entries for the fifteenth and sixteenth centuries of a similar nature. But, at any rate, when we arrive at the seventeenth century, we find entry after entry in the records of the company court indicating the great importance of marks to their owners and the methods of protecting and transmitting these marks. The regulatory antecedents of the mark appear in the still surviving objection of the Company to the use by its members of more than a single mark:[1]

(23rd May, 1620) William Sherebrook is warned not to strick the Crowne but onlie his marke w[ch] is the falchon w[ch] was formerlie by his owne Consent graunted to him and is enrolled to him in the howse. And if he do not reforme himself w[th]in xiiij daeis and betake him to his olde mark Then the howse do give him notic they will according to the rules of the howse lay such penaltie vppon him as by lawe they may.[2]

Chaffer to make or grynde, nor that eny persone of the seid Craft shall bere or sende his marke to eny fforeyn to be sette vpon eny worke by the seid foreyn to be made w[t]oute there be noman of the seid Craft that hath sufficient connyng to make the same vpon peyne to pay at euery tyme so offendyng xxd. to be employed in maner and fourme aboueseid. . . . And that nomaner persone enfraunchised in the seid Craft make eny maner wares of blades Excepte that he have a mark propre to hymself And the same his marke to be shewed in presence of the Wardeyns and by the same Wardeyns the seid marke to be entred in theldehall of Record in eschewyng further preiudice vpon peyne of forfaiture of xiijs. iiijd. at euery tyme so offendyng to be employed in maner & fourme as is aforeseid." (*Ibid.*, i, pp. 347–8.)

Upon the dissolution of the Bladesmiths as a separate "mistery", their authority over the craft passed to the Armourers, including the power to grant and oversee the makers' marks (*ibid.*, i, p. 118). To procure the necessary power to control the marks in use among the Bladesmiths attached to their "mistery," the Cutlers in 1519 obtained from the Court of Aldermen a grant providing: "It may therefor pleas the same to licence yo[r] seid Oratours and to graunt to theym power that they & their Successours beying Maister & Wardens of the same Craft as oft as nede shall be may appoynt & assign to euery Brother & freman of the seid Craft of Cutlers occupying makyng blads a Certen marke to be sett vppon their seuerall Blades which they shall make to thentent yt may be knowen who makyth good & perfite blads and who makyth disceytfull blads ffurthermore that when such marks be appoynted to suche makers of Blads their names w[t] the same marks to euerye of them assigned may be wretten Regestred & noted in the boks of this honorable Courte here to Remayne of Recorde to thentent aforeseid." (*Ibid.*, i, p. 350–1.) For facsimiles of eight cutlers' marks "entered of record" in *Letter Book N* of the City of London, Feb. 17th, 1519–20, see *ibid.*, i, opposite p. 118.

[1] *Ibid.*, ii, 342. *Cf.* R. Leader, *op. cit.*, ii, p. 3, Ordinances of the Sheffield Cutlers, 1590, No. 7; *ibid.*, ii, p. 5, "fine of 10[s] for striking two marks". *Cf.* similar pewterers' provisions, C. Welch, *Pewterers*, ii, pp. 75, 121, 162; also provision as to clothiers' marks in proclamation of Charles I quoted above, p. 95.

[2] Welch, *Cutlers*, ii, p. 342.

On the other hand, there is also the ordinance enacted in 1624 and repeatedly enforced that,

no man from hensforth shall have a proper marcke vnlesse he be a forger and be able of him self to fforge & temper his stuf as a worckman sholde do.[1]

This requirement not only prevented members from acquiring rights in gross in their trade-marks,[2] but compelled them to maintain a high standard of workmanship in order to be able to retain their marks:

(10th April, 1621) At this Court was graunted to . . . Raphe Leachwoorth the letter R for his marck if it shall appeare to the Court by the report of a worckinge forger that the said Raphe Leachewoorth can forge.[3]
(5th August, 1634) Jacob Ashe made sute to haue the A for a marke graunted vnto him to strike vppon Blades wch he intendeth God willing to forge the Answere of this Court is that first the Master wth Two or three worckmen shall make tryall of the sufficiencie of his worckmanship in forging by seeing the sayd Jacob forge a blade hymself and vppon his sufficiencie he shall haue the same graunted.[4]

Registration of marks was twofold, viz.: upon a plate kept at the Company Hall and in the official book kept by the Clerk of the Company.[5] Registration appears to have been at the risk of the applicant; that is to say, surety might be asked of him, holding the company harmless by reason of such registration.[6] Erroneous registration was corrected with much ceremony:

(24th June, 1681) Upon the Complaint of Mr. Garner who strikes the Flameing Sword That seuerall persons in and about the Cittie of London strucke his marke in whole the

[1] *Ibid.*, ii, p. 344.
[2] *Cf.* the decision of the Supreme Court of the United States in *United Drug Co.* v. *Rectanus Co.* (1918) 248 U. S. 90, at p. 97, where, referring to "the fundamental error of supposing that a trade-mark right is a right in gross or at large," the Court says: "There is no such thing as property in a trade-mark except as a right appurtenant to an established business or trade in connection with which the mark is employed." See also *Everett O. Fisk & Co* v. *Fisk Teachers' Agency* (1924) 3 F. (2d) 7, at p. 8.
[3] Welch, *Cutlers*, ii, p. 343.   [4] *Ibid.*, ii, p. 348.
[5] *Ibid.*, ii, p. 9.
[6] *Ibid.*, ii, p. 346, 6 October 1629; p. 352, 12 May 1669.

Master and Wardens were pleased to sumone before them att this Court who there appeared Thomas Walsingham who strikes the fflameing sword & starre Richard Piggott the fflameing sword and Ball Glemham Wheetcroft the fflameing sword & halfe moone Anthony Watson the fflameing sword & Diamond & Mr. Tindall the fflameing (sword & heart) whom the Court informed the said Mr. Garner haueing struck the said mark for 20 yeares and although some of their markes were enrolled in this Company's Bookes Yett they neither could nor would vindicate the said Enrollments thereof But were Resolved to deface them upon their plate being sensible (in case Mr. Garner can make his Enrollmᵗ good to anticipate the others) that both by Law and the Orders of this Company their strikeing their markes is illegall And thereupon forewarned them for euer hereafter of strikeing the said markes upon their perills.[1]

The widow's life estate in her husband's mark appears to have been firmly established, even as against her husband's surviving partner:

(5th May, 1612) It is ordered that where as Awsten Johnson & John Wesell were partners in the trade of knyf makynge which Awsten Johnson it hath pleased God to take to his mercy who in his leiftyme did betwene them stricke the Crosse & the said Wesell did to give more Cowntenaunce & trad to the same marcke discontynewe his owne proper marck beinge the flower de luce If the widow of the said Awsten shall or will hereafter vse the same trade of knyf makinge then the same widowe shall have it properlie for her self duringe her leif but if the said widowe shall clerelie discontynewe Then the Court hold it fitt & so do order that the said John Wesell shall have the same marke as survivor to the Said Awsten deceassed.[2]

(27th August, 1607) Widdow Harblet was admonished from hensforth not to strick or cause to be strucken the marke of the shepherds hooke but libertie is given her to make the best of her marcke by sellinge it to any person so it be don by consent of this howse . . . (1st December, 1607.) Widowe Harblet brought in her marck being the Sheppards hooke & dagger.[3]

(28th September, 1650) Elizabeth Robinson widowe

[1] Welch, *Cutlers*, ii, pp. 353-4.   [2] *Ibid.*, ii, p. 340.   [3] *Ibid.*, ii, p. 338.

surrendred her Marke Called the B and Crowne and att her request It was granted and enrolled to Clement Bell.[1]

(9th June, 1677) Elizabeth wife of Daniel Tredwell deceased surrendered the Bunch of Grapes his mark, which was enrolled in her presence to Peter Perkins.[2]

However, the records make it perfectly clear that at least at one time it was the Court's opinion that the widow's estate was solely a life estate and that, at any rate in the early seventeenth century, she had no right to dispose of the mark by will. The following entry involved a nice question concerning the innocent purchaser for value from the widow, as against one to whom the widow subsequently bequeathed the same mark:

(6th January 1622–3) One Lambert Williams formerly had grant of the Bunch of Grapes. After his death his widow continued to strike it by her servants & journeymen "bye the tolleracon of this howse." The widow in her life time did take upon her to sell the mark (which was out of her power to do) to John Hubberd free brother of this Mistery. Nevertheless on her death bed she again disposed of the mark by her will to one William Balser her man contrary to the orders of this house, for "the disposinge & allowing of all marcks to any person or persons vsinge the same mysterie of Cutlers is in the said Mr & Wardeins & Assistaunts. Now for so muche as the said John Hubberd is not capable of him self beinge no worckman to stricke or have the same marck allowed vnto him And yet to give the same John Hubberd some Content for the money he paid in his owne wronge for the same marke the Court" have at his request reserved the Bunch of Grapes for the use of the eldest son of John Jencks when he shall be capable so to strike the same. Meanwhile the said mark is "to lye dead & not to be struck by the allowaunce of this howse by any person or persons."[3]

It is difficult to reconcile this declaration of the Court as to its ultimate control or disposition of marks with the memoranda dated March 6th, 1627–8 and October 9th, 1628

[1] *Ibid.*, ii, p. 350.
[2] *Ibid.*, ii, p. 353. See also The Falchion Mark, "surrendered by Elizabeth, relict of Zachariah Sellers," *ibid.*, ii, p. 27.
[3] *Ibid.*, ii, p. 343 (long minute abridged).

concerning the purchase by William Bales of the Bunch of
Grapes mark "for euer" and the enrollment of that mark
"to him & his heires for euer in this Court."[1] Furthermore,
a prior entry shows the Court "entreating" the owner of a
mark to transfer it to another:

(2nd December, 1613) It is agreed that whereas the marke
of the morryon head was formerlie graunted to Mr. Olliver
Plucket the Court vppon entreatie to him made to passe the
same over to Little Haunce Smyth wold not be perswaded
but he was Contented to give the same over to the hands of
Mr Addams (the Master) for him to dispose of the same at
his pleasure So as if he did dispose it to the said Haunce it
maie if it please God the same Olliver Plucket shall over live
the said Haunce the same maie then be in the right agayne
of the said Olliver to dispose at his pleasure The said Mr
Addams excepting of the said grant of the said Olliver Plucket
hath vppon the Condicons aforesaid granted the said Morrian
head to the said Haunc in manner & forme aforesaid wᶜʰ the
said Haunc hath enrolled & paid for & also at this Court he
hath brought in the kingshead.[2]

This qualified system of trade-mark ownership worked out
by the cutlers of London involved not only a life estate for
the widow, as indicated in the litigation of January 6th, 1622–
3, concerning the Bunch of Grapes mark quoted above, but
also very often a reservation of the mark for the son:

(20th May, 1623) The Spur, his father's mark, granted to
Abraham Brock. He delivered up his own mark, the Spread
Eagle, which the Court promise shall not be granted to any
others without his consent.[3]
(28th February, 1642–3) Flower de luce and crown enrolled
to George Spencer duringe and vntill George Knolles, sonne of
Jeremy Knolles, shall atteyne the Age of xxj° yeares And
that hee bee mad a free brother of this Company.[4]

Several curious entries concerning the mark of the Cross
Keys indicate not only the prospective value of a mark in
the estimation of the family of its deceased owner, but also
the system of reservations:

[1] Welch, *Cutlers*, ii, p. 345.   [2] *Ibid.*, ii, p. 341.
[3] *Ibid.*, ii, p. 343.   [4] *Ibid.*, ii, p. 349.

(5th August, 1630)   Whereas John Bushell a free brother of
this howse made sute to haue the marke of the Crossekeys
enrowled vnto him for seaven yeares to come vntill the sonne
of his late deceased vncle shall come to the Age of Twentye
and one yeares   To hould vp the reputacon of the same this
Court ordered that the Master in being and Mr Tuck shall
come some tymes before the next Court ouerlooke and
sprooue of the worckmanship of the sayd John Busshell in
the forging & finishing of a knyfe or knyves and accordingly
proseed the next Court.

(10th August, 1630)   The marke of the Crosskeyes was
surrendred to the Mr Wardeins & Assistants of this Company
to be disposed of according to their discretion & good likeing.
Vppon the humble sute of John Busshell a free brother of this
howse to haue the sayd marke of the Crossekeyes enrouled to
him for the terme of Seaven yeares to come to maynteyne
the reputacon of the sayd marke for the benefitt of the sonne
of John Bushell late one of the Assistants of this Companie
deceassed   The sayd Mr Wardens & assistants & the rather
at the request of Elizabeth the late weif & executrix of the
said John Busshell by letter directed to the Mr & Wardens
the Coopie shereof doth hereafter more playnely appeare
doth referr the enrowling thereof vntill the next Court of
assistants.

To our loueing frendes the Master and Wardens of the
Companie of Cutlers giue theis
Gents I haue receaved a letter from my Cosen John Busshell
wherein he intreats mee either be present wth you to morrow
morning or write to Certifie my intention and my weifes that
our desier is that my Cossen John Busshell should inioye and
make vse of the marke for Seaven yeares to the end that it
might be of the more vse and advantadg to my wifes sonne
John Busshell when he shall Come of Age whome wee intende
betweene this and Michaellmas to bynd to the trad   And
wee are boath verie confident (howsoeuer the malice of some
Ill disposed men haue indeavored to prevent itt) that you are
soe Just and honest to whome the Cheif Gouerment of that
societie is Committed That noe indirect way nor perswation
shall leade you to Iniure the memory of soe honest a man and
sometymes a good member of that Company by giueing assent
to any that may preiudice his posteritie especially when you
shall Consider that what is his Case nowe may in tyme by
some of yo   If therefore out of your loue to Justice and

willingnesse to satisfye our request you shall Confer it vppon
my Cossen John Busshell for this Seaven yeares you shall doe
yourselves much right and oblidge me and my weif to remayne

Your affectionat frendes
Fra Conninesbye
Elizabeth Connigsbye

Detford the 9th of
    August, 1630.

At this meeting the marke of the Croskeyes was enrowled to
John Busshell according to the request of Mr Connigesby
and his weif to the Company by their letter to haue and to
hould from this Tenth daye of August 1630 for Seaven yeares
to come.[1]

Conditional transfers and registrations are frequent. In
the following entry one receiving a mark upon a condition
subsequent gives a bond to secure his performance of his
agreement to return the mark upon the occurrence of the
condition in question:

(17th April, 1610) At this Court Thomas Browne of the
parish of Clarckenwell in St Johns Street London came in
Court and was a suter to have the letter B graunted to him
for his marke wch said Romaine B was formerlie graunted to
John Branckston who nowe is gone to dwell in Barwick w^ch
said Romaine B the court agree the said Tho. Browne shall
strick vppon this condicon that if the said John Branckston
shall at any time hereafter retorne for London and shall requir
that the said Tho. Browne shall surceasse to strick his marke
then the said Tho. Browne shall forthwith give over stricking
the same mark & to take him self to some other marke by the
appointment of this howse. And herevppon the said Tho.
Browne did faithfully assure & promise to John Johnson (the
Junior Warden) to performe the said promise and took of the
said John Johnson a penny to give to the said John Johnson
ffortie pounds if he do not performe this assumption vppon
request to him mad in forme aforesaid.[2]

Other conditions imposed are difficult to reconcile with the
rule that a mark must be used in connection with a business:[3]

[1] Welch, *Cutlers*, ii, pp. 346–8. *Cf.* reservation of the Murrion's Head, 20
Jan. 1611–12 (*ibid.*, ii, p. 340).
[2] *Ibid.*, ii, p. 339.
[3] *Cf. United Drug Co.* v. *Rectanus, supra*, at p. 97: "The owner of a trade-
mark may not, like the proprietor of a patented invention, make a negative
and merely prohibitive use of it as a monopoly."

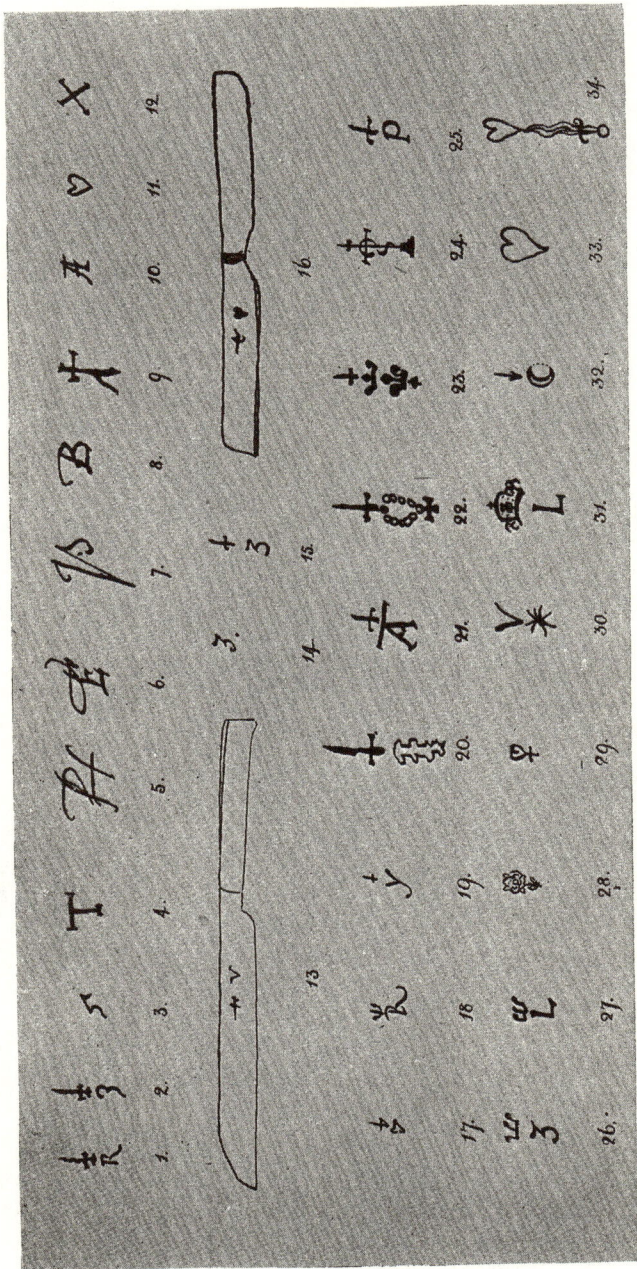

Reproduced from C. Welch's History of the Cutlers' Company of London

DRAWING OF LONDON CUTLERS' MARKS IN THE COURT MINUTE BOOKS OF THE COMPANY, 1606–1676

KEY TO MARKS

1. John Browne.
2. Peter Cornelius.
3. John Phillips.
4. Henry Stanus.
5. Robert Hobs.
6. Richard Ellarie.
7. William Hanwick.
8. John Branckston.
9. John Almond.
10. Sebright Orrenge.
11. Frederick Cheretree.
12. Gregorie Edwards.
13. Arnold Cornelius.
14. Peter and Arnold Cornelius.
15. Lawrence Sheppard.
16. Nathaniel Swayne.
17. John Wellam.
18. Samuel Swallow.
19. Joseph Surbut.
20. William Preston.
21. Jacob Ashe.
22. Philip Bowen.
23. Jeremy Knowles.
24. Henry King.
25. Robert Preston.
26. Robert Lister.
27. Enoch Taylor.
28. Daniel Treadwell.
29. Henry Letherland.
30. Zechariah Sellers.
31. William Laughton.
32. Jeremiah Holcroft.
33. Stephen Price.
34. Timothy Tindall.

(18th March, 1650–1) In regard Walter Powell Cutler hath purchased of George (Spencer) the flower de luce and Crowne It⁸ his desire neither to strike it himselfe nor that any other maie bee allowed to strike the same hereafter wch this Co^rt consented vnto.[1]

The ceremony surrounding the transfer of a mark is illustrated by the case of the mark of the Three Leaved Grass:

(24th February, 1606–7) At this Court Andrewe Roffe brought in his marke wch was allowed him by full consent of Court as that he also had & bought of Robert South being formerlie the marke of Wicker Bunt called the three leaved grasse. To the bargayne whereof came Wilson the Queens shoemaker and one other m(an) knowen to the Wardeins of this Company who was a goldsmith who testified that the said Andrewe Roffe did buy the same mark of the said South ffor the enrollinge of wch mark the said Andrewe paid ij⁸ vj^d.[2]

As may be seen from the illustration facing this page, cutlers' marks were small and easily mistaken for one another. That they were a constant source of litigation before the Court of the Company, is evidenced by the great number of cases cited by the historian of the Company:

The Broad Arrows were forbidden (February, 1609–10) for resembling the Cross Keys; the Helmet (August, 1610) for resembling the "murryonhead"; the Mulberry (October, 1612) which "on parte doth Counterfeyct other mens marks"; the Snuffers were altered (23rd May, 1620), and the Cross Arrows prohibited (August, 1622) for resembling the Cross Keys; the Pine Apple of John Knowlls was refused (August, 1624), being too much like the Pomegranate; The Pomegranate must adhere to the "stamp on the lead" (October, 1638), being too much like the Thistle; the Sceptre and O were prohibited (March, 1685–6), having too much resemblance to the Sceptre and Half Moon.[3]

Two entries will suffice to show the anxiety with which by this time owners of marks regarded the infringement thereof

---

[1] Welch, *Cutlers*, ii, p. 350. *Cf.* 4 June, 1664, *ibid.*, ii, p. 351.   [2] *Ibid.*, ii, p. 337.
[3] *Ibid.*, ii, pp. 15–16. For reproductions of Sheffield cutlers' marks, see R. Leader. *op. cit.*, i, pp. 107, 112.

and the method of the Court in dealing with such infringement:

(15th March, 1613–14)   George Lomely did deliver vp an old marke was formerlie graunted him beinge the G wth promise never to strick the same agayne wch he did give & surrender vp in regard as he saeith it hath ben Counterfeycted & discreadited by bad worcken vppon wch Consideracon The Company were Contented he shold stricke an other marck wch no man doth strick wch is the snuffers wch marke of the snuffers as this daie he brought in wch was graunted to him & inrolled in the hall.[1]

(23rd May, 1620)   At this Court appeared George Lomely who Contrarie to the orders of this howse w^thout warraunt hath struck the crose arrowes whereas formerlie his marck allowed vnto him by this howse by his owne Consent were the snuffers as by the lead in the howse where they are struck appearethe   And now sithenc he hath mad a marke wch he termeth the snuffers wch by the opinion of this Court resembleth the Croskeys   The Court therefore do enioyne the said Lomeley that from hensforth he do strick onlie his former marck beinge the snuffers in the manner he presented them wch if he do not The Court do signifie to him that they will according to the kings graunt pattent & rules of this howse graunted vnto him (them) laie the penalties vppon him for his Contempt & offenc that is for everie knyf he shall Conterfeyct & strick to forfeyct & paie xiijs. iiijd.[2]

Trade-mark infringement might involve the offender not merely in litigation before the Court of the Company, but even in criminal proceedings:

(6th October, 1612)   Tho. Hydden is enjoined to leave the stricking of his marke called the Mulberie vntill this Court shall give order therefore to allow him a mark wch as yet they can see no cause or allowe him any.

(10th November, 1612)   Tho. Hidden was Committed to prison vppon my Lord Maiors Commaundement for that he wold strick a marke not allowed him wch on parte doth Counterfeyct other mens.marks.

(10th December, 1612)   Tho. Hedden brought in his marke beinge a Hammer wch is allowed vnto him.[3]

[1] Welch, Cutlers, ii, p. 341.   [2] *Ibid.*, ii, p. 342.   [3] *Ibid.*, ii, pp. 340-1.

In concluding this study of the Cutlers of London it is interesting to note that one of their number appears to have been one of the first owners of a trade-mark to engage in newspaper advertising specifically in order to repress the piracy of his mark. Ephraim How, against whom complaints were made by his fellow-cutlers, had grievances of his own which he set forth in the *London Gazette*, May 24th–27th, 1703, as follows:

Whereas several Cutlers, in the disuse of their own Marks, do imitate the mark of Ephraim HOW, of Saffron-hill, which is the Heart and Crown, by stamping a playing Spade and a Crown, and also in Imitation of his Sirname they stamp NOW: Many having been deceived by this undermining Invention, all Persons who would buy Knives of his making, are desired to observe his Name and Mark narrowly, that they may not be imposed upon; for there is no Cutler whose name is NOW.[1]

In 1712 How again advertised in the *Daily Courant:*
Whereas several persons who sell knives, for the better vending their bad wares spread reports that Ephraim How, Cutler of London is deceased. This is to certify that he is living, and keeps his business as formerly, with his son in partnership, at the Heart and Crown on Saffron Hill; there being divers imitations, you are desired to observe the mark, which is the Heart, Crown and Dagger, with HOW under it.[2]

Having dealt with the London cutlers' marks at so great length it would be quite supererogatory to cover the same ground with regard to the Sheffield marks, the law of which developed substantially along the same lines, starting very much later than that in London. The cutlers of Hallamshire obtained their initial protection, not as in the case of London, from the municipal authorities and the Crown, but from the Lord of the Manor of Hallamshire. The granting of marks was part of the function of the jurors of the court of frankpledge, the administrators of the local law of the community. Although, early in the reign of Queen Elizabeth, cutlers,

---

[1] *Ibid.*, ii, p. 357.
[2] H. Sampson, *The History of Advertising from the Earliest Times*, p. 160.

customs in Hallamshire were spoken of as "ancient" and the trade described as subject to "ordinances made aforetime by men of the cutler's occupation,"[1] the first recorded grant of a mark occurs on November 7th, 1564 when "to this court . . . came Robert Boure, and took of the Lord a separate mark (*sepalem signum*) for himself for marking (*signandum*) iron knives, to wit, such a mark ƆH to have and to employ (*occupandum*) by himself. And if any other strike this mark and be convicted thereof by verdict, he shall forefeit to the Lord xx[s] and make amends to the offended party, and he gives to the Lord one penny of rent each year."[2]

This method of granting marks through the Lord's court and of paying "mark rent" to the Lord probably continued until the incorporation of the Company in 1624,[3] when the Company itself assumed the functions of the registration of marks and the supervision of the industry within a radius of six miles from the city of Sheffield. The Sheffield marks, in common with other production marks, were in their origin compulsory police marks and, as in the case of the London cutlers' marks, the "elevation of many marks into a valuable property was incidental, rather than designed . . . What as aimed at was not the protection of purchasers but a mutually understood trade indication, for the guidance of those exercising control or working in rivalry."[4] The Sheffield cutlers' records of the eighteenth century show much the same conceptions of the nature and legal implications of marks as do the London records of the seventeenth century. There is the same system of reservation of marks for the son of a deceased cutler and of a life estate in the mark for his widow.[5] In one case, where rival applicants for a dead freeman's mark were his son and the man who had married his widow, the Com-

[1] R. Leader, *op. cit.*, i, p. 6.
[2] *Ibid.*, i, p. 7. The 7th Article of the Orders for the Company in 1590 provided that "noe person usinge the said mysterye or crafte of Cutlers within the said Lordshippe shall stryke any marke upon his knyves except the marke be assyned to him before in the lordes Courte nor shall strike anye other marke butt his owne accustomed marke upon payne of forfayture for everye tyme doinge contrarye to this article tenne shillings to the said Erle and his heires. . . ." (*ibid.*, ii, p. 3).
[3] *Ibid.*, i, p. 18.   [4] *Ibid.*, i, p. 106.   [5] *Ibid.*, i, p. 110.

pany decided in favor of the latter, on condition that he give "for the benefit of the poor of the Corporation" the sum of three pounds.[1] There was the same insistence that, once a mark was granted by the Company, the grantee might use no other mark,[2] but, at the end of the century, there was a conspicuous "weakening of the old insistence on one man, one mark."[3]

An entry in the records of the Sheffield Cutlers' Company in 1749 indicates a tacit acknowledgment of the power of a mark-holder to transmit his mark on his death to another.[4] However, it was not until 1801 that for the first time this right of transmission was definitely recognized or at any rate confirmed by statute. Under the Act of 1801 [5] any freeman of the Cutlers' Company was empowered "to bequeath his mark, as his other personalty, by his will, his widow thereby not to be thereby prevented from carrying on the trade, or selling the right to the mark, for her lifetime, to any other person carrying on the trade." [6]

To recapitulate, the history of cutlers' marks shows the evolution of a mark from a typical regulatory compulsory mark of the Middle Ages to the modern trade-mark. The records of the cutlers show as early as the fifteenth century a sense of property in and the value of a mark, and by the seventeenth century we see the actual working of at least a qualified system of ownership in trade-marks, which may, to at any rate a limited extent — be "bought and sold and transmitted," and which are the subject of rigorous protection. The Act of 1801 crystallizes the development of the law of cutlers' marks and completes the process which had already commenced long before the case of the mark of the "Double Crescent" in 1452.

[1] *Ibid.*, i, p. 109.
[2] See entries 27 November 1731 and 29 January 1731, *Ibid.*, i, p. 108.
[3] *Ibid.*, i, p. 113.   [4] *Ibid.*, i, p. 114.   [5] 41 Geo. III, c. 97, local.
[6] Kerly on *Trademarks*, (5th ed.), p. 127; R. Leader, *op. cit.*, i, p. 114. For the history of Sheffield marks and the Cutlers' Company from the Cutlers' Company Act of 1801 until the present Trademark Act, see Kerly on *Trademarks* (5th ed. by F. G. Underhay), p. 126. See also references to this subject, *infra*, ch. vi.

CHAPTER VI

THE GENESIS OF THE MODERN LAW RELATING TO TRADE-MARKS

THREADING our way through the "dim, historic trails" from the Middle Ages we have arrived at the threshold of modern trade-mark law. We have found the starting points of these "trails" to be two in number, viz.: the proprietary mark or "merchant's mark," as it was known, indicating ownership of the goods to which it was affixed, and the regulatory or production mark indicating the source or origin of manufacture. We have seen that this classification of medieval marks into proprietary and regulatory marks was often one of function rather than of form or nature. The same mark might be used simultaneously by the gildsman on the one hand, voluntarily, as his "merchant's mark" and on the other, compulsorily, as his craftsman's or production mark, or two d'fferent marks might serve these purposes. Furthermore, especially in the cloth and cutlery trades, we have observed the evolution of the production mark from what we have termed a "liability mark" to an "asset mark," and we have noted the difficulty, during the process of transformation, of any rigid classification of production marks from the standpoint of their asset or liability nature. The modern manufacturer may use a mark or several marks or no mark just as he pleases; his forerunner, even as late as in the seventeenth century, was compelled to use a mark, and no more than a single mark. Nevertheless, as has appeared in the preceding pages, while the affixing of that mark may have worked to the detriment of its user, since thereby defective workmanship could be traced and punished, long before the use of marks ceased to be compulsory, their users began to realize the possibility of those marks as an asset, *i.e.*, as a symbol of good-will.

At the beginning of this essay we have noted that the case of *Southern* v. *How* is almost invariably regarded as the starting point of our present law of trade-marks. We have seen to what extent learned judges and writers have relied on *Southern* v. *How* to establish the antiquity of protection of trade-marks by English law. In this connection it is interesting to find that even Holdsworth, in demonstrating that in the early seventeenth century "the common law and the common lawyers were beginning to acquire some knowledge of the law applied by the merchants to regulate their commercial relations" has recently cited *Southern* v. *How*, — and, incidentally, the version of that case as given in *Croke's Reports*, — as an instance of "cases turning on such topics as . . . merchants' marks."[1] But in our analysis of *Southern* v. *How* and of the subsequent history of that case,[2] it was demonstrated that the sole contribution of that case was at best an irrelevant dictum of a reminiscent judge that he remembered an action in 22 Elizabeth by one clothier against another for the mis-use of the former's trade-mark.

It is possible that some day in some moldering mass of unpublished records of the common law may be found a report of a case in the reign of Elizabeth by a clothier for infringement of his trade-mark that will justify the authority with which *Southern* v. *How* has been so unanimously endowed. Until that day, however, *Southern* v. *How* will give no slight support to Dean Pound's complaint against courts and text-writers by whom "a principle was found latent in some meagrely reported, ambiguous and fragmentary pronouncement of a mediæval court which had culminated in the latest decisions of English and American courts."[3]

Southern v. *How* will then at best prove a most fragile link between the Middle Ages and the modern commercial

---

[1] W. S. Holdsworth, *op. cit.*, v, p. 144 and n. 8 thereto.
[2] See *supra*, pp. 6–10.
[3] R. Pound, *Interpretations of Legal History*, p. 28.

law of trade-marks. At any rate a careful investigation has not disclosed any contemporary reliance thereon or indeed any reference thereto. Only four years after the utterance of Dodderidge's dictum there appeared (1622) the first edition of Gerard Malynes' *Consvetvdo vel Lex Mercatoria*, Chapter 38 of which treats "Of Merchants Markes set upon Commodities." That chapter deals with the merchants' marks solely from the proprietary standpoint.

The marking of Merchants Commodities, either packt vp in Bundles, Trusses, Cafes, Coffers or Packes, is of great importance; for not onely by the Custome of Merchants, but also by the Civil Law, the propertie of the goods and Merchandises is adjudged to him, by whose marke they are marked or sealed. It is dangerous therefore to vse another mans marke, as many times Merchants doe in time of war, when they lend their names and markes for the preservation of their goods, betweene two or more contending Princes, both by Sea and Land. Every Merchant is to set downe his marke vpon his Bookes of account, wherewith his commodities are marked. . . . For even as Merchants doe saile betweene the two dangerous rockes of Scylla and Charibdis in their course of trafficke, when Princes are at variance; So is the danger to vse another Merchants marke without leaue; because the partie owner of the said marke is to defend the said goods, if they bee taken, or to countenance the persuers of the sute in Law for them, as farre as they in reason may require, otherwise the said goods may be lost as soone as taken. For as Ships are knowne by their Flags, and so taken to be at the Seas; so are Merchants goods marked with another mans marke, to bee that mans goods, although it were not, and will be so adjudged in the Courts of any Admirall of the Seas; . . . [1]

In the course of our investigation we have watched the development of sporadic doctrines and even systems of trade-mark law in the regulations promulgated by or for the gilds and in the adjudication by gild officials and gild courts or assemblies of questions arising in the course of the administration of these regulations. Although by the middle of the fifteenth century the disintegration of the gilds had begun,[2]

[1] pp. 190–200.   [2] See *supra*, p. 81.

and while the common law in the sixteenth and seventeenth
centuries was beginning to take cognizance of many cases
of a commercial nature,[1] the administration of such laws and
regulations as then existed with regard to trade-marks, was
a matter that still vitally affected the discipline and monopolistic aims of the gilds and companies. Trade-mark law
consequently remained to a great degree the concern of the
gilds and companies rather than of the common law courts.
Furthermore, as part of the scheme of the national control
of industry the gilds and companies were still useful "as
the local agents for carrying out a national industrial
policy." [2]

In addition to the law developed by the gilds and companies or, as Stubbs has aptly termed such law, "gild jurisprudence," [3] we have seen germs of modern trade-mark law in
statute law and also in the conciliar law, i.e. the law developed
by the King's Council and the Star Chamber. All three of
these sources of modern trade-mark law, and especially
"gild jurisprudence," had by the seventeenth century, made
contributions to trade-mark law of much greater significance
than that of the common law itself.

What, then, is the connecting link in the development of
trade-mark jurisprudence between gild, statute and conciliar
law on the one hand and the common law on the other? Of
course the simplest solution of this problem is to adopt
Seligman's theory that "the gild rules were . . . only part and
parcel of the common laws, and not merely the independent
work of the crafts themselves." [4] However, the question as
to the extent of the autonomy and separate judicial authority
of the gilds is still a mooted one,[5] upon which no theory of the
continuity of trade-mark law can safely be predicated. More-

[1] See W. S. Holdsworth, *op. cit.*, v, pp. 143 *et seq.*
[2] W. Cunningham, *op. cit.*, ii, p. 36, quoted by W. S. Holdsworth, *op. cit.*,
iv, p. 322, n. 4. See *ibid.*, iv, p. 360.
[3] W. Stubbs, *Constitutional History of England* (4th ed.) iii, p. 592.
[4] E. R. A. Seligman, *Two Chapters on the Mediaeval Guilds of England*,
p. 76. *Cf.* W. S. Holdsworth, *op. cit.*, iv, p. 311.
[5] For a summary of the conflicting views on this point, see A. P. Evans,
op. cit., pp. 612–615.

over, even if gild law should be regarded as a form or phase of common law, there still remains to be determined the actual point of contact between the fragmentary law of trade-marks as developed in the gilds and the modern common law and equitable doctrines of trade-mark law.

Further researches into the history of the clothier's case mentioned in *Southern* v. *How* on the one hand, and into the contemporaneous activity of the conciliar courts in the protection of trade-marks on the other, may possibly ultimately furnish a satisfactory solution of our problem. Such researches may indicate that the very judge or judges who sat in the clothier's case in the reign of Elizabeth were either identical or at any rate closely associated with the royal officials charged, in an administrative capacity, as members of the Council or Star Chamber, with the repression of commercial fraud. The Justices of "the clothing counties" were, in their administrative capacity, directly concerned with the clothing industry; they not merely obtained information,[1] but personally investigated conditions of the industry.[2] However, in the absence of specific evidence on the precise point in question, all that can be said is that from the standpoint of the crystallization and unification of theories and doctrines of trade-mark law, the activities and decisions of the Star Chamber and King's Council in the repression of the piracy of collective or geographical as well as of individual trade-marks, — especially in the cloth-making industry — in the sixteenth and seventeenth centuries, were in marked accord with the result that may have been reached, in the reign of Elizabeth, by a common-law court in a case involving the infringement of a mark upon cloth.

With the endeavors of the Tudors and the Stuarts to organize both external and internal trade came also the effort by the Crown to repress, through the Privy Council and the Star Chamber, various forms of commercial fraud including

[1] For an instance of the use by the Privy Council of the Justices of Assize to obtain information as to the cloth industry, see *Acts of the Privy Council, 1613–1614*, pp. 35, 191, 310, 351 *et seq.*
[2] See *History of Gloucestershire* (Victoria County Histories), ii, p. 159.

the infringement of trade-marks.[1] As we have seen in our study of the clothing and cutlery trades, the Star Chamber and Privy Council as well as the Crown itself by royal proclamation repeatedly intervened in the sixteenth and seventeenth centuries, to protect individual and collective marks.

However, despite the various tendencies towards the crystallization of the modern concepts of trade-marks and of trade-mark law indicated above, it was not until the beginning of the eighteenth century that the lawyers or at any rate law-writers and lexicographers were evidently beginning to think at all in general terms of trade-marks and when they did so, their definitions of trade-marks indicated a still very considerable uncertainty on their part as to the exact function of a mark and as to the basis of complaint for the mis-use of a mark. For instance, John Kersey in his *Dictionarium Anglo-Britannicum* of 1715 still regarded a trade-mark from the same proprietary standpoint as had Gerard Malynes almost a century before. Kersey defines "mark of goods" as a "distinguishing mark whereby every Merchant or Trader knows his own goods." On the other hand, the early law lexicographer, Giles Jacob in his *Lex Mercatoria or Merchant's Companion* published in 1718, says of marks:

If one Man shall set the Mark of another upon his Goods, to the Intent to bring him into any Trouble or Damage, or to put him to any Expence, by the Common Law, an Action of the Case will lye; for both the Common Law and the Civil Law hath great Respect to the marking of Goods, in relation to the settling the Property of the Merchandise under the right Owners and the *Cutlers* of *London* give to each Member a particular Mark, which cannot be appropriated without a particular Order and Leave of the Company and Party, and so other Companies. 2 *Cro. fol.* 471.[2]

Jacob's definition is an interesting fusion or rather confusion of all the prior and contemporaneous notions of trade-marks and of trade-mark rights and liabilities. It commences with

---

[1] See W. S. Holdsworth, *op. cit.*, iv, p. 360.
[2] *Lex Mercatoria or The Merchants Companion* (London 1718), pp. 26–27.

the regulatory mark, the infringement of which would bring "Trouble or Damage" to the owner of the mark; it next mentions the proprietary mark for which "both the Common Law and the Civil Law hath great Respect," after which it reverts to the regulatory mark of the cutlers of London, subject to the control of the Company, and winds up with a citation of *Southern* v. *How* in Croke's version of that case. In 1732 Jacob, in his *New Law Dictionary*, again says that a "mark of goods" "is what ascertains the Property or Goodness thereof &c. And if one Man shall use the Mark of another, to the intent to do him Damage, Action upon the Case lieth. 2 *Cro.* 471."

A statute of this period (13 George I, c. 26, 1726), enacted to protect the Scottish marks on linen, indicates that Parliament had by this time [1] arrived at the notion that the affixing of a mark to goods was a privilege rather than a duty and that, for the infringement of such a mark, reparation should be made to the owner thereof:

That it shall and may be lawful to and for every trader, dealer and weaver of linen manufacture, to weave his name, or fix some known mark in any piece of linen manufacture by him made, if he shall so think fit; and if any other person or persons shall counterfeit such mark or name, being thereof lawfully convicted upon the oath of one or more credible witness or witnesses before any two or more justices of the peace, or magistrates within any borough, he shall forfeit the sum of one hundred pounds, for the use of the person, whose mark shall be so counterfeited, to be raised, levied and paid in such manner as is hereinafter mentioned.[2]

The paucity of references to trade-marks in the legal literature of the seventeenth and eighteenth centuries has of course an economic aspect, that may perhaps also throw some light

---

[1] *Cf.* the language of the "Acte for the true . . . working of Waxe," 23 Eliz. c. 8, 1581, (*Stat. of the Realm*, iv., pt. 1, p. 670) requiring the marking of wax "to the intent that yf any deceipte bee used or done, it may be known who were the workers thereof. . . ." This statute was probably enacted to prevent the frauds indicated by the entry in *Cal. State Papers*, Dom., 1547–80, p. 635, No. 45, Oct. 18, 1579, "touching the sale of counterfeit and false wax."

[2] Clause XXX, 5 *Stat. at Large*, 634.

on the first trade-mark case in equity, *Blanchard* v. *Hill*, which we are about to consider. The slight degree of national economic significance acquired by trade-marks prior to the middle of the nineteenth century accounts for much of the tardiness in the growth of modern trade-mark law both in England and in the United States. As we have several times observed,[1] trade-marks did not develop as valuable symbols of good-will so long as producer and consumer were in close contact. Describing the economic situation in England at the beginning of the Industrial Revolution, Cunningham says:

> . . . the whole face of the country was changed by the Industrial Revolution. In 1770 there was no Black Country, blighted by the conjunction of coal and iron trades; there were no canals, or railways, and no factory towns with their masses of population . . . All the familiar features of our modern life and of its most pressing problems have come to the front within the last century and a quarter.[2]

It is worthy of note that the second volume of *Blackstone's Commentaries*, which appeared in 1766, contains no reference whatsoever to the subject of trade-marks in his discussion (Bk. II, Chap. XXVI) of "Titles to Things Personal by Occupancy," although among the "things personal" there enumerated are patents and copyrights.[3] Close upon the

---

[1] See *supra*, pp. 41, 48, 63, 78.

[2] W. Cunningham, *The Growth of English Industry and Commerce*, iii, p. 613.

[3] See Cooley's *Blackstone* (4th ed., by Andrews, Chicago 1899), i, p. 754, n. 1. In striking contrast is the *corpus* of commercial law, *Systema Jurisprudentiae Opificariae*, published by F. G. Struve (or *Struvius*) at Lemgo in 1738, based largely upon the unpublished works of Adrian Beier. Book ii of Volume III of this work contains three chapters devoted to trade-marks and trade-mark law, — chapters viii, ix and x, entitled respectively "*De signaturis & marchis mechanicis atque signis*," "*De signis collegiorum opificalium universalibus*," and "*De marchis singulorum*." These chapters are based mainly upon the edicts and decisions of various German ducal and other tribunals and authorities of the sixteenth, seventeenth and early eighteenth centuries. They represent, not a mere antiquarian interest in trade-marks or fragmentary references to the legal aspect of such marks, but an attempt at a systematic presentation of what were evidently then currently accepted and operative principles of trade-mark law in Germany. The "Introduction Historique" to Braune and Capitaine, *Les marques de fabriques*, pp. xxvi–xxvii, contains an analysis of these chapters; J. Kohler, *Das Recht des Markenschutzes* (p. 53), quotes from *Struvius* (p. 127): "*recte jus prohibendi competit contra illum, qui nostro signo utitur.*"

Industrial Revolution came a tremendous expansion not
only in the means of production and distribution but, pro-
portionately, in the advertising of goods, in which process
trade-marks for the first time acquired a national and not
merely local significance. Despite Dr. Johnson's observation
in 1759 that "the trade of advertising is now so near to perfection that it is not easy to propose any improvement," [1]
it was not until late in the eighteenth century that newspaper advertising began to be fairly common,[2] nor was it until
1871 that the pictorial poster was first used with great success in England.[3]

In the United States, just as in England, trade-marks did
not begin to acquire importance as assets of value in the
commerce of the nation in contra-distinction to local trade
until the second half of the nineteenth century. The origin
of the movement for trade-mark protection in America would
appear to have had some connection with the sail cloth or
duck industry in Massachusetts. As early as 1788 the
General Court of Massachusetts offered a bounty of "eight
shillings for every piece of Top Sail Duck and other stouter
sail cloth manufactured within this Commonwealth,"[4] and
this subsidy, accompanied by governmental relation of
standards of workmanship, was several times renewed.[5]

That competition in the manufacture of sail cloth was
accompanied by the infringement of trade-marks is evident
from an Act of the General Court (February 3, 1789) in-
corporating "The Beverly Cotton Manufactory," Sec. 5 of
which provided: [6]

[1] Quoted by G. W. Goodall, *Advertising: A Study of a Modern Business
Power* (London School of Economics Monographs, No. 41), p. 1.
[2] H. Sampson, *History of Advertising*, pp. 204 *et seq.*
[3] This was a design in black and white, originated by Frederick Walker to
advertise a dramatic representation of Wilkie Collins' novel, *The Woman in
White.* See G. W. Goodall, *op. cit.*, p. 22; S. R. Jones, *Posters*, pp. 2-3.
[4] *Mass. Laws & Resolves* 1787, c. 102, March 28, 1788 (ed. 1893, pp. 880-1).
[5] See J. L. Bishop, *History of American Manufacturers*, i, p. 419-20; Justin
Winsor, *Memorial History of Boston*, iv, 78 for further information concerning
Governmental relations with the sail-cloth industry, also *Resolves* of 1788,
c. 80, pp. 333-4; *Resolves* of 1791, c. 91, p.483. For many of these references,
I am indebted to Mr. Edward H. Redstone, State Librarian of the Commonwealth of Massachusetts.
[6] *Mass. Private and Special Laws*, 1789, c. 43 (ed. 1805, i, p. 226). Con-

That all goods which may be manufactured by the said Corporation, shall have a label of lead affixed to the one end thereof, which shall have the same impression with the seal of the said Corporation and that if any person shall knowingly use a like seal or label with that used by said Corporation, with a view of vending or disposing thereof, every person so offending shall forfeit and pay treble the value of such goods, to be used for and recovered for the use of the said Corporation, by action of debt, in any court of record proper to try the same.

By 1791 an echo of the need for the protection of trade-marks on sail-cloth is to be found in a petition by Samuel Breck [1] and other Boston sail-makers to the Second Congress asking that they be given the exclusive right to use certain marks for designating the sail-cloth of their manufacture, on which petition Thomas Jefferson, then Secretary of State, made the following report: [2]

December 9, 1791.

The Secretary of State, to whom was referred by the House of Representatives the petition of Samuel Breck and others, proprietors of a sail-cloth manufactory in Boston, praying that they may have the exclusive privilege of using particular marks for designating the sail-cloth of their manufactory, has had the same under consideration, and thereupon

Reports, That it would, in his opinion, contribute to fidelity in the execution of manufacturers to secure to every manufactory, an exclusive right to some mark on its wares proper to itself.

That this should be done by general laws, extending equal

cerning this cotton mill, see E. M. Stone, *History of Beverly*, pp. 85–6 and references in preceding note.

[1] Samuel Breck was an eminent merchant of Boston and agent of the army and fleets of Louis XVI. Investigation thus far has not disclosed the exact nature of his trade-mark difficulties. According to his son, he removed to Philadelphia in 1792 "in consequence of excessive and unequal taxation." (See Samuel Breck, *Genealogy of the Breck Family* (Omaha 1889) p. 40 and Appendix, pp. 205 *et seq.*, *Recollections of Samuel Breck*, ed. H. E. Scudder, p. 186.)

[2] T. Jefferson, *Complete Works* (Washington 1854), vii, 563; *Am. State Papers*, xiv, p. 48. (*Report of The Commissioners Appointed to Revise the Statutes Relating to Patents, Trades and Other Marks, and Trade and Commercial Names*, Senate Documents, vol. 3, No. 20, Washington, 1902, [hereinafter cited as *Report of United States Commissioners*], p. 92, quoted by E. S. Rogers, "Some Historical Matter Concerning Trade-Marks," 9 *Michigan Law Review*, 41.)

right to every case to which the authority of the Legislature should be competent.

That these cases are of divided jurisdiction: Manufactures made and consumed within a State being subject to State legislation, while those which are exported to foreign nations, or to another State, or into the Indian Territory, are alone within the legislation of the General Government.

That it will, therefore be reasonable for the General Government to provide in this behalf by law for those cases of manufacture generally, and those only which relate to commerce with foreign nations, and among the several States, and within the Indian Tribes.

And that this may be done by permitting the owner of every manufactory to enter in the records of the court of the district wherein his manufactory is, the name with which he chooses to mark or designate his wares, and rendering it penal in others to put the same mark to any other wares.

The references in contemporary newspapers to Breck's petition and Jefferson's report would indicate much interest in the commercial centers of the United States in the subject of trade-mark protection.[1] A letter from a Philadelphia manufacturer printed in the *Columbian Centinel* of Boston on December 24, 1791, is worthy of quotation at length:

It is with real pleasure and satisfaction that I behold the application of the proprietors of the sail cloth manufactory in the town of Boston to the Congress of the United States, for an act to secure them against the losses they are likely to sustain by persons counterfeiting their marks on sail cloth of an inferior quality. It is a subject which materially concerns every friend to the real prosperity and advancement of his country; and I entirely agree with those gentlemen in opinion, that it is a subject which loudly calls for the immediate interposition of the legislatures of these states. For it is of the greatest importance to the rising prosperity, commerce, opulency, and of course greatness of this country, that the manufacturer should be secured in the benefit and profit of his ingenuity, labour and industry, being an incitement to that industrious, enterprising, and useful set of

---

[1] E.g.: *Boston Gazette*, December 26, 1791, under "Report of the Proceedings of Congress" for December 9th; *Dunlap's American Daily Advertiser* (Philadelphia), December 12, 1791.

men, to carry on, persevere in, and bring to the greatest
possible perfection the various goods and articles by them
undertaken and manufactured.

There is no greater check to this laudable spirit of enterprise, industry and home manufacture, than that of im-
posters fraudulently counterfeiting of marks, and imposing
and selling bad and spurious articles for good, real and
genuine. It effectually cools the ambition of excelling and
becoming serviceable to one's country, and is highly preju-
dicial to the good repute of our manufactures in foreign
parts, consequently has a tendency to lessen instead of to
increase our commerce. I might enumerate many of its
baneful tendencies and effects, were it necessary, but it is a
subject which needs no comment. And although this offence
is one of the most heinous against the manufactures and
commerce of this country, being absolutely a species of
forgery, and meriting condign punishment, yet there is not
one of the states in which impositions and frauds of this
nature are properly guarded against, as much as is necessary,
and the publick good requires. Hence when a person thus
injured, discovers and brings to publick notice the aggressor,
he can obtain no redress adequate to the magnitude of the
injury he has sustained, although he may go to an enormous
expense and deal of trouble in the business, as well as a waste
of time, and after all is perhaps allowed by a jury, moderate
damages by no means equivalent to the loss sustained, much
less does it prove a salutary remedy against future offences
of the like nature.

A general act of Congress obviating these difficulties, and
providing for the prevention of offences of this kind, and for
the due punishment of the perpetrators of such infamy and
baseness, experience daily convinces me would be of universal
utility, and is a very desirable thing in this country.

The statement of the Philadelphia manufacturer just
quoted to the effect that statutory provision for trade-mark
protection was necessary because the remedy of damages,
which was the only remedy then afforded by the common law,
was ineffective, indicates that there must have been a certain amount of litigation in the state courts in the early
nineteenth century. It is therefore somewhat surprising that
the first reported case of trade-mark infringement did not

come before a state court of record until 1837 [1] and that it was not until 1844 that the first case was brought before a United States court.[2] It is interesting to note that in that first federal decision, Judge Story, in granting an injunction, said: "I do not quote cases to establish the principles above stated. They are very familiar to the profession; and are not now susceptible to any judicial doubt." [3] Up to 1870 only sixty-two trade-mark cases in all were decided by American courts.[4] An idea of the growth of the importance of trade-marks to their owners may be gathered from the fact that in 1870 only one hundred and twenty-one trade-marks were registered under the Trademark Act, to which we shall again refer later on in connection with the subject of trade-mark registration, while in 1923 almost fifteen thousand were registered.[5]

From a brief digression into the economic background of the genesis of modern trade-mark law, we return to a consideration of the reasons impelling Lord Hardwicke to deny emphatically, — indeed almost indignantly, — in *Blanchard* v. *Hill* the first recorded request for injunctive relief against trade-mark piracy. Even the citation by the Attorney-General of *Southern* v. *How*, which appears to have impressed so many of the later judges, failed to move the Lord Chancellor who declared: "The objection has been made, that the defendant in using this mark prejudices the plaintiff, by taking away his customers. But there is no more weight in this, than there would be in an objection to one innkeeper setting up the same sign with another." [6]

[1] *Thompson* v. *Winchester*, Sup. Ct. Mass. 1837, 19 Pick. 214; *Report of United States Commissioners*, p. 93.

[2] *Taylor* v. *Carpenter*, U. S. Cir. Ct., Dist. of Mass., 3 Story, 458; *Report of United States Commissioners*, p. 93.

[3] 3 Story 464.

[4] *Report of United States Commissioners*, p. 93.

[5] See "Report of Commissioner of Patents, 1923," in *U. S. Official Gazette* (1924), vol. 319, p. 231.

[6] 2 Atkyns p. 487. The infringement of signs or signboards appears, as a matter of fact, to have been quite common and unrepressed even in the early 18th century. In their *History of Signboards* (3rd ed., 12th impression, 1908, pp. 31-2) Larwood and Hotten, quoting from *Memorials of Nature and Art Collected on a Journey in Great Britain during the Years 1802 and 1803* by an observant foreigner, C. A. G. Goede (vol. i., London 1808, p. 68), give the follow-

Even in the light of the relative economic unimportance of trade-marks touched upon above, the decision in *Blanchard v. Hill* is especially difficult to understand when one re-members that Lord Hardwicke showed himself otherwise particularly keen to utilize the weapons of equity for the repression of new forms of commercial fraud. Writing a few years later to Lord Kames, he said:

As to relief against fraud, no invariable rules can be es-tablished. Fraud is infinite, and were a court of equity once to lay down rules, how far they would go, and no further, in extending their relief against it, or to define strictly the species or evidence of it, the jurisdiction would be cramped and perpetually eluded by new schemes which the fertility of man's invention would continue. To this fertility of inven-tion and the luxuriant growth of fraud is owing the increase of causes in courts of equity, and not to that encroachment upon the law, which my Lord Bacon in his forty-third apho-rism, calls an over-flowing of the bank of Pretorian Courts.[1]

ing interesting picture of the "appropriation of trade values" at the beginning of the 19th century: "As it is one of the principal secrets of the trade to attract the attention of that tide of people which is constantly ebbing and flowing in the streets, it may easily be conceived that great pains are taken to give a striking form to the signs and devices hanging out before their shops. The whole front of a house is frequently employed for this purpose. Thus, in the vicinity of Ludgate Hill, the house of S——, who has amassed a fortune of £40,000 by selling razors, is daubed with large capitals three feet high, acquaint-ing the public that 'the most excellent and superb patent razors are sold here.' As soon, therefore, as a shop has acquired some degree of reputation; the younger brethren of the trade copy its device. A grocer in the city who had a large *Beehive* for his sign hanging out before his shop, had allured a great many customers. No sooner were the people seen swarming about this hive than the old signs suddenly disappeared, and Beehives, elegantly gilt, were substituted in their places. Hence the grocer was obliged to insert an adver-tisement in the newspapers, importing 'that he was the sole proprietor of the original and celebrated *Beehive*.' A similar accident befell the shop of one E—— in Cheapside, who has a considerable demand for his goods on account of their cheapness and excellence. The sign of this gentleman consists in a prodigious *Grasshopper*, and as this insect had quickly propagated its species through every part of the city, Mr. E—— has in his advertisements repeatedly requested the public to observe that 'the genuine Grasshopper is only to be found before his warehouse.' He has, however, been so successful as to per-suade several young beginners to enter into engagements with him, on con-ditions very advantageous to himself, by which they have obtained a licence for hanging out the sign of a Grasshopper before their shops, expressly adding this clause in large capitals, that 'they are genuine descendants of the renowned and matchless Grasshopper of Mr. E—— in Cheapside.' " For an early New York case on this point see *Howard v. Henriques* 3 Sandf. (N. Y.) Super. 725; Cox, *Manual of Trademark Cases*, 2nd ed., No. 108, p. 60.
[1] P. C. Yorke, *Life and Correspondence of Philip Yorke, Earl of Hardwicke,* ii, p. 554.

Furthermore, Lord Hardwicke, one year after his denial of equitable protection to trade-marks—the symbol of good-will —handed down the first decision in the books protecting good-will itself as an asset of value in the hands of an administrator.[1]

The true *ratio decidendi* in *Blanchard* v. *Hill* is to be found in the emphasis placed by Lord Hardwicke upon the claim of the plaintiff to an exclusive right to the use of the "Great Mogul" as a stamp upon his cards in a charter granted to the Card-makers' Company of Charles I. It should be remembered that not only was the thought of monopoly at that time still abhorrent to English law and business, but that a monopoly on playing cards was the classic example of a monopoly and had been the subject of the famous "Case of Monopolies," *Darcy* v. *Allen*.[2] While the particular charter mentioned in *Blanchard* v. *Hill* was not identical with that which had been the subject of the litigation of 1603,[3] "Lord Hardwicke seems to have thought it impossible to grant an injunction without incurring the risk of countenancing the old system which had been condemned and declared illegal."[4]

Blanchard v. *Hill*, though described a century later by an English judge "as a leading case on the subject,"[5] appears to

---

[1] *Gibblett* v. *Reed* 9 Mod. 459; Cox, *Manual of Trade-Mark Cases* (2nd ed.), p. 2; also C. E. Allan, *The Law Relating to Good-Will*, p. 56.

[2] 11 Co. Rep. 84 b; for a full account of this case, see J. W. Gordon, *Monopolies by Patents*, appendix II, pp. 193 *et seq*. For a thorough analysis of the case, see W. S. Holdsworth, *op. cit.*, iv, pp. 349 *et seq*.

[3] W. H. Price, *The English Patents of Monopoly*, pp. 22–24. How great was the resentment then at the enforcement of playing card monopolies appears in the recently published *Journal of Sir Simonds D'Ewes*, containing the following entry of an occurrence in the "Starre-Chamber" Nov. 25, 1604; "After wee weere risen I went into the Howse where sate the grand Committee for Grievances, and there weere diverse witnesses in examination about Mr. Squibs patent for cardes, being a monopolie how he had violentlie brooken into ther howses taken away cardes readie made, and ther stampes to make them by: and raised the price of cards from 3d. a packe to 9d. a packe. Then was Mr. Squibb and one Mr. Thomas May a messenger whome Squibb had imploied called in: and ordered that they should noe further prosecute." (*Journal of Sir Simonds D'Ewes* [D'Ewes' second "Journal," — of the Long Parliament], ed. by W. Notenstein, 1923, p. 68).

[4] F. M. Adams, *Treatise on the Law of Trade-Marks*, p. 7.

[5] Wood, V. C., in *Farina* v. *Silverlock* (1855) 24 Law Journal, Ch., N.S. 632. Again in *Collins Co.* v. *Brown* (1857) 3 K. & J. 423, 428, Wood, V.C., cited the reasoning of Lord Hardwicke in *Blanchard* v. *Hill* as "the true foundation of the jurisdiction in these cases."

have created no contemporary comment, adverse or otherwise, and later on was either ignored or repudiated by courts of law and equity both in England and in this country.[1] In 1777 there was tried before Lord Mansfield in the Court of King's Bench a case then recorded as "remarkable . . . and the first of its kind," [2] *Cabrier* v. *Anderson*, in which a verdict of £100 was awarded to the plaintiff under a statute of William III for defendant's putting his (Cabrier's) name to five watches made by the defendant.[3] It is not surprising, therefore, that in 1783, when, in the case of *Singelton* v. *Bolton*, the issue of trade-mark piracy at common law was touched upon before Lord Mansfield, he, with his great sense of commercial necessities and equities, held that "if the defendant had sold a medicine of his own under the plaintiff's name or mark, there would be a fraud for which an action would lie.[4]

The first reported case squarely involving the protection of trade-marks by an English common law court did not come until 1824 when Abbott, C.J., in *Sykes* v. *Sykes* [5] appears

[1] In 1883 Romilly, M. R., declared: "I doubt very much, notwithstanding the high authority of Lord Hardwicke's name, whether this case would be followed at this day to the extent to which it is there carried and on the grounds it is there recited." (*Hall* v. *Barrows* 32 Law Journal, N.S. Equity, p. 550.)
In this connection, see *Charles Goodall & Son Ld.* v. *John Waddington Ld.*, 41 Rep. Pat. Cas. 658, decided by the Court of Appeal in October, 1924. The trade-mark there involved was on playing cards. The court took cognizance of the division of the entire playing card manufacturing industry between plaintiff, defendant and one other firm (p. 655, lines 36 *et seq.*); nevertheless, the court based its denial of an injunction solely on the ground of the absence of the probability of deception. *Blanchard* v. *Hill* was cited neither by counsel nor by the court.
In the leading American case of *Dixon Crucible Co.* v. *Guggenheim* 2 Brewster (Phila.) 321, 327, the Court, criticizing the fears of monopoly expressed in *Blanchard* v. *Hill*, said: "The modern, if not the more enlightened opinion, would seem to be, that the protection of a trademark by a court of equity has just the opposite tendency, as it is an encouragement to men to embark in manufacturing." See also *Amoskeag Mfg. Co.* v. *Spear*, 2 Sandf. (N. Y.) Super. 599, 605, and the recent case of *Scandinavia Belting Co.* v. *Asbestos Rubber Works* 257 Fed. 937, 941; also *Monthly Law Magazine* for December 1840, article on "Trademarks," reprinted in 25 *American Jurist* (1841), p. 269, 277.
[2] *St. James Chronicle*, Dec. 4, 1777.
[3] Atkyns and Overall, *Some Account of the Worshipful Company of Clockmakers of the City of London*, p. 259. The statute (9 & 10 Wm. III, c. 28, *Stat. at Large* iii, 713) prohibited the export of empty watchcases engraved with counterfeit names (to be filled abroad with inferior movements) "to the great prejudice of the buyers and the disreputation of the art at home and abroad."
[4] 3 Doug. 293; Cox, *Manual of Trade-Mark Cases*, No. 4, p. 3.
[5] 3 B. & C. 541.

to have regarded the law as settled and the citation of authorities as consequently unnecessary. The declaration in that case alleged that the plaintiff

made and sold for profit a large quantity of shot-belts and powder-flasks &c, which he was accustomed to mark " Sykes Patent," in order to denote that they were manufactured by him, the plaintiff, and to distinguish them from articles of the same description manufactured by other persons. That plaintiff enjoyed great reputation with the public on account of the good quality of the such articles and made great gains by the sale of them, and that defendant, knowing the premises, and contriving, &c., did wrongfully, knowing (*sic*), and fraudulently, against the will and without licence and consent of the plaintiff, make a great quantity of shot-belts and powder-flasks and caused them to be marked with the words of "*Sykes Patent*," in imitation of the said mark so made by the plaintiff . . .; and did knowingly and deceitfully sell for their own lucre and gain the said articles so made and marked as aforesaid, *as and for* shot-belts and powder flasks, &c. of the manufacture of the plaintiff; whereby plaintiff was prevented from selling a great quantity of shot-belts and powder flasks &c. and greatly injured in reputation, the articles so manufactured and sold by the defendant being greatly inferior to those manufactured by the plaintiff.[1]

We shall have occasion to refer to this pleading again when discussing the basis of the modern action for trade-mark infringement.[2]

It is unfortunate that in the first instance of the issuance of an injunction restraining trade-mark infringement, *Day* v. *Day*, there appears to be no record of the reasoning of the Lord Chancellor Lord Eldon, the case being merely noted by Eden in the 1821 edition of his work on *Injunctions*.[3]

In the great case of *Millington* v. *Fox*[4] (1838) the Lord Chancellor, Lord Cottenham, without citing any authorities and ignoring *Blanchard* v. *Hill*, held that equity would enjoin trade-mark infringement even though such infringement was without intent to defraud and in ignorance of the plain-

---

[1] 3 B. & C., pp. 451–2.   [2] See *infra*, ch. vii, p. 142.
[3] P. 314.   See Kerly, *op. cit.*, p. 2, n. 8.
[4] 3 Myl. & Cr. 338.

tiff's ownership of the trade-mark involved. Plaintiff's bill in equity after setting forth long user of the trade-marks in question by plaintiff and their predecessors without pleading any fraud on the part of defendants, merely alleged that the latter "had manufactured considerable quantities of steel which they had marked with the plaintiff's beforementioned marks; in order that it might be sold in the market as steel manufactured by the plaintiffs." Lord Cottenham while differentiating this case from one in which fraud was involved, held "that there was sufficient in the case to show that the Plaintiffs had a title to the marks in question; and they undoubtedly had a right to the assistance of a Court of Equity to enforce that title . . . That circumstance [defendant's innocence] however, does not deprive the Plaintiffs of their exclusive use of those names . . ."[1]

We shall glance but cursorily at the history of the development of trade-mark law subsequent to the initial instances of the protection of trade-marks by both law and equity. We shall rather endeavor to indicate in what way the historical origins indicated in the foregoing chapters have influenced and are still influencing the development of the law. But in order that we may appreciate the historical preconceptions and difficulties with which the courts and text-writers both in this country and in England are still wrestling, we must refer briefly to certain phases of legislative and judicial trade-mark protection in both countries.

The tardiness with which the law has given adequate protection to trade-marks and the lack of general legislative recognition of the beneficial effects of such protection are indicated by the fact that in England no parliamentary consideration of a broad and general nature was given to the matter until 1862. At that time the necessity for a trademark registration act was urged [2] but for reasons referred to hereafter the only statute then enacted [3] did not provide for

[1] *Ibid.*, p. 352.
[2] See *Report from the Select Committee on Trade-Marks Bill* in *Reports of Committees*, 1862, Session Papers xii, Index, p. 178, *s.v.* "Registration", No. 1.
[3] 25 & 26 Vict., c. 88.

the registration of trade-marks but merely made a counter-feiting of these marks a penal offence. It was not until 1875 that the ignorance or indifference of Parliament [1] in this matter of registration was finally overcome and that the first British trade-mark registration statute [2] was enacted. In 1870 the first United States statute providing for the registration of marks was passed [3] and, this statute being held unconstitutional,[4] a similar one was re-enacted with the objectionable features eliminated in 1876.[5]

A perusal of the report of the British Parliamentary Committee on Trade-marks of 1862 and of the various early debates in the Congress of the United States on the subject of trade-marks [6] will be disappointing reading to the student of comparative jurisprudence with preconceptions as to the superiority and rapidity of progress of Anglo-Saxon law, for they clearly indicate that both here and in England registration statutes were enacted, not so much for the protection of manufacturers at home, but in order to enable these manufacturers to obtain the advantages of reciprocal statutes in foreign countries.[7]

[1] See James Bryce, Introd. to Suppl. to Ludlow and Jenkyns *Treatise on the Law of Trademarks* (2nd. ed. London 1877) p. vii. Also Hansard, *Parliamentary Debates* 3rd Series, Vol. 217, 1874, column 702; *ibid.*, 3rd Series, vol. 223, 1875, column 139.
[2] 38 & 39 Vict., c. 91.   [3] 16 *Stat. L.* 198.
[4] *Trade-Mark Cases*, 100 U. S. 82.
[5] 19 *Stat. L.* 141. See *Report of United States Commissioners*, pp. 105 *et seq.*
[6] See *Report of United States Commissioners*, Chapter XXV, pp. 380 *et seq.*
[7] See remarks of Mr. Jenckes in United States Congress, April 14, 1870, in part as follows: "Concerning trademarks, we are at present in an anomalous condition, which perhaps is not understood by the House generally. By certain treaties or conventions with Belgium, France, and Russia, we have agreed to recognize the validity of the trademarks of those countries upon their being registered in the Patent Office of the United States, and to give them the same effect throughout the United States that they have in the country where they originated; and trademarks recognized by the law of this country have the same effect throughout those European countries as the trademarks secured by the citizens or subjects of those countries. Thus by treaties, which are a part of the supreme law of the land, we have secured to subjects of those three nations rights which are not by national law secured to citizens of the United States. The rights which it is proposed to protect by registration of trademarks are not greater in any sense than those which are secured to citizens of foreign countries. In fact, these provisions are substantially those of the continental nations, and also those of the trademarks statute of Great Britain, with which country I believe we are also engaged in negotiations for a similar treaty." (*Report of United States Commissioners*, p. 392). See also *ibid.*, pp. 100, 383, 421, 441, of *Report from the Select Committee on Trade-Marks Bill*, Q. Nos. 1142,

The report of the Parliamentary Committee of 1862 and
the debates of Congress in 1870 throw an interesting light on
the then current conceptions of the nature of a trade-mark
and the purpose of and necessity for a national trade-mark
law. In England the main difficulty seems to have been in a
refusal or inability of legislators, lawyers and merchants to
regard a trade-mark as a normal and ordinary asset or subject
of property. The most dire consequences, such as fraudulent
uses and sales of trade-marks and the creation of monopolies,
it was prophesied, must ensue from the recognition of trade-
marks as property.[1] In the American Congress the objections
to federal trade-mark legislation appear to have been based
partly on considerations of "States' Rights,"[2] partly upon a
feeling that the subject was of trivial importance.[3]

The extreme reluctance of the witnesses before the Parliamentary Committee of 1862 to interpret trade-mark rights
in terms of property has been shared both by English and
American Courts. We have seen that, in the abridgments
and digests, as well as in decisions citing *Southern* v. *How*,
the clothier's action for the misuse of his mark referred to by
Justice Dodderidge, has been uniformly classified as an
action in deceit.[4] But quite apart from *Southern* v. *How*,
there is a steady stream of substantial English authority
holding the common law action for trade-mark infringement
to be one of deceit, although the plaintiff in such cases is as

1143, 2461: "We have obtained legal opinions in Germany and are told that
the law with respect to . . . trademarks . . . only protects manufacturers
of such countries as have reciprocal treaties or laws to protect German manufacturers, and that as no such law exists in our case, we can do nothing."
(Q. No. 2461.) See also *Trade-Mark Cases*, 100 U. S. 82, 88.
    [1] See *Report from the Select Committee on Trade Marks Bill* (1862) Questions
Nos. 206, 224, 620, 2825, 2826.
    [2] Mr. Hammond of Georgia: "It is claimed that the States cannot ade-
quately protect trademarks. Why not? Their judges are as honest and as
learned in law as those upon the United States benches. The jurors, if different
in the two courts, are not better in those of the Federal Courts; in some parts
of the country they are much below the State standard of intelligence and virtue.
States' officers are more numerous, and equally faithful; their courts more
numerous and more accessible; justice can be had cheaper and quicker in the
State courts." (*Report of United States Commissioners*, p. 446.) See also *ibid.*,
pp. 474 *et seq.*
    [3] *Ibid.*, pp. 436, 447.
    [4] See *supra*. ch. i, p. 9 and n. 1 thereto.

a matter of fact never deceived, but defrauded. In *Blofeld*
v. *Payne*[1] (1833), just as in *Sykes* v. *Sykes* and *Millington* v.
Fox, an important advance in trade-mark law was effected
without any extended reasoning or citation of prior authorities. In *Blofeld* v. *Payne*, an action in King's Bench, the
declaration stated:

that the plaintiff enjoyed a great reputation for the good
quality of his hones, and made great profit by the sale
thereof; that the defendant wrongfully and without his
consent caused . . . hones to be . . . wrapped in envelopes
resembling those of the plaintiff, and containing the same
words, thereby denoting that they were of his manufacture,
which hones the defendant so wrapped up as aforesaid *as and
for* the plaintiff's for their own gain, whereby the plaintiff
was prevented from disposing of a great number of his hones
and they were depreciated in value and injured in reputation,
those sold by the defendant being greatly inferior.[2]

The jury found for the plaintiff with one farthing damages,
but stated that they thought the defendant's hones were not
inferior to his. The four judges unanimously upheld the
verdict, Littledale, J., holding that the act of the defendant
was a fraud against the plaintiff, and that, if it occasioned him
no substantial damage, it was still, to a certain extent, an
injury of his right.

In *Crawshay* v. *Thompson*[3] (1842), also an action on the
case for "wrongfully, knowingly and fraudulently" stamping
bars of iron made by defendant with a stamp resembling one
used by the plaintiff, it was held:[4]

this is in the nature of an action for deceit; and it is laid down
in Com. Dig., tit. Action upon the case for a deceipt (F3), that
"the declaration regularly ought to charge that the defendant
was *sciens* of the matter by which he deceived; and that he
did it *falsò et fraudulenter*."

In subsequent English decisions at common law the courts,
while continuing to describe the action for trade-mark in-

---

[1] 4 B. & Ad. 410.
[2] *Ibid.*, p. 410. (Italics, the writer's.)
[3] 4 Man. & G. 357.
[4] *Ibid.*, p. 385, per Cresswell, J.

fringement as being an action in deceit or "action on the case in the nature of a writ of deceit," have from time to time let fall expressions of doubt as to the propriety of this classification.[1] In 1902 in *Addley Bourne* v. *Swan & Edgar, Ld.*[2] the leading authorities on this point were reviewed by Farwell, J., who concluded that, although in cases of trade-mark infringement no fraudulent misrepresentation had been made to the *plaintiff*, nevertheless, whether correctly or not, the law was definitely settled that the proper common law action for trade-mark infringement is an action in deceit.[3]

The American courts in approaching the question of redress for trade-mark infringements did not proceed upon

[1] In *Crawshay* v. *Thompson* 4 Man. & G. 357 (1842) Maule J. said of such an action at p. 385: "This is in the nature of an action for deceit." In *Rodgers* v. *Nowill* 5 C.B. 109 (1847), described in the report as an "action on the case, for an alleged piracy by the defendants, of a certain mark," the same judge asked (at p. 116): "Is this an action on the case for a deceit?" Counsel, insisting that "there is no other title under which such an action can be classed," and arguing that intent to deceive as well as damage must be proven to sustain plaintiff's case, cited *Baily* v. *Merrell* 3 Bulstr. 95 and *Pasley* v. *Freeman* 3 T.R. 51. It must be noted that both cases cited by plaintiff involved direct misrepresentation to the plaintiff and not to the third party, as is the case in trade-mark piracy. The four judges appear to have avoided an exact definition of the nature of the action, though they emphatically permitted recovery. In *Edelsten* v. *Edelsten* (1863) 1 De G. J. & S. 185, 199 Lord Westbury, L.C., held that in actions for trademark infringement "at law the proper remedy is by an action on the case for deceit; and proof of fraud on the part of the defendant is of the essence of the action. . . ." In *Leather Cloth Co.* v. *American Leather Cloth Co.* (1865) 4 De G. J. & S. 137 (1863) at pp. 139–140, Lord Westbury, L.C., likewise said again: "At law, the remedy for the piracy of a trademark is by an action on the case in the nature of a writ of deceit. This remedy is founded on fraud, and originally it seems that an action was given not only to the trader whose mark has been pirated but also to the buyer in the market if he had been induced by the fraud to buy goods of an inferior quality." In *Jamieson & Co.* v. *Jamieson* (1898) 15 Rep. Pat. Cas. 169, C.A., Vaughan Williams, L.J., said at p. 191: "This is an action for a wrong. It is an action for deceit; for fraudulently pretending that the Defendant's goods were the Plaintiff's goods and so trying to pass them off. That is not a breach of any right of property in the Plaintiffs. It is merely an exercise by the Plaintiff of a right that he has that he should not be injured by the fraud of the Defendant in pretending that the goods manufactured by him, the Defendant, are of Plaintiff's manufacture." In *London, General Omnibus Co.* v. *Lavell* (1899) 70 L.J. Ch. 17, Alverstone, L.J., stated that "the action is for deceit upon the ground that the defendant has run an omnibus which is likely to divert the passengers from the plaintiffs' omnibuses." Furthermore, Vaughan Williams, L.J., said (at p. 20): "These actions, which in their origin undoubtedly are actions of deceit, actions based upon an allegation of deceit by the defendants, have in course of time come to be treated very much as actions brought against defendants for having trenched upon the private rights of the plaintiffs."

[2] 20 Rep. Pat. Cas. 105.

[3] See also Pollock on *Torts* (12th ed.) p. 314 n. Z; Kerly on *Trademarks* (5th ed.), p. 567.

the English common law theory of deceit but gave their protection upon substantially the same equitable grounds that had been thus expressed in England in 1842 in the oft quoted dictum of Lord Langdale, M.R.,:

A man is not to sell his goods under the pretense that they are the goods of another man . . . He cannot therefore be allowed to use names, marks, letters or other *indicia*, by which he may induce purchasers to believe that the goods which he is selling are the manufacture of another person. . . . I have no doubt that another person has not a right to use that name or mark for the purpose of deception, and in order to attract to himself that course of trade, or that custom, which, without that improper act, would have flowed to the person who first used, or alone was in the habit of using the trade name or mark.[1]

A typical statement of the early reaction of the American courts towards trade-mark piracy is contained in the authoritative opinion of Justice Duer of the Superior Court of New York in *Amoskeag Mfg. Co.* v. *Spear* decided in 1849. Justice Duer said:

When we consider the nature of the wrong that is committed when the right of an owner of a trade-mark is invaded, the necessity for the interposition of a court of equity becomes still more apparent. He who affixes to his own goods an imitation of an original trade-mark, by which those of another are distinguished and owned, seeks, by deceiving the public, to divert and appropriate to his own use, the profits to which the superior skill and enterprise of the other had given him a prior and exclusive title. He *endeavors*, by a false representation, to effect a dishonest purpose; he commits a fraud upon the public and upon the true owner of the trade-mark. The purchaser has imposed upon him an article that he never meant to buy, and the owner is robbed of the fruits of the reputation that he had successfully labored to earn. In his case there is a fraud coupled with damage, and a court of equity in refusing to restrain the wrongdoer by an injunction, would violate the principles upon which a large portion of its jurisdiction is founded and abjure the exercise of its most important functions, the suppression of fraud and the preven-

---

[1] *Perry* v. *Truefitt* (1842), 6 Beavan 66, 73.

tion of the mischief that otherwise may prove to be irreparable.[1]

With the merger of law and equity both in this country and
in England, and also in view of the fact that injunctive relief
is more effective than pecuniary reparation, the repression of
trade-mark infringement has in recent years fallen more and
more within the scope of equity and the principles governing
relief in such cases have accordingly been those of equity
rather than of law. What those principles are and to what
extent they have been shaped and are still being influenced
by historical antecedents will form the subject of our concluding chapter.

[1] *Amoskeag Mfg. Co.* v. *Spear* 2 Sandf. (N.Y.) Super. 599, 605–6. See
also *Marsh* v. *Billings* (1851) 61 Mass. 322, 330; *Miller Tobacco Manufactory*
v. *Commerce* (1883) 45 N.J.L. 18; *Smith* v. *Walker* (1865) 57 Mich. 456, 474;
Falkinburg v. *Lucy* (1868) 35 Cal. 52, 64; *Dixon Crucible Co.* v. *Guggenheim*
(1870) 2 Brewster, Phila., 321, 333; *Stonebraker* v. *Stonebraker* (1870) 35 Md.
252, 268; *Candee, Swan & Co.* v. *Deere & Co.* (1870) 54 Ill. 439, 457.

CHAPTER VII

THE PROBLEMS OF THE MODERN LAW
HISTORICALLY CONSIDERED

AT the beginning of this essay we have referred [1] to the difficulties experienced by courts both in this country and in England in determining those principles by which they should be governed in the adjudication of cases involving trade-mark infringement and unfair competition. The problem seems simple enough. "The redress that is accorded in trade-mark cases," says a leading decision of the Supreme Court of the United States in 1915,

is based upon the party's right to be protected in the good-will of a trade or business. The primary and proper function of a trade-mark is to identify the origin or ownership of the article to which it is affixed. . . . Courts afford redress or relief upon the ground that a party has valuable interest in the good-will of his trade or business, and in the trade-marks adopted to maintain and extend it. The essence of the wrong consists in the sale of the goods of one manufacturer or vendor for those of another. [2]

This statement of "general principles" does not differ materially from that made in England three-quarters of a century previously in *Perry* v. *Truefitt* quoted at the end of the preceding chapter [3] to the effect that "the principle on which the courts both of law and of equity proceed" is that "a man is not to sell his own goods under the pretense that they are the goods of another man." But in the application of this principle the courts have encountered a number of difficulties which to a considerable extent are traceable to the historical background described in the preceding chapters.

[1] See *supra*, ch. i, pp. 4–6.
[2] *Hanover Milling Co.* v. *Metcalf* 240 U. S. 403, 412–413, per Pitney, J.
[3] See *supra*, p. 144.

In the first place many courts appear to have been unable to free themselves from certain historical preconceptions as to the functions of trade-marks. Legal evolution has not kept pace with functional change. "Life casts the moulds of conduct, which will some day become fixed as law. Law preserves the moulds — which have taken form and shape from life."[1] As recently as 1870, the Supreme Court of Illinois, treating the subject of trade-mark protection as "*novus hospes*,"[2] described the nature of a trade-mark in language as confused as that of Giles Jacob, the lexicographer, and that might even well have come from the fifteenth century:

A trade-mark is similar in some respects to the marks or brands owners of live stock which run at large put upon each one of them. The object of the one is to distinguish the property bearing it from another. . . . A trade-mark denotes the origin of the article. *No one man can have more than one mark or brand, and it is required to be recorded. If the owner could have more than one mark by which to distinguish his property, great confusion and uncertainty would be produced to such an extent as to defeat the object in view. We have found no case where a proprietor has claimed more than one trade-mark . . .*[3]

To say, as courts frequently do,[4] that a trade-mark indicates either origin or ownership may have been an adequate explanation of its function to Gerard Malynes and his contemporaries, but today only by ignoring realities can one say that to the consuming public a trade-mark actually indicates the specific ownership or origin of goods to which such trade-mark is affixed. Given a popular product with an international or at any rate a consumption through the complicated channels of modern distribution, a knowledge of its specific source can by no means generally be attributed to those who purchase it. The very courts that still describe trade-marks as symbols indicating "origin or ownership" at the same

[1] B. Cardozo, *The Nature of the Judicial Process*, p. 64.
[2] *Candee, Swan & Co.* v. *Deere & Co.*, 54 Ill. 439, 453.
[3] *Ibid.*, pp. 456–7. (Italics, the writer's.)
[4] See *supra*, p. 19 and n. 2 thereto.

time concede the indifference of the public to the actual physical origin or ownership of the goods in question. Twenty years ago it was pointed out by the Circuit Court of Appeals for the Seventh Circuit, that "we may safely take it for granted that not one in a thousand knowing of or desiring to purchase 'Baker's Cocoa' or 'Baker's Chocolate,' know of Walter Baker & Co., Limited. The name 'Baker' is identified with the product, and known, in connection with the product of the appellant, as a badge and guaranty of excellence." [1] And, as was recently remarked by Mr. Justice Holmes with regard to the trade-mark "Coca Cola," " . . . it would hardly be too much to say that the drink characterizes the name as much as the name the drink." [2]

The same thought has been frequently expressed by the English Courts. "Persons," they say,

may be misled and may mistake one class of goods for another, although they do not know the names of the makers of either. A person whose name is not known but whose mark is imitated, is just as much injured in his trade as if his name was known as well as his mark. His mark, as used by him, has given a reputation to his goods. His trade depends greatly on such reputation. His mark sells his goods.[3]

"The reference to the maker only arises when there is superadded to the thought of the thing the thought of the person who makes it; a thought which seldom arises in the mind of the purchaser, who cares nothing about the maker, but only about the thing which he is buying." [4] "Thirsty folk want beer, not explanations. If the public get the thing they want, or something near it, and get it under the old name — the name with which they are familiar — they are likely to be supremely indifferent to the character and conduct of the brewer, and the equitable rights of rival traders." [5]

[1] *Walter Baker & Co.* v. *Slack* 130 Fed. 514, 518. See also *Shredded Wheat Co.* v. *Humphrey Cornell Co.*, 250 Fed. 960, 963.
[2] *Coca Cola Co.* v. *Koke Co.* 254 U. S. 143, 146.
[3] *Powell* v. *The Birmingham Vinegar Brewery Company, Ld.* 13 Rep. Pat. Cas. 235, 250, per Lindley, L.J.
[4] *Siegert* v. *Findlater* L.R., 7 Ch. Div. 801, 813, per Fry, J.
[5] *Montgomery* v. *Thompson* 1891 A.C. 217, 225, per Lord Macnaghten.

The Courts, in their desire to preserve historical definitions intact while keeping pace with the exigencies of the modern mechanism of trade, have been compelled to strain to the utmost their interpretations of "origin and ownership." "It is not essential to property in a trade-mark," said the New York Court of Appeals,

that it should indicate any particular person as the maker of the article to which it is attached. It may represent to the purchaser the quality of the thing offered for sale, and in that case is of value to any person interested in putting the commodity to which it is applied upon the market.[1]

"The use of a trade-mark," likewise held the Massachusetts Supreme Court,

does not necessarily and as a matter of law import that the articles upon which it is used are manufactured by its user. It may be enough that they are manufactured for him, that he controls their production, *or even that they pass through his hands in the course of trade and that he gives to them the benefit of his reputation, or of his name and business style.*[2]

In a recent case before the Judicial Committee of the Privy Council involving the famous "Gold Flake" trade-mark on cigarettes, Lord Phillimore said:

It is possible for an importer to get a valuable reputation for himself and his wares by his care in selection or his precautions as to transit and storage, or because his local character is such as that the article acquires a value by his testimony to its genuineness; and if therefore goods, though of the same make are passed off by competitors as being imported by him, he will have a right of action.[3]

What then does a trade-mark indicate? Not that the article in question comes from any definite or particular source, the

---

[1] *Godillot* v. *Harris* 81 N. Y. 265, 266, per Danforth, J.

[2] *Nelson* v. *Winchell & Co.*, 203 Mass. 75, 82, per Sheldon, J., citing decisions of the United States Supreme Court, New York Court of Appeals and English courts. (Italics, the writer's.) *Cf. A. Bourjois* v. *Katzel* 260 U. S. 689, 692 (trade-mark rights in United States purchased from foreign manufacturer by American distributor); *Hughes* v. *Alfred H. Smith Co.* 205 Fed. 302,311 (trade-mark affixed by English manufacturer for American dealer).

[3] *Imperial Tobacco Company of India, Ltd.* v. *Bonnan* (May 1924) 41 Rep. Pat. Cas. 441, 446, lines 36–41.

characteristics of which or personalities connected with which are favorably known to the purchaser. A trade-mark merely guarantees to the consumer that the goods in connection with which it is used emanate from the same source or have reached the consumer through the same channels of trade as certain other goods that have given the consumer satisfaction and that bore the same trade-mark. The distinction between saying that the consumer knows the specific source of a trade-marked article, and saying that he knows that two articles emanate from a single source may appear to be an exceedingly tenuous and insubstantial one until we consider that in the *Coca Cola* and *Baker's Chocolate* cases, as well as many others, infringers have sought to defend their acts on the ground that the consuming public did not know the specific source from which the article of the plaintiff emanated and that consequently the public was not deceived into buying the defendant's instead of the plaintiff's product. As stated above, from the standpoint of realities, the consumer does not regard the trade-mark as an indication of origin but rather as a guaranty that the goods purchased under the trade-mark will have the same meritorious qualities as those previously noted by him in his purchases of other goods bearing the same mark. The mark "sells the goods."

But the main difficulties of the courts and also of text-writers has been not so much with the nature of a trade-mark as with the nature of trade-mark rights and the proper bases for the protection of these rights. The principal obstruction to the development of the law in accordance with the necessities of business has been the uncertainty of those administering or commenting upon the law as to whether or not trade-marks are what they term "property."[1] This uncertainty, it will be recalled, was very noticeable in the deliberations of both the British Parliament and the Congress

---

[1] In this connection a similar difficulty is encountered by French courts and text-writers. For a discussion of the various views, see Etienne Arnal, *De la propriété des marques de fabrique* (Montpellier, 1909), pp. 28–42. For medieval and modern German and Italian views, see G. Lastig, *Markenrecht und Zeichenregister*, ch. ix.

of the United States concerning legislation providing for trade-mark registration,[1] and while a great deal of law has been made in the last half century and much commentary has been written in recent years upon that law, there still appears to be much confusion on the point.

The text-writers on equity and on the general principles of the law of torts usually speak of trade-mark infringement as the violation of a property right of one kind or another. Langdell, for instance, describes trade-mark infringement as a tort "clearly to property," "yet," he continues, " it is not a tort to any particular thing, nor has it properly any relation to any particular thing. It is, therefore, a tort to the estate of the person injured in the aggregate, — to the *universitas* of his estate (as the Romans called it), consisting as it does, in making him so much poorer." [2] Pomeroy's *Treatise on Equitable Remedies* states that "the basis of the right is a property right in the manufacturer or vendor to have his trade protected." [3] Kerr on *Injunctions* states that the jurisdiction of equity in such cases "is in aid of the legal right and is founded on the equity of protecting property from irreparable damage." [4] Halsbury's *Laws of England* likewise finds that "the jurisdiction of the court in the protection given to trade-marks rests upon property, and the court interferes by injunction, because that is the only mode by which property of this kind can be effectually protected." [5] Judge Salmond in his work on *Torts* intimates on the other hand that it is only by registration that a trade-mark becomes thereby a species of incorporeal property." [6]

The courts, however, have not been so dogmatic as these text-writers but have wavered between the two horns of a dilemma. While desiring to afford protection to trade-marks, they have at various times manifested a very strong disin-

---

[1] See *supra*, p. 141.
[2] C. C. Langdell *A Brief Survey of Equity Jurisdiction* (2nd ed.), p. 250.
[3] Pomeroy, *Treatise on Equitable Remedies, Supplementary to Pomeroy's Equity Jurisprudence*, vol. 2, p. 4528.
[4] Kerr on *Injunctions* (5th ed.), p. 357.
[5] Halsbury's *Laws of England*, vol. 17, Article "Injunctions," p. 259.
[6] Salmond on *Torts* (6th ed.), pp. 565-6.

clination to base their relief in such cases upon a theory of
the protection of property, although they have been able to
discover no sound alternative ground for relief. It will be
recalled that the pleadings in the early common law cases set
forth a reputation of the plaintiff that had been damaged by
the fraudulent act of the defendant.[1] The gist of the action
was fraud, although the fraud was really committed against
the purchaser and not against the owner of the trade-mark
in question. Equity on the other hand set out to protect the
plaintiff's "exclusive use" of marks, quite irrespective of the
question of fraud and even in the absence of fraud.[2] Equity
acted solely "in aid of" and "ancillary to" the legal right,[3]
which it defined as "a right to have a particular trade-mark."[4]
"At law" said Lord Westbury, L.C.,

the proper remedy is by an action on the case for deceit: and
proof of fraud on the part of the Defendant is of the essence
of the action: but this Court will act on the principle of
protecting property alone, and it is not necessary for the injunction to prove fraud in the defendent, or that the credit
of the Plaintiff is injured by the sale of an inferior article.
The injury done to the Plaintiff in his trade by loss of custom
is sufficient to support his title to relief.[5]

In the famous *American Leather Cloth Co.* case, decided in
the same year (1863), it was again held by the Lord Chancellor, to the same effect, that:

The true principle . . . would seem to be that the jurisdiction
of the Court in the protection given to trade-marks rests upon
property, and that the Court interferes by injunctions, because that is the only mode by which property of this description can be effectually protected.[6]

On the other hand it has been held by other English judges
that "it is now settled law, that there is no property whatever

[1] See *supra*, pp. 137–138, 141–143.
[2] See *supra*, pp. 138–139.
[3] *Motley* v. *Downman*, 3 Myl. & Cr. 1, 14.
[4] *Farina* v. *Silverlock*, 39 Law & Eq. 514, 516.
[5] *Edelstein* v. *Edelsten*, 1 De G. J. & S. 185, 199–200.
[6] *The Leather Cloth Co. Ltd.* v. *American Leather Cloth Co. Ltd.* 4 De G.
J. & S. 137, 142.

in a trade-mark,"[1] and that it is inaccurate to speak of there being property in a trade-mark.[2]

The American decisions as to the nature of trade-mark rights and of the remedy in cases of trade-mark infringement are as chaotic as those of England. The question was early presented to the courts of this country as a problem in constitutional law, *i.e.*, the jurisdiction of Congress and of the state legislatures to legislate concerning trade-marks and their registration. In a long line of decisions beginning even prior to the presentation of the issue to the Supreme Court of the United States it was held by a state court that

the right of property [in trade-marks] does not in any manner depend for its inceptive existence or support upon statutory law, though its enjoyment may be better secured and guarded, and infringements upon the right of the proprietor may be more effectually prevented or redressed by the aid of the statute than at common law. Its exercise may be limited or controlled by statute, as in case of other property, but, like the title to the good-will of a trade, which it in some respects resembles, the right of property in a trade-mark accrues without the aid of the statute . . .; the proprietor may assert and maintain his property right wherever the common law affords remedies for wrongs.[3]

In the *Trade-Mark Cases*, the Supreme Court of the United States said that the right to adopt and use a trade-mark

is a property right for the violation of which damages may be recovered in an action at law, and the continued violation of it will be enjoined by a court of equity, with compensation for past infringement. This exclusive right was not created by the act of Congress, and does not now depend upon it for its enforcement. The whole system of trade-mark property and the civil remedies for its protection existed long anterior to that act, and have remained in full force since its passage.[4]

[1] *Collins Company* v. *Brown*, 3 K. & J. 423, 6.
[2] See Lord Herschell in *Reddaway* v. *Banham* [1896] A.C. 199, 209, and other cases cited by the Supreme Court of the United States in *Hanover Milling Co.* v. *Metcalf*, 240 U. S. 403, 413; also cases cited in *Chadwick* v. *Covell* 151 Mass, 190, 194.
[3] *Derringer* v. *Plate* (1865) 29 Cal. 292, 295.
[4] *Trade-Mark Cases*, (1879) 100 U. S. 82, 92.

In an Indiana decision a few years later, Chief Justice Elliott said: " . . . Congress has no more power to deprive the State Courts of jurisdiction in trade-mark cases than it would have to deprive them of power to decide controversies concerning any other species of property." [1]

From the constitutional phase of law we pass to the tort aspect and find there a contrariety of opinion on the question as to the basis of trade-mark rights and remedies. The cases appear to be in irreconcilable conflict not only with each other but occasionally even with themselves.[2] We have quoted the view of the Supreme Court as expressed in the *Trade-Mark Cases* in 1879. Compare the sweeping decision there as to "the whole system of trade-mark property" with the cautious and qualified statement of the same court in 1915, that "the trade-mark is treated as merely a protection for the good-will, and is not the subject of property except in connection with an existing business." [3]

An interesting indication of the shifts and shadings of judicial thought on this point is to be found in three decisions of Mr. Justice Holmes, whose opinions constitute so notable and voluminous a contribution to the law of trade-marks as developed in the last quarter of a century. Writing in 1890, while still a junior judge of the Supreme Court of Massachusetts, he said,

When the common law developed the doctrine of trade-marks and trade names, it was not creating a property in advertisements more absolute than it would have allowed the author of "Paradise Lost"; but the meaning was to prevent one man

---

[1] *Smail v. Sanders* (1888) 118 Ind. 105, 106. See also annotations to *Trade-Mark Cases* in 10 *Rose's Notes of United States Reports* (Revised ed.), pp. 847–9, *United Drug Co.* v. *Rectanus Co.* 248 U. S. 90, 98–9; *Coca Cola Co.* v. *Stevenson* 276 Fed. 1010, 1016; *Louis Bergdoll Brewing Co.* v. *Bergdoll Brewing Co.* 218 Fed. 131, 132; *Apollo Bros.* v. *Perkins* 207 Fed. 530, 533; *Thomas G. Carroll & Son Co.* v. *M'Ilvaine & Baldwin*, 171 Fed. 125, 128; *Hennessy v. Braunschwerger & Co.* 89 Fed. 664, 667–8; *Re Gorham Mfg. Co.* 41 App. D.C. 263, 265; *Traiser* v. *J. W. Doty Cigar Co.* 198 Mass. 327, 328–9; *Kayser & Co.* v. *Italian Silk Underwear Co.* 160 N. Y. App. Div. 607, 610–12.

[2] E.g., *Thomas G. Carroll & Son Co.* v. *M'Ilvaine & Baldwin*, 171 Fed. 125. On page 128, Judge Hough states: "'Property right' in a trade-mark exists at common-law . . .", and in the next paragraph he states: "the owner of a trade-mark has no estate in the trade-mark as such . . ."

[3] *Hanover Milling Co.* v. *Metcalf* 240 U. S. 403, 414.

from palming off his goods as another's, from getting another's business or injuring his reputation by unfair means, and, perhaps, from defrauding the public.[1]

However, in a case decided in 1923, Mr. Justice Holmes writes for the Supreme Court of the United States,

The monopoly in that case [of a patent] is more extensive, but we see no sufficient reason for holding that the monopoly of trade-mark, so far as it goes, is less complete. It deals with a delicate matter that may be of great value but that easily is destroyed, and therefore should be protected with corresponding care.[2]

Finally in an opinion written only a few months ago, Mr. Justice Holmes states,

Then what new rights does the trade-mark confer? It does not confer the right to prohibit the use of the word or words. It is not a copyright . . . A trade-mark only gives the right to prohibit the use of it so far as to protect the owner's goodwill against the sale of another's product as his . . . When the mark is used in the way that does not deceive the public, we see no such sanctity in the word as to prevent its being used to tell the truth. It is not taboo.[3]

The conflict of opinion on the question whether trade-marks are property and what is the proper basis of their protection was carefully considered about a decade ago by the Circuit Court of Appeals for the Seventh Circuit in a leading case, *Hanover Star Milling Company* v. *Allen & Wheeler Co.* Judge Baker there said:

So it is evident that those who deny that trade-marks are property agree with the others that complainants are entitled to protection in the use of trade-marks. And both sides meet in finding that the cause of action in the injury done or threatened to a complainant's trade in which he has used the marks in question to designate the origin or ownership of his goods and that the appropriate relief is to enjoin the defendant

---

[1] *Chadwick* v. *Covell* 151 Mass. 190, 193–194.
[2] *A. Bourjois & Co., Inc.* v. *Katzel* 260 U. S. 689, 692.
[3] *Prestonettes, Inc.,* v. *Coty* 264 U. S. 359, 368.

from using the marks to divert trade that otherwise would
have gone or would go to the complainant. Whether trade-
marks are accurately called property or not, it is clear that
some of the rights that are incident to property do attach to
them; and therefore, just as courts sometimes state jurisdic-
tional facts by describing corporation parties as "citizens," it
may be convenient to speak of trade-marks as "property,"
as a short way of expressing a limited truth that requires
ampler means for a complete and accurate statement, and
that limited truth is as compactly defined as anywhere else
in *Weston* v. *Ketcham* 51 How. Prac. (N. Y.) 455: "There
is no such thing as a trade-mark 'in gross,' to use that term of
analogy. It must be 'appendant' to some particular business
in which it is actually used upon or in regard to specified
articles." It is not the trade-mark, but the trade, the business
reputation and good-will, that is injured; and the property
and right in the trade is protected from injury by preventing
a fraud-doer from stealing the complainant's trade by means
of using the complainant's "commercial signature." [1]

Without doubt many of the judicial perplexities concerning
the proper classification of trade-marks have been due to the
failure of the courts to keep pace not only with the functional
evolution of trade-marks, but also with the changing concepts
of property. "Delusive exactness," writes Mr. Justice
Holmes, "is a source of fallacy throughout the law. By
calling a business 'property' you make it seem like
land. . . ." [2] But is it essential that we associate property
with the dimensional? Professor Chafee has recently said:

The extension of equitable jurisdiction for the protection
of human dignity and peace of mind has been made much

---

[1] *Hanover Star Milling Co.* v. *Allen & Wheeler Co.* 208 Fed. 513, 516.

In several recent cases Federal Courts have used the terminology of the law
of real property in discussing questions involving trade-marks. They speak
of trade-mark infringement as a "trespass" upon the rights of the plaintiff
(*Louis Bergdoll Brewing Co.* v. *Bergdoll Brewing Co.*, 218 Fed. 131, 132), of
"infringers as trespassers" (*Hercules Powder Co.* v. *Newton*, 266 Fed. 169, 171;
National Picture Theatres v. *Foundation Film Corp.*, ibid., 209, 211). In *Coca-
Cola Co.* v. *Stevenson*, 276 Fed. 1010, 1013–14, Judge Fitzhenry held that a court
of equity had jurisdiction to order the Secretary of the State of Illinois to cancel
wrongful registrations of plaintiff's trade-mark by defendant "which constitute
a cloud upon the plaintiff's title . . .", citing as his authorities decisions of the
Illinois State Courts in cases of removal of cloud on title or of quieting title to
real property.

[2] *Truax* v. *Corrigan* 257 U. S. 312, 342.

easier through the ever widening meaning attached to the conception of property. The gulf between an acre of land and the right of privacy may have been too broad for equity to bridge, but its jurisdiction over property has now extended from land and chattels to far more intangible human interests. . . . Equity has long safeguarded such state-recognized mental property as patent, copyrights and trade-marks.[1]

"A large part of what is most valuable in modern life," writes Vice Chancellor Stevenson, "seems to depend more or less directly upon 'probable expectancies' . . . It would seem to be inevitable that courts of law, as our system of jurisprudence is evolved to meet the growing wants of an increasingly complex social order, will discover, define and protect from undue interference more of these 'probable expectancies'"[2] Among those "probable expectancies" which courts of law are being called upon with every increasing frequency to define and protect is good-will, i.e., the expectation of the trader or manufacturer that he will be undisturbed in the custom or trade which the merits of his wares or the ingenuity of his advertising have attracted from the consuming public. A trade-mark is a most important creative and also sustaining factor of that "probable expectancy" and, being "recognized by law and enforced by the power of a State,"[3] there appears to be no valid ground for excluding trade-mark rights from the category of property or property rights.

Reasoning along these lines, the New York Court of Appeals has recently said, speaking of trade-marks,

Any civil right not unlawful in itself nor against public policy, that has acquired a pecuniary value, becomes a property

[1] Zechariah Chafee, "The Progress of the Law, 1919–1920," 34 *Harvard Law Review* 388, 407–8. *Cf.* Arnal, *op. cit.*, p. 29: "Que le droit à la marque soit un droit immatériel, rien de plus juste; mais pourquoi, parce qu'il est immatériel, lui refuser le nom de propriété, ce n'est point une raison valable." *Cf. Das Firmenrecht des Kaufmanns und der Schutz anderer Bezeichnungen des gewerblichen Verkehrs* (p. 83): "Welcher Art dieses Recht ist, ist bestritten. Die französische Literatur nennt das Recht 'une propriété non absolue, mais relative.' Unser Recht kennt jedoch nicht die Ausdehnung des Begriffes 'Eigentum' auf unkörperliche Sachen, wir nennen vielmehr derartige Rechte 'immaterielle Güterrechte.'" See also G. Lastig, *op. cit.*, p. 193.
[2] *Jersey City Printing Company* v. *Cassidy* 63 N. J. Eq. 759, 765. *Cf. Booth & Bro.* v. *Burgess* 72 *ibid.*, 181, 187.
[3] T. E. Holland, *Elements of Jurisprudence* (13th ed.) p. 83.

right that is entitled to protection as such. The courts have frequently exercised this right. They have never refused to do so when the facts show that the failure to exercise equitable jurisdiction would permit unfair competition in trade or in any matter pertaining to a property right.[1]

The Supreme Court of the United States has likewise recently stated in a case of unfair competition: "The rule that a court of equity concerns itself only in the protection of property rights treats any civil right of a pecuniary nature as a property right. . . ."[2] The English Court of Appeals has likewise expressed the same thought within the last few months in a "passing-off" case, Lord Justice Sargant saying:

It seems to me that it is essential for an action of that sort that there should be tangible probability of injury to the property of the Plaintiffs, but I think that under the word "property" may well be included the trade reputation of the Plaintiffs, and that, if tangible injury is shown to the trade reputation of the Plaintiffs, that is enough.[3]

An objection usually made to speaking of trade-marks in terms of property is based upon the fear that by so doing a monopoly in language or in design may be created. This point was recently considered by Judge Dickinson of the District Court for the Eastern District of Pennsylvania, who wrote:[4]

Patents, copyrights, and trade-marks excite two deeply seated feelings. One is the feeling of any one who has originated anything of his right to claim an exclusive property in it and to the trade growing out of it. The other is a hatred of monopoly. The latter feeling gives way to the former so far as to grant limited monopolies through patents and copyrights. This is a concession made for the general good aptly expressed in the constitutional phrase. The purchasing public regards this as the concession of a privilege; inventors

[1] *Fisher* v. *Star Co.* (1921) 231 N. Y. 414, 428, per Chase, J.
[2] *International News Service* v. *Associated Press*, 248 U. S. 215, 236, per Pitney, J. See also *Peekskill Theatre, Inc.*, v. *Advance Theatrical Co.* 206 N. Y. App. Div. 138, 141.
[3] *Harrods Limited* v. *R. Harrod Limited*, 41 Rep. Pat. Cas. 74, 87.
[4] *Loughran* v. *Quaker City Chocolate & Confect. Co.* 286 Fed. 694, 697 (affirmed 296 Fed. 822). *Cf. Barton* v. *Rex-Oil Co.*, 2 F. (2d) 402, 3.

and authors look upon it as a right limited only as the price exacted for the aid of the law in enforcing it. Mere dealers in commodities are prone to think themselves entitled to a like monopoly unlimited in time. This is a mistake. The only right they have is their right to sell their goods as such and to protection against the goods of another being palmed off upon their customers as theirs. To aid them in the assertion of this right they are permitted to mark their goods so as to identify and designate them and to name them as their own.

The same thought has been thus tersely expressed in Mr. Rogers' work on trade-marks: [1]

Take, for example, the words "Gold Dust." If you should use these words in conversation with a friend on the street and a man should step up to you and say, "I own the words, 'Gold Dust' and I forbid you to use them," you and your friend would laugh at him and wonder when he escaped from the asylum. On the other hand, no one disputes the right of N. K. Fairbank Company to forbid the use of the words "Gold Dust" on a package of washing powder. What is the difference? They are ordinary English words. Why has the Fairbank Company any better right to them than the extraneous person you regarded as a lunatic? Simply this, that there is no property in a word or name as such. It is only when it symbolizes a business good-will that the attributes of property attach to it.

However, all that such a monopoly actually implies is the exclusive right of the owner of a going concern to sell goods under a valid trade-mark as long as and wherever he continues to sell goods under that mark. Without entering into any discussion as to the relative economic utility and value of trade-marks, which has no place in this essay,[2] it may be remarked that the dictionary is quite large enough to justify

[1] E. S. Rogers, *Good Will, Trade-Marks, and Unfair Trading*, pp. 99–100.
[2] For a discussion of the relation of trade-marks to the wealth of nations, see Thorstein Veblen, *The Theory of Business Enterprise*, pp. 139–140; Sidney Webb, *Industrial Democracy* (1920) p. 685, note i. Both of these references are cited in an interesting unpublished typewritten thesis in the library in the University of Chicago by Anna R. Van Meter, entitled *The Function of the Trade-Mark*. See also G. B. Hotchkiss, "An Economic Defence of Advertising" in *American Economic Review*, vol. xv (Supplement), 14, at p. 18, and discussion by M. A. Copeland, *ibid*, 38, at p. 40; G. W. Goodall, *Advertising*, p. 81.

such limited monopolies. As a Federal Court has recently said in enjoining infringement of a two-word mark, "Plaintiff's rights are limited at the most to two words. All the rest of infinity is open to the defendant." [1]

It may perhaps be thought that an over-emphasis has been placed upon the difficulties of the courts in classifying trade-mark rights as property rights. But, as intimated above,[2] the courts are confronted with this dilemma: on the one hand they are anxious to protect trade-marks for the simple reason that trade-mark piracy is repugnant to the judicial conscience;[3] on the other hand, they must feel their way to some legal theory of trade-mark protection which will avoid the necessity of invoking the only basis of equitable protection to which they have been accustomed to resort, viz., the protection of a property right. The problem is not solved by boldly describing trade-mark rights as property rights. To say that a trade-mark is property and therefore should be protected clarifies the situation no more than to say that a trade-mark is protected and is therefore property. A sounder basis of the repression of trade-mark infringement and of other forms of unfair competition is the protection of a merchant or a manufacturer from interference with "his

---

[1] *Coca Cola Co.* v. *Old Dominion Beverage Corp.* (C. C. A. 4th Cir.) 271 Fed. 600, 604, per Rose, D.J. See Hopkins, *op. cit.*, Sec. 24, pp. 56, 57.

[2] See *supra*, pp. 151–152.

[3] E.g.: "'Unfair Competition' consists in selling goods by means which shock judicial sensibilities; and the Second Circuit has long been very sensitive," — Hough, D. J., in *Margarete Steiff, Inc.* v. *Bing* (1914) 215 Fed. 204, 206. *Cf. International News Service* v. *Associated Press* 248 U. S. 215, 240.

"Mr. *Tucker* said, in answer to a question whether it would be fair, if he was asked for a 'Corona' cigar, to hand a cigar of the Partagas factory, that it would be improper to do this, for it would be giving a customer what he did not want. Mr. *Roberts* said an inquiry for a box of Coronas would be of misleading meaning to him, but that he could not deal fairly with such a customer until he had ascertained what he wanted. Mr. *Padro* said that, if a man asks for a 'Corona' cigar, it is doubtful without context what he wants. But he admitted that, as an honest man, he would inquire whether it was the brand or the size that was required." — Pollock, M.R., in *Havana Cigar & Tobacco Factories, Ld.* v. *Oddenino* (1923) 41 Rep. Pat. Cas. 47, 56.

"Such a practice is not merely inconsistent with that higher standard of honour or ethics which would be established by a specially conscientious trader, but directly violates those ordinary every-day principles of honest trading which the courts have consistently endeavored to enforce." — Sargent, L.J., in the same case at p. 60. See also E. S. Rogers, "Unfair Competition," 17 *Michigan Law Review*, 490, 494.

reasonable expectation of future patronage."[1] Assuming that it is undesirable or inaccurate that trade-mark rights be denominated property rights, there is no reason why on other equitable principles owners of trade-marks should not be fully protected by courts of equity. These courts are beginning to afford a greater degree of recognition and protection than formerly to personal rights,[2] and if historical antipathies or economic objections preclude their protecting trade-marks as property rights there is no reason they should not protect the owners of trade-marks in their personal right of freedom from or interference with their trade expectations.

The reluctance of the courts to regard trade-mark infringement purely and solely as a trespass upon a property right and at the same time their concurrently existing desire to do equity to the owner of trade-marks has led them into all sorts of subtleties and metaphysics. For instance, just as they have strained to the utmost the definition of the terms source and origin, so they have ceased to put upon the plaintiff seeking injunctive relief the well-nigh impossible burden of proving intent to defraud and *scienter* on the part of the defendant and, for such a personal intent, have substituted a so-called "constructive intent" which they describe as "inferable from the circumstances."[3] Practically the only way in which violations of trade-mark and trade name rights and other acts of unfair competition can be and almost invariably are established is by the evidence of detectives or other investigators, or by what are known in England as "trap orders." Of course those making such test purchases,

---

[1] E. S. Rogers, *Good-will, Trade-Marks, and Unfair Trading*, p. 13. See *International News Service* v. *Associated Press* 248 U. S. 215, 240; *Summerfield Co.* v. *Prime Furniture Co.* 242 Mass. 149, 155.

[2] See Joseph R. Long, "Equitable Jurisdiction to Protect Personal Rights," 32 *Yale Law Journal* 115; Roscoe Pound, "Equitable Relief against Defamation and Injury to Personalities," 29 *Harvard Law Review* 640; Note on *Witte* v. *Bauderer* (255 S.W. 1016), injunction restraining stranger from flirting with complainant's wife, in 24 *Columbia Law Review* 431.

[3] Hopkins, *op. cit.*, Sec. 118; Nims on *Unfair Competition* (3rd ed.), Secs. 318, 358; Kerly, *op. cit.*, p. 472; *Elgin National Watch Co.* v. *Illinois Watch Case Co.* 179 U. S. 685; *Saxlehner* v. *Siegel Cooper Company, ibid.*, p. 42; *Higgins Co.* v. *Higgins Soap Co.* 144 N. Y. 462; *Pennsylvania Central Brewing Co.* v. *Anthracite Beer Co.* 258 Pa. 45; *Millington* v. *Fox* 3 My. & Cr. 358.

far from being deceived, actually expect to be defrauded; nevertheless their evidence is held by the courts to disclose the defendant's fraudulent "intent and purpose exactly the same as if the sales were made to purchasers not buying in order to obtain evidence against the seller." [1] One court, in order to justify the enjoining of substitution, where no technical infringement of trade-mark was involved, has gone so far as to speak of "a sort of constructive application by defendant of complainant's trade name or mark, to the goods of another manufacturer." [2]

A great many courts desiring to base their protection of trade-marks upon a more substantial foundation than the refinements and subtleties of reasoning just described, and at the same time reluctant to place their intervention squarely on the ground of the protection of property rights, have made the protection of the public not merely a *test* of unfair competition or of trade-mark infringement, but a *basis* of their jurisdiction. The Circuit Court of Appeals for the Second Circuit has recently said: "The court acts to promote the honesty and fair dealing, and because no one has the right to sell his own goods as the goods of another. The court seeks to protect the purchasing public from deception and also the property rights of the complainant." [3]

The view that equity should protect the public as well as the property rights of the complainant was early refuted by Lord Chancellor Westbury who said:

Imposition on the public is indeed necessary for the Plaintiff's title, but in this way only, that it is a test of the invasion by the Defendant of the Plaintiff's right of property; . . . but the true ground of this Court's jurisdiction is property,

---

[1] See Nims, *op. cit.*, Sec. 337 and cases cited in note 45 thereto; *Burroughs Wellcome & Co.* v. *Thompson & Capper* 21 Rep. Pat. Cas. 69, 84; *Joseph Farrow & Co., Ld.* v. *J. F. Seyfried & Sons, Ld.*, 38 *ibid.* 114; *Havana Cigar & Tobacco Factories, Ld.* v. *Tiffin*, 26 *ibid.*, 473.

[2] *American Fibre Chamois Co.* v. *de Lee* 67 Fed. 329, 331.

[3] *Goldwyn Pictures Corporation* v. *Goldwyn* 296 Fed. 391, 401, per Rogers, Cir.J.; *Industrial Finance Corp.* v. *Community Finance Co.* 294 Fed. 870, 872; *Imperial Cotto Sales Co.* v. *N. K. Fairbanks Co.* 270 Fed. 686; *Coca Cola Co.* v. *J. G. Butler & Sons*, 229 Fed. 224, 229–230; *Wisconsin White Lily Paper Co.* v. *Safer* 182 Wis. 71; *B.V.D. Co.* v. *Kaufman & Baer* 272 Pa. 240, 242. Also cases cited *supra*, p. 5, n. 4.

and the necessity of interfering to protect it by reason of the inadequacy of the legal remedy.[1]

Many eminent American jurists have likewise rejected the idea of protection of the public as a basis of injunctive relief. "It is doubtless morally wrong and improper," said Mr. Justice Day, while still a Judge of the Circuit Court of Appeals for the Sixth Circuit,

> to impose upon the public by the sale of spurious goods, but this does not give rise to a private right of action unless the property rights of the plaintiff are thereby invaded. . . . Courts of equity in granting relief by injunction are concerned with the property rights of the plaintiff.[2]

An illuminating discussion of this point by Judge Veeder vigorously presents the necessity for clear thinking on this question:

> The fundamental basis of the private remedy is, however, not the protection of the public from imposition, but injury to the complainant. That the public is deceived may be evidence of the fact that the original proprietor's rights are being invaded. If, however, the rights of the original proprietor are in no wise interfered with, the deception of the public is no concern of a court of chancery. So, although fraudulent conduct which is calculated to deceive the public is a necessary element, it is the private loss of the complainant that is to be prevented, not the public injury arising to others. This is in conformity with general principles. A court of equity cannot enforce as such the police power of the state.[3]

The stressing of the deception of the public as a ground for trade-mark protection undoubtedly has historical justification. The element of "the deceit of the people" as the basis

---

[1] *Hall* v. *Barrows* 4 De G. J. & S. 150, 159.

[2] *American Washboard Co.* v. *Saginaw Mfg. Co.* 103 Fed. 281, 285.

[3] *Aunt Jemima Mills Co.* v. *Rigney & Co.* 234 Fed. 804, 806. See also *Florence Mfg. Co.* v. *J. C. Dowd & Co.* 178 Fed. 73; *Joseph Schlitz Brewing Co.* v. *Houston Ice & B. Co.* 241 Fed. 817, 820; *Munn & Co.* v. *Americana Co.* 83 N. J. Eq. 308; Hopkins, *op. cit.*, p. 44. 2 Pomeroy, *Equitable Remedies* (2nd ed.), p. 4529; E. S. Rogers, "Predatory Price Cutting as Unfair Trade" in 27 *Harvard Law Review* 139, 147.

of trade-mark law still found running through decisions may be traced to a far earlier period than Dodderidge's dictum in *Southern* v. *How i.e.*, to the regulatory and compulsory nature of trade-marks in the early days of gild life. The medieval craftsman who appropriated his fellow-craftsman's mark and affixed it to "false" or "naughty" or "deceyptfull" wares was — from the standpoint of the community — guilty, not of a tort against the owner of the mark, but of a crime against the king's people.[1] The medieval gild law and statute law of trade-marks, — if so we may term the regulation of trade through the use of compulsory marks, — was essentially a "police" rather than a civil law, promulgated by or for and administered by the gilds and companies on the one hand and by Parliament on the other. Apart from monopolistic considerations, and, at any rate from the standpoint of the recitals of formal law, the regulation of such marks as those prescribed for bakers and coopers kept the people's food and drink of proper quality and of good measure; the protection of goldsmiths' marks involved the stability of the coinage; the defence of the realm necessitated the provisions for bladesmiths' and other armorers' marks. The misuse of such marks rendered the owner thereof liable to the hurdle and the pillory if thereby false wares were erroneously traced to his workshop, while the infringer, if discovered, was punished with equal or greater severity.

From the standpoint of the public interest itself, there is perhaps no longer a need for regarding deception of the public as one of the bases for trade-mark protection. A large number of Federal and State statutes for the repression of misbranding and other forms of commercial charlatanry may now be invoked,[2] — some at any rate with much success[3] —

[1] If the subject of trade-mark infringement had at all come within the jurisdiction of the Royal civil courts of the fourteenth and fifteenth centuries, relief would have been obtained by a writ of deceit on the case rather than in trespass. See W. Holdsworth, *History of English Law* ii, 3rd ed., pp. 407-8.

[2] For a collection of such statutes, see Hopkins on *Trade-Marks* (4th ed.), Part II; also *Hygrade Provision Co.* v. *Sherman*, U. S. Sup. Ct. Adv. Opinions, Feb. 2, 1925, p. 169, *Hebe Co.* v. *Shaw*, 248 U. S. 297.

[3] See 20 *Bulletin U. S. Trade Mark Assn.* 12 for a description of the work of the "Commercial Frauds Court" of New York City.

for the protection of the public interest. Furthermore the Federal Trade Commission, specifically charged with the prevention of unfair methods of competition as they affect the public welfare,[1] is gradually formulating and enforcing canons of commercial ethics, which are already having a marked influence in the direction of the protection of the public from unfair business methods, including the mis-branding of goods.[2] The doubt that existed for some time as to the extent of the jurisdiction of the Federal Trade Commission over cases of trade-mark infringement has apparently been resolved in favor of the Commission,[3] and, whatever defects may exist in either the powers or the procedure of the Commission in such cases from the standpoint of the private litigant,[4] the public interest, whenever apparent, can doubtless in many instances be protected by the very fact of the publicity incidental to the intervention of the Commission.

However, the objection to holding deception of the public as not merely a test of unfair competition but in itself a basis of relief is stronger than the merely negative one that such protection of the public is supererogatory. The question as to whether the deception of the public should

[1] See statement of the Commission, March 17, 1925: "In all such cases there must be three parties involved, the respondent, the competitor injured and the public." (*Journal of Commerce*, March 18, 1925.)

[2] See *Federal Trade Commission* v. *Winsted Hosiery Co.*, 258 U. S. 483; *Federal Trade Commission* v. *Pure Silk Hosiery Mills, Inc.* 15 T. M. Rep. 63; *Royal Baking Powder Co.* v. *Federal Trade Commission*, 281 Fed. 744; W. Notz, "New Phases of Unfair Competition and Measures for Its Suppression," in 30 *Yale Law Journal* 384; J. L. Mechem, "Procedure and Practice Before the Federal Trade Commission," in 21 *Michigan Law Review* 125.

[3] Whatever may have been the "unfair methods of competition" that were originally intended by Congress to fall within the jurisdiction of the Federal Trade Commission (see dissenting opinion of Denison, Cir. J., in *L. B. Silver Co.* v. *Federal Trade Commission*, 289 Fed. 985, 992 *et seq.;* also H. P. Seligson, "The Extent of the Jurisdiction of the Federal Trade Commission Over Unfair Methods of Competition" in 9 *American Bar Assn. Journal* 698, in *Juvenile Shoe Co., Inc.* v. *Federal Trade Commission*, 289 Fed. 57, the Circuit Court of Appeals for the Ninth Circuit seems to have taken for granted the jurisdiction of the Federal Trade Commission to enjoin respondent from using petitioner's corporate name, — whether for the protection of petitioner rather than that of the public is not altogether clear. *Certiorari* was denied by the Supreme Court in 263 U. S. 706. *Cf. John Bene & Sons* v. *Federal Trade Commission*, 299 Fed. 468, 472.

[4] See G. C. Henderson, *The Federal Trade Commission* pp. 169 *et seq.*

be regarded as one of the·bases of trade-mark infringement is of course closely connected with that of the actual significance of trade-marks to the public itself. As we have already indicated,[1] the public is concerned with the trade-mark not so much as an indication of origin but as a guaranty of quality. Any theory of trade-mark protection which overlooks this fact and which does not focus the protective functions of the court upon the good-will of the owner of the trade-mark, inevitably renders such owner dependent for protection, not so much upon the normal agencies for the creation of good-will, such as the excellence of his product and the appeal of his advertising, as upon the judicial estimate of the state of the public mind. This psychological element is in any event at best an uncertain factor, and "the so-called ordinary purchaser changes his mental qualities with every judge;"[2] furthermore it may easily be vitally affected by the dishonest acts of competitors. No sooner does a trade-mark become well known than a host of commercial buccaneers are ready to "reap the fruits of its celebrity."[3] It has been repeatedly held that "the mere fact that the article has obtained such a wide sale that the mark has also become indicative of quality is not of itself sufficient to debar the owner of protection or make it the common property of the trade. To hold otherwise would be to deprive the owner of the exclusive use of his trade-mark just at the time when it had become most valuable and stood most in need of pro-

[1] See *supra*, pp. 147–148.

[2] H. Münsterberg, "The Market and Psychology" in *American Problems*, p. 171. See also the entertaining and instructive article of E. S. Rogers, "The Unwary Purchaser" in 8 *Michigan Law Review* 613, pointing out the "irreconcilable conflict" between cases as to the test of the likelihood of deception in cases of unfair competition involving trade-marks and trade names. For interesting recent psychological studies showing the discrepancy between the actual and the judicially determined confusion of the public, see R. H. Paynter, *A Psychological Study of Trade-Mark Infringement* (Columbia University Archives of Psychology, 1920, No. 42) and H. E. Burtt, "Measurement of Confusion Between Similar Trade Names" in 19 *Illinois Law Review* (1925), 320.

[3] For a glaring example of such piracy, see *Barton v. Rex-Oil Co.*, 2 F. (2d) 402, which also illustrates the phenomenally rapid development of trade in trade-marked articles, — from a small stock of leather polish peddled at Camp MacArthur, Texas, in 1918, to almost four million bottles sold throughout the country in 1921.

tection." [1] Or, as the New York Court of Appeals has said, "The value of a trade-mark consists in its becoming known to the trade as the mark of the manufacturer who has invented or adopted it, and in being known to the public as the name of an article which has met with popular favor. It cannot be that the very circumstances which give it value, operate at the same time to destroy it." [2]

The decisions just quoted, broad in the scope of their protection of trade-marks as property, were rendered over forty years ago and before the courts had begun to take judicial notice of the large investments in advertising that were then only just beginning to be made by manufacturers and merchants. However, with the enormous development of large scale national advertising, have come intimations from the courts that the investment in advertising a trade-mark in itself creates a distinct equity in favor of the advertiser, supplementing or enlarging the previously existing equities protecting good-will. [3] The initial decision pointing out the equities arising from investment in trade-mark advertising was that of Judge Coxe who said: [4]

Where the goods of a manufacturer have become popular not only because of their intrinsic worth, but also by reason of the

[1] *Burton* v. *Stratton* 12 Fed. 696, 702.
[2] *Selchow* v. *Baker* 93 N. Y. 59, 66. See also *Menendez* v. *Holt* 128 U. S. 514, 520; *N. K. Fairbank Co.* v. *Central Lard Company* 64 Fed. 133; *Schendel* v. *Silver* 63 Hun (N. Y.) 230; *In the Matter of Trademarks of Kodak, Ld.* 20 *Rep. Pat. Cas.* 337, 350.
[3] See *Coca Cola Co.* v. *Koke Co.* 254 U. S. 143; *A. Bourjois & Co.* v. *Katzel* 260 U. S. 689; *Coca Cola Co.* v. *Old Dominion Beverage Corporation* 271 Fed. 600, 602; *Coca-Cola Co.* v. *Stevenson* 267 Fed. 1010, 1018; *Anheuser Busch* v. *Budweiser Malt Products Corp.* 287 Fed. 243; *Jacob Ruppert* v. *Knickerbocker Food Specialty Co.* 295 Fed. 381, 383; *Potter-Wrightington* v. *Ward Baking Co.* 288 Fed. 597, 599–600; *Henry Mfg. Co.* v. *Henry Screen Mfg. Co.* 204 N. Y. App. Div. 27, 29; *Fishel & Sons Inc.* v. *Distinctive Jewelry Co. Inc.* 196 N. Y. App. Div. 779, 788; *George G. Fox Co.* v. *Hathaway* 199 Mass. 99, 101, *Harkert Cigar Co.* v. *Herman* 196 N.W. (Sup. Ct. Ia.) 986, 987; *France Milling Co.* v. *Washburn-Crosby Co.* 3 F. (2d) 321, 326; *Oppenheim, Obendorf & Co., Inc.*, v. *President Suspender Co.*, 3 F. (2d) 88, 89.
In administrative law, for the purpose of taxation, an investment in advertising a trade-mark is regarded as capital investment independent of, and often in excess of the actual fiscal assets of many a concern. (See *Treasury Dept. B.I.R. Cumulative Bulletin* No. 2, 1920, p. 292; Holmes on *Federal Taxes*, 6th ed., pp. 621 *et seq.*) For valuation placed upon the trade-marks of ten leading industrial concerns by the Bureau of Internal Revenue, see *Bulletin U. S. Trademark Association*, New Ser., vol. 16 (Feb. 1921) pp. 23 to 25.
[4] *Hilson Co.* v. *Foster* (1897) 80 Fed. 896, 897.

ingenious, attractive and persistent manner in which they have
been advertised, the good-will thus acquired is entitled to
protection. The money invested in advertising is as much a
part of the business as if invested in buildings, or machinery,
and a rival in business has no more right to use the one than
the other, — no more right to use the machinery by which
the goods are placed on the market than the machinery which
originally created them. No one should be permitted to step
in at the eleventh hour and appropriate advantages resulting
from years of toil on the part of another.

: The recent decision of the English Court of Appeals involving the famous "Corona" cigar trade-mark is worthy of
careful study in connection with this subject.[1] In that case
the owners of the "Corona" cigar brand sought to enjoin the
delivery of cigars of other brands in response to requests for
"a Corona." Defendant, whose defence was financed by the
large cigar manufacturing interests of Havana, while admitting
the validity of the "Corona" trade-mark and conceding
plaintiff's title to that mark, claimed that in the course of
time "Corona" had come to mean in the public mind not
merely a brand but also — and to a greater extent — a size
and shape of cigar. The Court of Appeals would appear to
have based its decision sustaining plaintiff's right to an
injunction on the ground that the trial court had found as a
fact that to the *majority* of the public, "Corona" still meant a
brand and not merely a size or shape of cigar.

This reasoning of the English Court of Appeals of course
goes to the very root of the question as to the proper basis
of trade-mark protection. There was in that case no claim
such as was made recently in the "Asperin" case, *Bayer
Co.* v. *United Drug Co.*,[2] of any abandonment of the word
"Corona" to the public domain, nor was it shown that the
plaintiff had ever acquiesced in the use of its mark "Corona"
to designate a size or shape. Nevertheless, followed to its
logical conclusion, the reasoning of the Court would imply

[1] *Havana Cigar & Tobacco Company, Ltd.* v. *Oddenino*, 41 Rep. Pat. Cas.
47. See especially portions of opinions of Pollock, M.R., at p. 55; of War-
rington, L.J., at pp. 58–59 and of Sargent, L.J., at p. 60.
[2] 272 Fed. 505.

that if a sufficient number of infringers were able to becloud in the public mind, "Corona" would thereby become a size or shape and would cease to be a brand, and thus plaintiffs, without fault on their part, would, by this very fraud, ultimately be debarred from protection of their trade-mark. The American decisions, such as *Selchow* v. *Baker*, quoted above,[1] would appear to offer a greater degree of protection to trade-marks.

There are indications that the question as to the logical and effective basis of the law of trade-marks and unfair competition will have to be decided by the highest courts of both this country and England within the next few years in connection with the problem of the protection which is being sought against the use of infringing marks upon non-competing goods. In 1898 an English Court of Chancery took a radical step in the direction of the protection of symbols of good-will, in holding that the trade-mark "Kodak" on cameras was infringed by "Kodak" on bicycles, because "'Kodak cameras' are especially available for use on cycles" and "many shops sell . . . both bicycles and photographic cameras . . ."[2] Again in 1917 the United States Circuit Court of Appeals for the Second Circuit decided that the trade-mark "Aunt Jemima's" for flour was infringed by "Aunt Jemima's" for syrup because "syrup and flour are both food products, and good products commonly used together."[3] Within recent months the Circuit Court of Appeals for the Sixth Circuit has held that a trade-mark for a magazine might be infringed by a similar mark on hats, although there was no actual market competition between the product of the plaintiff and the defendants. Explaining the doctrine of unfair competition, Judge Denison said:

. . . there is no fetish in the word competition. The invocation of equity rests more vitally upon the unfairness. If

---

[1] *Supra*, p. 167.

[2] *Eastman Photographic Materials Co., Ld.* v. *John Griffiths Cycle Corporation, Ld.* (1898) 15 Rep. Pat. Cas. 105, 110. *Cf.* Walter v. Ashton [1902] 2 Ch. 282.

[3] *Aunt Jemima Mills Co.* v. *Rigney & Co.* (1917) 247 Fed. 407, 410. But *cf. France Milling Co.* v. *Washburn Crosby Co.* (U. S. C. C. A., 2nd Cir., April 6, 1925 not yet reported).

B. represents that his goods are made by A. and if damage therefrom to A. is to be seen, we are aware of no consideration which makes it controlling whether this damage to A. will come from market competition with some article which A. is then manufacturing or will come in some other way.[1]

Shortly after the filing of the decision just quoted a United States District Court held the use of the trade-mark "Rolls-Royce" for automobiles to be infringed by the use of the mark upon radio tubes. The Court brushed aside all citations of precedents, remarking,

I am more impressed with the broad equities in this matter as it is presented in this individual case than I am perhaps by certain collateral citations . . . I can't see, even in the citations that have been given that which leads me to determine otherwise than I am minded to determine.[2]

The *ratio decidendi* in such cases would appear to be simply a reluctance on the part of the Court to permit defendants "to get the benefit of complainant's reputation or of its advertisement or to forestall the extension of its trade." [3] It discards entirely the archaic theories of the Middle Ages and of "gild jurisprudence," predicated upon the proprietary, regulatory and monopolistic significance of trade symbols and is a salutary, if somewhat belated, recognition of the actual nature and function of the trade-mark under modern conditions of production and distribution. Such reasoning, unhampered by medieval preconceptions and present misconceptions, will give adequate protection to both existent and potential good-will, and will prove the most effective

---

[1] *Vogue Co.* v. *Thompson-Hudson Co.*, 300 Fed. 509, 512.

[2] Runyon, D. J., in *Rolls-Royce of America, Inc.* v. *Howard Wall, Inc.* (Oct., 1924) 15 T. M. Rep. 12, 13. See also, *contra*, the decision of Judge Dickinson U.S.D.C., E.D., Pa.) in *Rosenberg Brothers and Company* v. *John F. Elliott* (June 1924) 3 F. (2d) 682, that "Fashion-Park" as a trade-mark on "overcoats, coats, vests, trousers and the like kind of clothing," sold to the wholesale trade, was not infringed by "Fashion-Park" on men's hats sold only at retail. *Cf. France Milling Co.* v. *Washburn Crosby Co., supra*, p. 169, n. 3.

[3] *Aunt Jemima Mills Co.* v. *Rigney & Co., supra*, at p. 410. For a further discussion of the appropriation of trade symbols by non-competitors, see 25 *Columbia Law Review* (1925) 199; 23 *Michigan Law Review* (1925) 433.

means of combating trade-mark pirates who lurk ever-watchful on the fringes of the field of trade.

To summarize briefly the conclusions reached in this chapter:

(1) The development of the law of unfair competition with respect to trade-marks has been hampered by the failure of the law to keep pace with the functional evolution of trade-marks themselves.

(2) Using the term property in its modern legal sense, viz., as a right having a pecuniary value which will be protected by the legal agencies of society, rights in or pertaining to trade-marks may be classified as property.

(3) However, the classification of trade-marks as property is not essential to their protection since equity should, in any event, prevent the destruction or impairment of the probable expectancy of trade or custom, of which the trade-mark is a symbol as well as a creative factor.

(4) The owner of a trade-mark who expends large sums of money in making his mark known to the public as a symbol and guarantee of the excellence of the quality of his product should receive the same protection from the courts for his investment in advertising his trade-mark that he would undoubtedly be entitled to receive for investment in plant or materials.

BIBLIOGRAPHY

A. LEGAL SOURCES

(1) Treatises, Articles, Reports, etc. Relating to Trade-marks, Unfair Competition and Patents

NOTE: Valuable bibliographies of treatises and articles relating to trade-mark law are to be found in E. Pouillet, *Traité des marques de fabrique et de concurrence déloyale* (6th ed. by A. Taillefer and C. Claro, Paris, 1912), pp. xiii–xxiii; T. Braun and A. Capitaine, *Les marques de fabrique et de commerce* (Paris and Brussels, 1908) pp. 709–727; "Catalogue of the Library of the United States Trade-Mark Association" in *Bulletin of the United States Trade-Mark Association*. vol. vi (1910), pp. 37–57.

ADAMS, F. M. *Treatise on the Law of Trade-marks.* London, 1876.
ALLAN, C. E. *The Law Relating to Good-Will.* London, 1889.
ARNAL, E. *De la propriété des marques de fabrique.* Montpellier, 1909.
BLUMENTHAL, C. *Das Firmenrecht des Kaufmanns und der Schutz anderer Bezeichnungen des gewerblichen Verkehrs.* Greifswald, 1916.
BRAUN, T. and CAPITAINE, A. *Les Marques de fabrique et de commerce.* Paris and Brussels, 1908.
BROWNE, W. H. *A Treatise on the Law of Trade-Marks.* 2nd ed. Boston, 1898.
BRYCE, J. Supplement to Ludlow, Sir H., and Jenkyns, H., *Treatise on the Law of Trade-marks*, 2nd ed. London, 1877.
BURTT, H. E. "Measurement of Confusion Between Similar Trade Names" in *Illinois Law Review*, vol. xix (1925), p. 320.
CHAFEE, Z. JR. *Cases on Equitable Relief Against Torts.* Cambridge, 1924. Pp. 100 *et seq.* deal with trade-mark infringement and unfair competition.
COLUMBIA LAW REVIEW. Note on *Vogue v. Thompson-Hudson Co.* (300 Fed. 509) in vol. xxv (1925) p. 199.
COLUMBIAN CENTINEL. Boston, Dec. 24, 1791. "Letter from a Philadelphia Manufacturer" concerning trade-marks and their infringement.
COX, R. *Manual of Trade-Mark Cases*, 2nd ed. Boston, 1892.
DANIELS, L. E. "History of the Trademark" in *Bulletin of the United States Trade-Mark Association*, vol. 7, New Series, (1911) p. 239.
DIETZEL, G. "Das Handelszeichen und die Firma" in *Jahrbuch des gemeinen deutschen Rechts*, vol. iv, p. 227. Leipzig, 1860.
DUNANT, P. *Traité des marques de fabrique et de commerce en Suisse.* Geneva, 1898.
EDMUNDS, L. H. *The Law and Practice of Letters Patent.* 2nd. ed. by T. M. Stevens. London, 1897.

FEDERAL TRADE COMMISSION. *Memorandum on Unfair Competition at Common Law*. Washington, 1916.

GOLD, J. L. "Equity: Trade-Marks: Nature of Infringement" in Notes and Comment, *Cornell Law Quarterly*, vol. vii (1921–2), p. 373.

GORDON, J. W. *Monopolies by Patents and The Statutory Remedies Available To the Public*. London, 1897.

HAINES, C. G. "Efforts to Define Unfair Competition" in *Yale Law Journal*, vol. xxix (1919–20), p. 1.

HARVARD LAW REVIEW. Note on *A. Bourjois & Co., Inc. v. Katzel* (275 Fed. 539) in vol. xxxv (1921–2), p. 624.

HENDERSON, G. C. *The Federal Trade Commission: A Study in Administrative Law and Procedure*. New Haven, 1924.

HOPKINS, J. L. *The Law of Trade-marks, Trade Names and Unfair Competition* . . ., 4th ed. Cincinnati, 1924.

KERLY, D. M. *The Law of Trade Marks and Trade Name*. 5th ed., by F. G. UNDERHAY. London, 1923.

KOHLER, J. *Das Recht des Markenschutzes*. Wurzburg, 1884.

LASTIG, G. *Markenrecht und Zeichenregister*. Halle, 1889.

MECHEM, J. L. "Procedure and Practice. Before the Federal Trade Commission" in *Michigan Law Review*, vol. xxi (1922–3), p. 125.

MICHIGAN LAW REVIEW. Note on *Vogue v. Thompson-Hudson Co.* (300 Fed. 509) in vol. xxiii (1925), p. 434.

MONTHLY LAW MAGAZINE. Article on Trade-Marks, vol. ix (1840–41), p. 201. Reprinted in *American Jurist*, vol. xxv (1841), p. 269.

MÜNSTERBERG, H. "The Market and Psychology" in *American Problems*, p. 151. New York, 1912.

NIMS, H. D. *The Law of Unfair Competition and Trade-Marks*. 2nd ed. New York, 1917.

NOTZ, W. "New Phases of Unfair Competition and Measures for Its Suppression — National and International" in *Yale Law Journal*, vol. xxx (1920–1), p. 384.

OLSHAUSEN, T. *Das Verhältniss des Namenrechts zum Firmenrecht*. Berlin, 1900.

OLIPHANT, H. *Cases on Trade Regulation Selected from Decisions of English and American Courts* (American Case Book Series). St. Paul, 1923.

——, "Trade Regulation" in *American Bar Association Journal*, vol. ix (1923), p. 311.

PATENT AND TRADE MARK REVIEW, vols. i–xxiii. New York.

PAYNTER, R. H. JR. *A Psychological Study of Trade-Mark Infringement* (Columbia University Archives of Psychology, No. 42, Jan. 1920). New York, 1919.

PAUL, A. C. *The Law of Trade-Marks Including Trade Names and Unfair Competition*. St. Paul, 1903.

PELLA, D. R. *Marcas de Fábrica y de Comercio en España*. Madrid, 1911.

POUILLET, E. *Traité des marques de fabrique et de concurrence déloyale en tous genres*. 6th ed. by A. TAILLEFER and C. CLARO. Paris, 1912.

PRICE, W. H. *English Patents of Monopoly* (Harvard Economic Studies, vol. i). Cambridge, 1913.

REPORT OF THE COMMISSIONER OF PATENTS to Congress for the Year Ended December 31, 1923. *Official Gazette of the United States Patent Office*, vol. 319, Feb. 1924, p. 225. Washington, 1924.

REPORT OF THE COMMISSIONERS APPOINTED TO REVISE THE STATUTES RELATING TO PATENTS, TRADE AND OTHER MARKS, and Trade and Commercial Names, Under Act of Congress Approved June 4, 1898. (Senate Documents, 56th Congress, 2nd Session, Document No. 2). Washington, 1902.

REPORT FROM THE SELECT COMMITTEE ON TRADE-MARKS BILL AND MERCHANDISE MARKS BILL: Together with the Proceedings of the Committee, Minutes of Evidence, etc. (*Session Papers, Reports from Committees*, [7], Session Feb. 6–Aug. 7, 1862), vol. xii. London, 1862.

REPORTS OF PATENT, DESIGN AND TRADE MARK CASES. Vols. i to xlii (Advance Sheets). London, 1884–1925.

ROGERS, E. S. *Good Will, Trade Marks and Unfair Trading*. Chicago, 1919.

——, "Predatory Price Cutting as Unfair Trade" in *Harvard Law Review*, vol. xxvii (1913–14), p. 139.

——, "Some Historical Matter Concerning Trade-marks" in *Michigan Law Review*, vol. ix (1910–11), p. 29.

——, "Unfair Competition" in *Michigan Law Review*, vol. xvii (1918–19), p. 490.

SEBASTIAN, L. B. *The Law of Trade Mark Registration*. 2nd ed. by L. B. SEBASTIAN, F. E. BRAY and J. Q. HENRIQUES. London, 1922.

SELIGSON, H. P. "The Extent of the Jurisdiction of the Federal Trade Commission Over Unfair Methods of Competition" in *American Bar Association Journal*, vol. ix (1923), p. 698.

STRUVE or STRUVIUS, F. G. *Systema Jurisprudentiae Opificariae . . . additis Documentis . . . ex Scriptis & Manuscriptis Adriani Beieri . . .* 3 vols. in 1. Lemgo, 1737. Copy in Harvard Law Library.

UNITED STATES TRADE-MARK ASSOCIATION, *Bulletin*. New Ser. vols. 1 to 20. New York, 1904–25.

——, *Reporter*, vols. 1 to 15. New York, 1911–25.

UNITED STATES TREASURY DEPT. *B.I.R. Cumulative Bulletin* No. 2. Washington, 1920.

UPTON, F. H. *A Treatise on the Law of Trade Marks*. Albany, 1860.

VAN METER, A. R. *The Function of the Trade-Mark*. Unpublished typewritten thesis in library of University of Chicago Law School.

(2) LEGAL LITERATURE OTHER THAN THAT RELATING TO TRADE-
MARKS, UNFAIR COMPETITION AND PATENTS.

(*a*) STATUTES, RECORDS, REPORTS AND COLLECTIONS OF CASES:

ACTS OF THE PRIVY COUNCIL OF ENGLAND. New Series, vols. 1–32, ed.
J. R. DASENT; vol. 1613–14, ed. E. G. ATKINSON. *Record Commission*, London, 1890–1917, 1921.

CALENDAR OF THE CHARTER ROLLS PRESERVED IN THE PUBLIC RECORD
OFFICE. (London)

CALENDAR OF THE CLOSE ROLLS PRESERVED IN THE PUBLIC RECORD
OFFICE. (London)

CALENDAR OF THE PATENT ROLLS PRESERVED IN THE PUBLIC RECORD
OFFICE. (London)

CALENDAR OF THE STATE PAPERS PRESERVED IN THE PUBLIC RECORD
OFFICE. (London)

DECREE OF THE STAR CHAMBER, October 12, 1632, concerning counterfeiting of seals to Colchester baize by Thomas Jupp. Imprinted
by Robert Barker. London, 1632. Copy in the Duke of Northumberland's library.

PROCEEDINGS AND ORDINANCES OF THE PRIVY COUNCIL OF ENGLAND
[1386–1542], vols. 1–7, ed. H. NICOLAS. Record Commission,
London, 1834–37.

PROCLAMATION OF CHARLES I, April 16, 1633, "Against frauds and
deceits used in Draperie. . ." Imprinted by Robert Barker.
London, 1633. Copy in the British Museum (506. h. 12 [19])

ROTULI PARLIAMENTORUM; UT ET PETITIONES ET PLACITA IN PARLIA-
MENTO [1278–1503]. 6 vols. London, no date. Index 1832.

RYMER, T. *Foedera, Conventiones, Litterae* . . . 4 vols. in 7. (*Record
Commission* and *Rolls Series*). London, 1816–69.

STATUTES OF THE REALM [1235–1713] ed. A. LUDERS and others. 11
vols., *Record Commission*, London, 1810–28.

YEAR BOOKS: (1) Of 20–22, 30–35 Edw. I; of 11–12 Edw. III (6 vols.);
of 12–20 Edw. III (14 vols.) *Rolls Series*. London, 1863–83; 1885–
1911.

(2) Of Edw. II: *Selden Society* (*Year Book Series*) *Publications*, vols.
xvii, xix, xxii, xxiv, xxvi, xxvii, xxix, xxxi, xxxiii, xxxiv, xxxvi–xxxix.
London, 1903–23.

(3) Of Ric. II, ed. G. F. DEIER (Ames Foundation). Cambridge,
1914.

ACTS AND LAWS OF THE COMMONWEALTH OF MASSACHUSETTS [1780–
1805], Boston, 1890–98.

PRIVATE AND SPECIAL STATUTES OF THE COMMONWEALTH OF MASSA-
CHUSETTS, vol. i. Boston, 1805.

Particularly useful collections of cases were the following:

MARSDEN, R. G. *Select Pleas in the Court of Admiralty*, vol. i (Selden

Society Publications, vol. vi) and vol. ii (Selden Society Publications, vol. xi). London, 1894–97.

GROSS, C. *Select Cases Concerning the Law Merchant*, vol. i (Selden Society Publications, vol. xxiii). London, 1908.

CARR, C. T. *Select Charters of Trading Companies, A.D. 1530–1707* (Selden Society Publications, vol. xxviii). London, 1913.

LEADAM, I. S. & BALDWIN, J. F. *Select Cases Before the King's Council* (Selden Society Publications, vol. xxxv). London, 1918.

(b) TREATISES AND ARTICLES

BACON, M. *A New Abridgement of the Law* . . . 5 vols. London, 1768–70.

BENNETT, W. P. *The History and Present Position of the Bill of Lading.* Cambridge, 1914.

BEWES, W. A. *The Romance of the Law Merchant.* London, 1923.

BIRREL, A. *The Law and History of Copyrighting Books.* London, 1899.

BLACKSTONE, SIR W. *Commentaries on the Laws of England*, by T. M. COOLEY, 4th ed. by J. de W. ANDREWS. 2 vols. Chicago, 1899.

BRACTON, H. *De Legibus et Consuetudinibus Angliae.* Ed. T. TWISS (Rolls Series), 6 vols. London, 1878–1883.

BRITTON. Tr. M. NICHOLS, ed. S. E. BALDWIN. Washington, 1901.

BRODHURST, B. E. S. "The Merchants of the Staple" in *Select Essays in Anglo-American Legal History*, vol. iii, p. 16.

CARDOZO, B. H. *The Nature of the Judicial Process.* New Haven, 1922.

CHAFEE, Z. JR. "The Progress of the Law, 1919–1920" in *Harvard Law Review*, vol. xxxiv (1920–21) p. 388.

COLUMBIA LAW REVIEW. Note on *Witte v. Bauderer* (225 S. W. [Tex.] 1016) in vol. xxiv (1924), p. 431.

COMYNS, SIR J. *A Digest of the Laws of England*, 5 vols. London, 1780.

EDEN, R. H. *A Treatise on the Law of Injunctions.* London, 1821.

ENCYCLOPÆDIA BRITANNICA. 11th ed., Article "Law Merchant," vol. 16, p. 300. Cambridge, 1911.

FLETA SEU COMMENTARIUS JURIS ANGLICANI. London, 1647.

GLANVILL, R. DE. *Tractatus de Legibus et Consuetudinibus Regni Angliae.* Tr. J. Beames, ed. J. H. Beale, Jr. Washington, 1900.

HALSBURY, EARL OF. Article, "Injunctions" in *The Laws of England*, vol. xvii, p. 197. London, 1911.

HOLDSWORTH, W. S. *History of English Law.* Vols. i, ii, and iii, 3rd ed. London, 1923–3. Vols. iv, v, and vi, London, 1924.

HOLLAND, T. E. *The Elements of Jurisprudence.* 13th ed. Oxford, 1924.

HOLMES, G. E. *Federal Income Tax.* 6th ed. Indianapolis, 1925.

JACOB, G. *Lex Mercatoria* or *Merchant's Companion.* London, 1718.

JEUDWINE, J. W. *Tort, Crime and Police.* London, 1917.

KENT, J. *Commentaries on American Law.* 7th ed. 4 vols. New York, 1851.

KERR, W. W. *Treatise on the Law and Practice of Injunctions.* 5th ed. by
J. M. PATTERSON. London, 1914.

LANGDELL, C. C. *A Brief Survey of Equity Jurisdiction.* 2nd ed. Cambridge, 1908.

LONG, J. R. "Equitable Jurisdiction to Protect Personal Rights" in
Yale Law Journal, vol. xxxiii (1923–4), p. 115.

MALYNES, G. DE. *Consuetudo, vel, Lex Mercatoria:* or *The Ancient
Law-Merchant, in Three Parts.* London, 1622.

MEARS, T. L. "The History of the Admiralty Jurisdiction" in *Select
Essays in Anglo-American Legal History,* vol. ii, p. 312.

MITCHELL, W. *An Essay on The Early History of the Law Merchant.*
Cambridge, 1904.

MOLLOY, C. *De Jure Maritimo et Navali:* or *A Treatise of Affaires Maritime, and of Commerce.* London, 1676.

NELSON, W. *An Abridgement of the Common Law.* 3 vols. London,
1725–6.

POLLOCK, SIR F. *The Law of Torts.* 12th ed. London, 1923.

POMEROY, J. N. JR. *Treatise on Equitable Remedies,* 2nd ed., San Fran-
cisco, 1919, vols. i and ii, being vols. v and vi of J. N. POMEROY'S
Equity Jurisprudence and *Equitable Remedies.*

POUND, R. "Equitable Relief Against Defamation and Injury to
Personality" in *Harvard Law Review,* vol. xxix (1915–16), p. 640.

——, *Interpretations of Legal History.* Cambridge, 1923.

SALMOND, SIR J. *The Law of Torts.* 6th ed. London, 1924.

SCRUTTON, SIR T. E. "General Survey of the History of the Law
Merchant" in *Select Essays in Anglo-American Legal History,*
vol. iii, p. 7.

——, *The Contract of Affreightment as Expressed in Charterparties and
Bills of Lading.* 11th ed. by SIR T. E. SCRUTTON and F. D.
MACKINNON. London, 1923.

SELDEN SOCIETY PUBLICATIONS, vols. i. to xl. London, 1887–1923.
See also CARR, C. T.; GROSS, C.; LEADAM, I. S.; MARSDEN, R. G.
in this Section, also HUDSON, W. and LEACH, A. F. in Section *B.* of
this bibliography, *infra,* p. 181. See also YEAR BOOKS.

SELECT ESSAYS IN ANGLO-AMERICAN LEGAL HISTORY. By various
authors. 3 vols. Boston, 1907–09.

STEPHEN, H. J. *New Commentaries on the Laws of England,* 16th ed. by
E. JENKS. 4 vols. London, 1914.

VANCE, W. R. "The Early History of Insurance" in *Select Essays in
Anglo-American Legal History,* vol. iii, p. 99.

VINER, C. *A General Abridgement of Law and Equity.* 24 vols. London,
1791–5.

VINOGRADOFF, SIR P. *Introduction to Historical Jurisprudence.* Oxford,
1920.

B. VOLUMES AND ARTICLES ON SOCIAL AND ECONOMIC HISTORY INCLUDING GILD AND MUNICIPAL RECORDS

NOTE: The bibliographical starting-points of any investigation in this field are C. Gross, *The Sources and Literature of English History from the Earliest Times to About 1485* (2nd ed., London and New York, 1915), the same author's *A Bibliography of Municipal History Including Gilds and Parliamentary Representation* (New York, 1897), and the *Select Bibliography for the Study, Sources and Literature of English Mediaeval Economic History*, compiled under the supervision of Hubert Hall (London, 1914). Material suggested in these bibliographies has been supplemented by works and articles found elsewhere, or that have appeared subsequently, especially in the field of the history of gilds and livery companies.

ANDERSON, R. C. *The Assize of Bread Book, 1477–1517.* (Publications of the Southampton Record Society, vol. 23). Southampton, 1923.

ASHLEY, W. J., SIR *Introduction to English Economic History and Theory.* Vol. i, parts I and II. 4th ed., 10th impression. London and New York, 1919.

ATKYNS, S. E. and OVERALL, W. H. *Some Account of the Worshipful Company of Clockmakers of the City of London.* London, 1881.

BAIN, E. *Merchant and Craft Guilds.* Aberdeen, 1887.

BATESON, M. *Records of the Borough of Leicester.* Vols. 1 to 3 (1103–1603). Cambridge, 1899–1905. For vol. 4 (1603–1688) see STOCKS, H.

BENHAM, W. G. *The Red Paper Book of Colchester.* Colchester, 1902.

BENSON, R. and HATCHER, H. *Old and New Sarum.* Vol. 6 of *Modern History of Wiltshire*, 6 vols. in 3. Ed. R. C. Hoare. London, 1822–44.

BERRY, H. F. "The Dublin Gild of Carpenters, Millers, Masons and Heliers, in the Sixteenth Century" in *Journal of the Royal Society of Antiquaries of Ireland*, vol. 35 [5th Ser. vol. xv] p. 321. Dublin, 1905.

BERRY, H. F. "The Records of the Dublin Gild of Merchants, Known as the Gild of the Holy Trinity, 1438–1674" in *Journal of the Royal Society of Antiquaries of Ireland*, vol. 30 [5th Ser. vol. x] p. 44. Dublin, 1900.

BICKLEY, F. B. *The Little Red Book of Bristol.* 2 vols. Bristol, 1900.

BLAIR, C. H. *Northumbrian Monuments.* (Newcastle-upon-Tyne Records Committee Publications, vol. iv). Newcastle-upon-Tyne, 1924.

BLOMEFIELD, F. *An Essay Towards a Topographical History of the County of Norfolk, 1739–75.* 2nd ed., 11 vols. London, 1805–10.

BOILEAU, ETIENNE. *Le Livre de Métiers.* (Ed. R. de Lespinasse and F. Bonnardot). Paris, 1879.

CHAPMAN, A. B. W. *The Black Book of Southampton*, vols. i and ii.

(Publications of the Southampton Record Society, vols. 13–14)· Southampton, 1912.

CHEAL, H. *The Story of Shoreham*. Hove, Combridges, 1921.

COLLINS, F. *Wills and Administration from the Knaresborough Court Rolls*, vols. i and ii. (Publications of the Surtees Society, vols. cix, cx). Durham and London, 1902, 1905.

COOTE, H. C. "The Ordinances of Some Secular Guilds of London, 1354 to 1496" in *Transactions of London and Middlesex Archæological Society*, vol. iv, p. 1. London, 1871.

COTTON, W. "Some Account of the Ancient Guilds of the City of Exeter" in *Transactions of the Devonshire Assqciation for the Advancement of Science, Literature and Art*, vol. v, p. 117. Plymouth, 1872.

CROMWELL, T. [K.] *History and Description of the Ancient Town and Borough of Colchester, in Essex*. 2 vols. London, 1825.

CUNNINGHAM, W. *The Growth of English Industry and Commerce*, vol. 1 (*During the Early and Middle Ages*), 5th ed. Cambridge, 1910. Vols. 2 and 3 (*Modern Times*, Parts I and II). Cambridge, 1912, 1917.

DENDY, F. W. *Extracts from the Records of the Merchant Adventurers of Newcastle-upon-Tyne*, vol. i, ii. (Publications of the Surtees Society, vols. xciii, ci). Durham and London, 1895, 1899.

DIXON, R. W. "Thaxted" in *The Antiquary*, vol. xvii, pp. 10–12; 57–62. London, 1888.

DOUBLEDAY, H. A., PAGE, W. and ROUND, J. H. *History of Essex* (Victoria County Histories), vol. i, ed. H. A. Doubleday and W. Page; vol. ii, ed. W. Page and H. Round. London, 1903–07.

DUKE, E. *Prolusiones Historicae*. Salisbury, 1837.

EARWAKER, J. P. *Court Leet Records of the Manor of Manchester* [1552–1686; 1731–1846], 12 vols. Manchester, 1884–90.

EVANS, A. P. "The Problem of Control in Medieval Industry" in *Political Science Quarterly*, vol. xxxvi, p. 603. New York, 1921.

FIRTH, J. F. *Coopers' Company, London, Historical Memoranda, Charters, Documents, and Extracts from the Records of the Corporation and the Books of the Company, 1396–1848*. London, 1848.

FITCH, R. "Notices of Norwich Brewers' Marks and Trade Regulations" in *Norfolk Archæology: Norfolk and Norwich Archæological Society*, vol. v, p. 313. Norwich, 1859. Plates reproducing 40 brewers' marks.

FURLEY, J. S. *City Government of Winchester from the Records of the XIVth and XVth Centuries*. Oxford, 1923.

GAILHARD-BANCEL, M. DE. *Les anciennes corporations de métiers et la lutte contre la fraude dans le commerce et la petite industrie*. Paris, 1912.

GROSS, C. *The Gild Merchant. A Contribution to British Municipal History*. 2 vols. Oxford, 1890.

GUILDING, J. M. *Reading Records: Diary of the Corporation, 14311–654*. 4 vols. London, 1892–96.

HARDY, W. J. "Foreign Settlers at Colchester and Halstead" in *Proceedings of the Huguenot Society of London*, vol. ii, 1887–8, p. 182. London, 1889.

HARRIS, M. D. *Life in an Old English Town.* London, 1898.

——, *Coventry Leet Book (The) or Mayor's Register, 1420–1555.* 4 parts. (Early English Text Society). London, 1907–13.

HARROD, H. "Notes on the Records of the Corporation of Great Yarmouth" in *Norfolk Archæology; Norfolk and Norwich Archæological Society Publications*, vol. iv, p. 239. Norwich, 1855.

HEARNSHAW, F. J. C. *Leet Jurisdiction in England, Especially as Illustrated by the Records of the Court Leet of Southampton.* (Southampton Record Society Publications, No. 5). Southampton, 1908.

——, and HEARNSHAW, D. M. *Court Leet Records* [of Southampton], vol. i, Part I, II, III and Supplement. (Publications of the Southampton Record Society, vols. 1, 2, 4, 6). Southampton, 1905–8.

HEATH, J. B. *Some Account of the Worshipful Company of Grocers of the City of London*, 3rd ed. London, 1869.

HERBERT, W. *The History of the Twelve Great Livery Companies of London.* 2 vols. London, 1836–37.

HIBBERT, F. A. *Influence and Development of English Guilds.* Cambridge, 1891.

HILLS, G. M. "On the Ancient Company of Stitchmen of Ludlow: Their Account-Book and Money-Box" in *Journal of the British Archæological Association*, vol. xxiv, p. 327. London, 1868.

HUDSON, W. *Leet Jurisdiction in Norwich* (Selden Society Publications, vol. v). London, 1892.

——, and TINGEY, J. C. *Records of the City of Norwich.* 2 vols. Norwich, 1906–10.

HUNTER, J. *Hallamshire; the History and Topography of the Parish of Sheffield in the County of York.* Ed. and enlarged by A. Gatty. London, 1869.

JEAYES, I. H. and BENHAM, W. G. *Court Rolls of the Borough of Colchester, 1310–1352.* Colchester, 1921.

JOHNSON, A. H. *History of the Worshipful Company of the Drapers of London.* 5 vols. Oxford, 1914–22.

KINGDON, J. A. *Facsimile of First Volume of MS. Archives of the Worshipful Company of Grocers of the City of London.* 2 parts. London, 1886.

KRAMER, S. *The English Craft Gilds and the Government.* New York, 1905.

LAMBERT, J. M. "The Trade Gilds of Beverley," in *Transactions of the East Riding Antiquarian Society*, vol. xix, p. 91. Hull, 1913.

LAMBERT, J. M. *Two Thousand Years of Gild Life.* Hull, 1891.

LAMOND, E. *A Discourse of the Common Weal of this Realm of England.* Cambridge, 1893.

LEACH, A. F. *Beverley Town Documents* (Selden Society Publications, vol. xiv). London, 1900.

LEADER, R. E. *History of the Company of Cutlers in Hallamshire.*
2 vols. Sheffield, 1905–6.

LEIGHTON, W. A. "The Guilds of Shrewsbury" in *Transactions of the
Shropshire Archæological and Natural History Society*, vol. v, p. 265.
Shrewsbury, 1882.

LETTS, M. "Law and Order in a Medieval Town" in *Law Quarterly
Review*, vol. xxxix. London, 1923.

LIPSON, E. *An Introduction to the Economic History of England*, vol. i
(The Middle Ages). London, 1920.

LLOYD, G. I. H. *The Cutlery Trades.* London, 1913.

LOWER, M. A. "Memorials of the Town Parish, and Cinque-Port of
Seaford" in *Sussex Archæological Collections*, vol. vii, p. 73. London, 1854.

MAITLAND, F. W. "Review of 'The Gild Merchant'" in *The Collected
Papers of Frederic William Maitland*, ed. by H. A. L. FISHER, vol. ii,
p. 223. Cambridge, 1911.

MALDEN, H. E. *History of the County of Surrey* (Victoria History of the
Counties of England). 4 vols. London, 1902–14.

MACADEM, J. H. *Baxter Books of St. Andrews.* Leith, 1903.

MARKHAM, C. A. and COX, J. C. *Records of the Borough of Northampton.*
Introd. by W. L. D. Adkins. 2 vols. London, 1898.

MATTHEWS, J. H. *Cardiff Records.* 6 vols. Cardiff, etc., 1898–1911.

MORRIS, B. *The Stirling Merchant Gild.* Stirling, 1919.

NICHOLL, J. *Some Account of the Worshipful Company of Ironmongers
of London*, 2nd ed. London, 1866.

NICHOLS, J. G. "Bakers' Hall and the Muniments of the Company"
in *Transactions of the London and Middlesex Archaeological Society*,
vol. iii, p. 54. London, 1870.

OVERALL, W. H. "Some Account of the Ward of Vintry and the
Vintners' Company" in *Transactions of the London and Middlesex
Archæological Society*, vol. iii, p. 404. London, 1870.

PAGE, W. *History of the County of Somerset* (Victoria History of the
Counties of England). 2 vols. 1906–1911.

——, *History of the County of Gloucestershire* (Victoria County Histories).
Only vol. ii issued. London, 1907.

——, *London. Its Origin and Early Development.* London, 1923.

PAULI, R. *Drei Volkswirthschaftliche Denkschriften aus der Zeit Heinrichs VIII von England.* Gottingen, 1878.

PENTY, A. J. *A Guildsman's Interpretation of History.* London, 1920.

POTTHOFF, H. *Die Leinenleggen in der Grafschaft Ravensberg.* Bielefeld,
1900.

REES, J. A. *The Worshipful Company of Grocers.* London, 1923.

RENARD, G. *Guilds in the Middle Ages.* (Tr. by D. Terry, ed. by
G. D. H. Cole). London, 1919.

RILEY, H. T. *The French Chronicle of London.* London, 1863.

——, *Memorials of London and London Life in the XIIIth, XIVth and
XVth Centuries.* London, 1868.

——, Munimenta Guildhallae Londoniensis. *Liber Albus* . . .; *Liber*

Custumarum et Liber Horn (Chronicles and Memorials of Great Britain, Rolls Series, No. 12). 3 vols. London, 1859–62.

SALTER, H. E. *Records of Medieval Oxford*. Oxford, 1912.

SARGEANT, F. "The Wine Trade in Gascony" in *Finance and Trade Under Edward III*, ed. G. Unwin. (Publications of the University of Manchester, Historical Series, No. xxxii). Manchester, 1918.

SELLERS, M. *York Memorandum Book*, Part I (1376–1419); Part II (1388–1493). (Publications of the Surtees Society, vols. cxx, cxxv). London and Durham, 1912, 1915.

——, *York Mercers and Merchant Adventurers, 1356–1917*. (Publications of the Surtees Society, vol. cxxix). Durham and London, 1918.

SHARPE, R. R. *Calendar of Letters from the Mayor and Corporation of the City of London, circa A.D. 1350–70*, etc. London, 1885.

——, *Calendar of Letter Books Among the Archives of the Corporation of the City of London at the Guildhall*. Letter-Books A–L [Edw. I–Hen. VII]. 11 vols. London, 1899–1912.

SHERWELL, J. W. *A Descriptive and Historical Account of the Guild of Saddlers of the City of London*. London, 1889.

SLASKI, W. VON. *Danziger Handel im XVten Jahrhundertauf Grund eines in Danziger Stadtarchiv befindlichen handlungsbuches geschildert*. Heidelberg, 1905.

SMITH, L. T. "The Bakers of York and Their Ancient Ordinary" in *Archæological Review*, vol. i. London, 1888.

SMITH, T. *English Gilds* (Early English Text Society). London, 1870.

STALEY, E. *The Guilds of Florence*, 2nd ed. London, 1906.

STEVENSON, W. H., BAKER, W. T. and GUILFORD, E. L. *Records of the Borough of Nottingham*. 6 vols. Vols. i–iv ed. by W. H. Stevenson; vol. v ed. by W. T. Baker; vol. vi ed. by E. L. Guilford. London and Nottingham, 1882–1914.

STOCKS, H. and STEVENSON, W. H. *Records of Borough of Leicester, 1603–1688*, vol. 4. (Continuation of vols. 1 to 3, ed. by M. Bateson). Cambridge, 1923.

STONE, E. M. *History of Beverly* . . . Boston, 1843.

STOW, J. *A Survey of London*. Ed. C. L. Kingsford. 2 vols. Oxford, 1908.

STUBBS, W. *Constitutional History of England*. 4th ed. 3 vols. Oxford, 1896.

STUDER, P. *The Oak Book of Southampton of c. A.D. 1300*, vols. i, ii and Supplement. (Publications of the Southampton Record Society, vols. 10–12). Southampton, 1910–11.

SYMONDS, G. E. "Thaxted And Its Cutlers' Guild" in *Transactions of Essex Archæological Society*, vol. iii, New Series, p. 255. Colchester, 1889.

THOMAS, A. H. *Calendar of Early Mayor's Court Rolls* . . . *1298–1307*. Cambridge, 1924.

TOULMIN, J. *The History of Taunton in the County of Somerset*. Ed. by J. Savage. Taunton, 1822.

TURNER, W. H. *Selections from the Records of the City of Oxford* . . . Oxford and London, 1880.

UNWIN, G. *Finance and Trade Under Edward III.* (Publications of the University of Manchester, Historical Series, No. XXXII). Manchester, 1918.

——, *Industrial Organization in the Sixteenth and Seventeenth Centuries.* Oxford, 1904.

——, *The Gilds and Companies of London.* London, 1908.

WALDO, F. J. *Short History of the Worshipful Company of Plumbers of the City of London.* 2nd ed. London, 1923.

WEBB, S. and B. "The Assize of Bread" in *Economic Journal*, vol. xiv, p. 196. London, 1904.

WELCH, C. *History of the Worshipful Company of Pewterers of the City of London.* 2 vols. London, 1902.

——, *History of the Worshipful Company of Paviors of* . . . *London.* London, 1919.

——, *History of the Worshipful Company of the Cutlers of London.* 2 vols. London, 1916–23.

WHEELER, J. *A Treatise of Commerce.* London, 1601.

WILLIAMS, W. M. *Annals of the Worshipful Company of Founders of the City of London.* London, 1867.

WINSOR, J. *Memorial History of Boston.* 4 vols. Boston, 1881.

YOUNG, S. *Annals of the Barber-Surgeons of London.* London, 1890.

C. VOLUMES AND ARTICLES ON ART, ARCHÆOLOGY AND NUMISMATICS

BANKS, J. "Ordinances Respecting Swans on the River Witham" [1570] in *Archæologia*, vol. xvi, p. 155. London, 1810.

BAUR, P. V. C. *Catalogue of the Rebecca Darlington Stoddard Collection of Greek and Italian Vases in Yale University.* (Yale Oriental Series: Researches, vol. viii). New Haven, 1922.

BLEGEN, C. W. *Korakou, a Prehistoric Settlement Near Corinth.* (American School of Classical Studies at Athens). Boston, 1921.

BOEHEIM, W. "Die Mailänder Nigroli und der Augsburger Desiderius Colman, die Waffenkünstler Karl's V" in *Repertorium für Kunstwissenschaft*, viii, 185. Berlin, 1885.

——, *Handbuch der Waffenkunde.* Leipzig, 1890. pp. 648–80 are devoted to a list and reproductions of armourers' marks.

——, "Werke Mailänder Waffenschmiede in der Kaiserlichen Sammlungen" in *Jahrbuch der Kunsthistorischen Sammlungen der oesterreichischen Kaisershauses*, vol. ix. Vienna, 1899.

BOUTELL, C. *Heraldry.* London, 1864.

BOYNE, W. *Trade Tokens Issued in the Seventeenth Century in England, Wales and Ireland by Corporations, Merchants, Tradesmen, etc.* Revised ed. by G. C. WILLIAMSON. 2 vols. London, 1889–91.

BRULLIOT, F. *Dictionnaire des monogrammes* . . . New ed. 3 vols. in
    1. Munich, 1832–34. Reproduces artists' signatures and symbols.
BUCK, J. H. "Historical Sketch of Makers' Marks" in *Trade Marks
    of the Jewelry and Hundred Trades*, published by Jewelers Circular
    Publishing Co. (3rd ed.) New York, 1915.
BUMPUS, T. F. *London Churches, Ancient and Modern*. London,
    1905.
CHAFFERS, W. *Handbook to Hall Marks on Gold & Silver Plate*. Ed.
    C. A. MARKHAM (4th ed.) London, 1913.
——, *Marks and Monograms on Pottery and Porcelain of the Renaissance
    and Modern Periods* . . . 3rd ed. revised & enlarged. London,
    1872.
CHRIST, M. *Dictionnaire des monogrammes* (French tr. from German).
    Paris, 1762.
CHRISTY, M. *The Trade Signs of Essex*. Chelmsford and London, 1887.
COOPER, T. P. "The Armorial Bearings of Gilds and Livery Com-
    panies" in *The Antiquary*, vol. xlix [New Series, vol. ix] pp. 287–91;
    345–49. London, 1913.
COSSON, A. DE "Arsenals and Armouries in Southern Germany and
    Austria" in *Archæological Journal*, vol. xlviii, p. 117. London,
    1891.
COTMAN, J. S. *Engravings of Sepulchral Brasses in Norfolk and Suffolk.*
    2nd ed. by Sir S. R. MEYRICK, 2 vols. London, 1839.
CROSSLEY, F. H. *English Church Monuments, A.D. 1150–1550*. London,
    1921. Reproduces merchant's mark on tomb (p. 159).
DANIELS, L. E. "The History of the Trademark" in *Bulletin U. S.
    Trademark Assn.*, vol. 7 (New Series), p. 239. New York, 1911.
DAVIS, C. T. *Monumental Brasses of Gloucestershire*. London, 1899.
DEAN, B. *Catalogue of a Loan Exhibition of Arms and Armor*. New
    York, 1916.
——, *The Collection of Arms and Armor of Rutherford Stuyvesant*. New
    York, 1914.
DRUITT, H. *Manual of Costume as Illustrated by Monumental Brasses.*
    Philadelphia, 1907.
DUNKIN, E. H. W. *Monumental Brasses of Cornwall*. London, 1882.
EWING, W. C. "Notices of the Norwich Merchant Marks" in *Norfolk
    Archæology; Norfolk and Norwich Archæological Society Publica-
    tions*, vol. iii, p. 177. Norwich, 1852.
FAIRHOLT, F. W. "Marks of Gold and Silver Smiths" in *Trade Marks
    of the Jewelry and Hundred Trades*, published by Jewelers Circular
    Publishing Co. (3rd ed.) New York, 1915.
FFOULKES, C. J. *Inventory and Survey of the Armouries of the Tower of
    London*. 2 vols. London, 1916.
——, *The Armourer and His Craft from the XIth to the XVIth Century.*
    London, 1912. Pp. 62–73 deal with the relation of armourers'
    marks to "the proof of armour"; pp. 147–152 contain list of
    armourers' marks with illustrations. Appendices also have regula-
    tions concerning armourers' marks.

FFOULKES, C. J. "The Armourers of Italy" in *The Connoisseur*, vol. xxv, pp. 28, 167. London, 1909.
——, "The Craft of the Armourer" in *The Connoisseur*, vol. xxiv, p. 99. London, 1909.
GAWTHORP, W. E. *The Brasses of Our Homeland Churches*. London, 1923. Ch. viii deals with merchants' marks.
GERSTUNG, W. *Das Zeichenbuch*. Offenbach am Main, 1923. Contains excellent reproductions of medieval marks and symbols, unfortunately without adequate explanations and references.
GILBERT, W. "The Token Coinage in Essex in the Seventeenth Century" in *Essex Archæological Society Transactions*, vol. xiii, New Series, p. 184. Colchester, 1915.
GILCHRIST, H. I. *Catalogue of the Collection of Arms and Armor Presented to Cleveland Museum of Art by Mr. and Mrs. John Long Severance*, pp. 265–78. Cleveland, 1924.
GRAESSE, J. G. T. and JAENNICKE, E. *Führer für Sammler von Porzellan und Fayence* . . . 15th ed., by E. ZIMMERMAN. Berlin, 1919. Reproduces European, Japanese and Chinese porcelain and pottery marks.
GRAY, H. ST. G. and SYMONDS, H. "Somerset Trade Tokens, XVII Century" in *Proceedings of the Somersetshire Archæological and Natural History Society*, vol. lxi, p. 115. Taunton, 1916.
HAINES, H. *Manual of Monumental Brasses*. 2 vols. London, 1861.
HAMY, E. T. "Un Naufrage en 1332" in *Études historiques et géographiques*. Paris, 1896.
HANNOVER, E. *Pottery and Porcelain, a Handbook for Collectors*. Ed. and tr. by B. RACKHAM, 3 vols. London, 1924. A very important work, containing much information concerning pottery and porcelain marks and their infringement, also valuable bibliographies.
HEARNE, T. See THYNNE, F.
HOMEYER, K. G. *Die Haus- und Hofmarken*. Berlin, 1853.
JACKSON, C. J. *English Goldsmiths and Their Marks*. 2nd ed. London, 1921. Very comprehensive in scope and thorough in treatment.
JONES, S. R. *Posters and Their Designers*. London, 1924.
LAKING, G. F. *A Record of European Armour and Arms*. 5 vols. London, 1920.
LARWOOD, J. and HOTTEN, J. C. *History of Signboards*, 3rd ed. London, 1908.
LEEDS, E. T. "Oxford Tradesmen's Tokens" in *Surveys and Tokens* (Oxford Historical Society, vol. lxxv), ed. by H. E. SALTER. Oxford, 1923.
MACKLIN, H. W. *The Brasses of England*, 2nd ed. London, 1907.
MANNING, C. R. "Monumental Brass Inscriptions &c. in Norfolk" in *Norfolk Archæology: Norfolk and Norwich Archæological Society Publications*, vol. xi, p. 182. Norwich, 1892.
MARKHAM, C. A. *Pewter Marks and Old Pewter Ware*. London, 1907.
MAYO, C. H. "Swans on the Salisbury, Avon and The Dorset Stour"

in *Notes & Queries for Somerset and Dorset*, vol. xiii, p. 297. Sherborne, 1913. Contains excellent reproductions of swan-marks.

MÉLY, F. DE. *La céramique italienne, marques et monogrammes.* Paris, 1884.

——, *Les primitifs et leurs signatures.* Paris, 1913.

METROPOLITAN MUSEUM OF ART, NEW YORK. *Bulletin*, vol. xix, No. 5. New York, 1924.

NEALE, J. M. *Illustrations of Monumental Brasses.* (Cambridge Camden Society, 1846.)

NEWTON, W. *A Display of Heraldry.* London, 1846.

PEACOCK, E. "Swan Marks" in *Archæological Journal . . . of the Royal Archæological Institute*, vol. xli, p. 290. London, 1884.

RAINE, J. JR. *A Volume of English Miscellanies Illustrating the History and Language of the Northern Counties of England.* (Publications of the Surtees Society, vol. lxxxv [vol. ii for 1888]). Durham and London, 1890.

ROGERS, E. S. *Good Will, Trade-Marks and Unfair Trade.* Chicago, 1919.

——, "Some Historical Matter Concerning Trade-Marks" in *Michigan Law Review*, vol. ix (1910–11), p. 29.

ROTH-SCHOLTZ, F. *Thesaurus Symbolorum Ac Emblematum.* Nuremberg and Altdorf, 1730. See ROTH-SCHOLTZ in Section *D* of this bibliography, *infra*, p. 190.

RYLANDS, J. P. "Merchants' Marks and other Mediaeval Personal Marks" in *Transactions of the Historical Society of Lancashire and Cheshire for the Year 1910*, vol. lxii [New Series, vol. xxvi] p. 1. Liverpool, 1911.

SAMPSON, H. *The History of Advertising from the Earliest Times.* London, 1875.

STIRLING-MAXWELL, W. *Annals of the Artists of Spain.* 4 vols. New ed. London, 1891. Vol. iv, p. 1642, reproduces Spanish artists' monograms.

SUFFLING, E. R. *English Church Brasses from the 13th to the 17th Century.* London, 1910.

THORNELEY, J. L. *Monumental Brasses of Lancashire and Cheshire.* Hull, 1893.

THYNNE, F. "A Discourse of the Duty and Office of an Herald at Arms," 1605, reprinted in *A Collection of Curious Discourses*, ed. T. HEARNE, 2nd ed. 2 vols. London, 1775.

WATTERS, H. B. *History of Ancient Pottery* (Based on the Work of Samuel Birch). London, 1905.

D. EARLY PRINTERS' AND PUBLISHERS' DEVICES

NOTE: A good general Bibliography of bibliography and of the history of typography and of printers and publishers will be found in A. W. Pollard, *Fine Books*, (London, 1912) pp. 309–318.

ALDIS, H. G. *The Printed Book.* Cambridge, 1921.

AMES, J. *Typographical Antiquities.* Enlarged by T. F. Dibdin, 4 vols. London, 1810–19.

ARBER, E. *A Transcript of the Registers of the Company of Stationers of London, 1554–1640.* 5 vols. London, 1875–94.

BAILLET, A. *Jugemens des savans sur les principaux ouvrages des auteurs.* Ed. by B. de la Monnoye. 8 vols. Paris, 1722–30.

BARACK, K. A. See Introd. to *Elsässische Bückermarken* in Heitz's BÜCHERMARKEN series.

BAYLEY, H. *A New Light on the Renaissance.* London, 1909.

BERNOUILLÉ, C. See Introd. to *Die Basler Büchermarken* in Heitz, BÜCHERMARKEN series.

BIBLIOGRAPHICA. Review of P. Kristeller's *Die Italienischen Buchdrucker- und Verlegerzeichen,* vol. i, pp. 123–5. London, 1895.

BIBLIOGRAPHICAL SOCIETY. *Illustrated Monographs.*

BIBLIOGRAPHICAL SOCIETY. *Transactions.* London, 1893, etc.

BIRRELL, A., *The Law and History of Copyrighting Books.* London, 1899.

BRESCIANO, G. "Insegne di typografi e librai napoletani del XV e XVI secolo," in *Bolletino del Bibliofilo,* vol. i, pp. 94–6, 129–56. Naples, 1918–19.

BRIQUET, C. M. *Les Filigranes.* 4 vols. Paris, 1907.

BROWN, H. F. *The Venetian Printing Press.* New York, 1891.

BROWNE, W. H. *Treatise on the Law of Trademarks,* 2nd ed. Boston, 1898.

BÜCHERMARKEN. *Die Büchermarken oder Buchdrucker- und Verlegerzeichen.* Strassburg, 1892, etc.

  1. *Elsässische Büchermarken bis Anfang des 18. Jahrhunderts.* Herausgeg. von P. HEITZ, 1892.

  2. *Die Italienischen Buchdrucker- und Verlegerzeichen bis 1525.* Herausgeg. von P. KRISTELLER, 1893.

  3. *Die Basler Büchermarken bis Anfang des 17. Jahrhunderts.* Herausgeg. von P. HEITZ, 1895.

  4. *Die Frankfurter Drucker und Verlegerzeichen bis Anfang des 17. Jahrhunderts.* Herausgeg. von P. HEITZ, 1896.

  5. *Spanische und Portugiesische Bücherzeichen des xv. und xvi. Jahrhunderts.* Herausgeg. von K. HAEBLER, 1898.

  6. *Kölner Büchermarken bis zum Anfang des xvii. Jahrhunderts.* Herausgeg. von DR. ZARETZKY, 1898.

  7. *Genfer Buchdrucker- und Verlegerzeichen vom xv. xvi. und xvii. Jahrhundert.* Herausgeg. von P. HEITZ, 1908.

BURNHAM, L. "Harold Bayley's 'A New Light on the Renaissance,'" in *The Bookman,* p. 531, vol. xxix. New York, 1909.

CAMBRIDGE MODERN HISTORY. See TILLEY, A.

CHEVILLIER, A. *L'Origine de l'imprimerie de Paris*. Paris, 1694.

DANIELS, L. E.. "The History of the Trade-Mark" in *Bulletin of the United States Trade-Mark Association*, New Series, vol. 7, p. 239. New York, 1910.

DELALAIN, M. P. *Inventaire des marques d'imprimeurs et de libraires*, 2nd ed. Paris, 1892.

DE VINNE, T. L. *Notable Printers of Italy during the fifteenth century*. New York, 1910.

DIBDIN, T. F. *Typographical Antiquities*. 4 vols. London, 1810–19.

DUFF, E. G. *A Century of the English Book Trade*. London, 1905.

DUPONT, P. *Histoire de l'imprimerie*. 2 vols. Paris, 1854.

ENCYCLOPÆDIA BRITANNICA. 11th ed. vol. xxvii (Cambridge, 1911) pp. 509–548.

EYRE, G. E. B. and RIVINGTON, C. R. *A Transcript of the Registers of the Worshipful Company of Stationers from 1640–1708, A.D.* 3 vols. London, 1913–14.

FIRMIN-DIDOT, A. *Alde Manuce*. Paris, 1875.

——, Article "Typographie" in *Encyclopédie Moderne*, vol. xxvi. Paris, 1851, pp. 558–922.

FREIMANN, A. Article "Printers' Marks" in *Jewish Encyclopedia*, vol. x (New York, 1905) pp. 200–204.

GIBSON, S. *Abstracts from the Wills of Oxford Printers*. London, 1907.

GRAY, G. J. and PALMER, W. M. *Abstracts from the Wills and Testamentary Documents of Printers, Binders and Stationers of Cambridge, from 1504 to 1699*. (Bibliographical Society, London), London, 1915.

GRESWELL, W. P. *Annals of Parisian Typography*. London, 1818.

GROLIER CLUB. *A Description of the Early Printed Books owned by the Grolier Club*. New York, 1895.

HAEBLER, K. *The Early Printers of Spain and Portugal*. (Bibliographical Society Illustrated Monographs, No. IV). London, 1897

HEITZ, P. See BÜCHERMARKEN.

ISAMBERT, F. A. *Recueil général des anciennes lois françaises*. Vol. xii. Paris, 1828.

JOHNSON, H. L. *Historic Design in Printing*. Boston, 1923.

KOHLER, J. *Das Recht des Markenschutzes*. Würzburg, 1884.

KRISTELLER, P. See *Die Italienischen Buchdrucker- und Verlegerzeichen* in Heitz, BÜCHERMARKEN Series.

MCKERROW, R. B. *Printers' and Publishers' Devices in England and Scotland, 1485–1640*. (Bibliographical Society Illustrated Monographs, No. XVI.). London, 1913.

MACFARLANE, J. *Antoine Verard* (Bibliographical Society Illustrated Monographs, No. VII). London, 1900.

MADAN, F. "Early Representations of the Printing Press" in *Bibliographica*, vol. i. London, 1895.

PLOMER, H. R. *Abstract from the Wills of English Printers and Stationers, 1492–1630*. (Bibliographical Society, London.) London, 1903.

PLOMER, H. R. "Eliot's Court Printing House, The (1584–1674)" in *The Library*, 4th Series, vol. ii (Transactions of the Bibliographical Society, London, 2nd Series, vol. ii), pp. 175–184. Oxford, 1922.

——, *English Printers' Ornaments*. London, 1924. See review in *London Times Literary Supplement*, March 13, 1924, p. 159, criticizing exclusion of printers' devices from this work.

——, *Short History of English Printing*, 2nd ed. London, 1915.

POLLARD, A. W. *An Essay on Colophons*, The Caxton Club, Chicago, 1915.

——, *Fine Books*. London, 1912.

——, *Early Illustrated Books*, 2nd ed. London, 1917.

——, *Last Words on the History of the Title-Page*. London, 1891.

——, "Printers' Marks of the XVth and XVIth Centuries" in *The Connoisseur*, vol. ii (London, 1902), p. 262.

——, "Some Notes on English Illustrated Books" in *Transactions of the Bibliographical Society, London* vol. vi, p. 29. London 1900–01.

——, "Some Notes on the History of Copyright in England," 1622–1674 in *The Library*, 4th Series, vol. iii (Transactions of the Bibliographical Society, London, vol. iii), p. 97. Oxford, 1923.

PROCTOR, R. *Jan Van Doesborgh* (Bibliographical Society, Illustrated Monographs, No. XI). London, 1894.

PUTNAM, G. H. *The Censorship of the Church of Rome*. 2 vols. New York, 1906. .

REED, T. B. *History of Old English Letter Foundries*. London, 1887.

RENOUARD, P. *Bibliographie des impressions et des œuvres de Josse Badius Ascencius*. 3 vols. Paris, 1908.

REUSCH, H. *Die Indices Librorum Prohibitorum des sechzehnten Jahrhunderts* (Bibliothek des Litterarischen Vereins in Stuttgart, vol. clxxvi). Tübingen, 1886.

ROBERTS, W. *Printers' Marks*. London, 1893.

ROGERS, E. S. *Good Will, Trade-Marks and Unfair Trading*. Chicago, 1919.

——, "Some Historical Matter Concerning Trademarks" in *Michigan Law Review*, vol. ix (1910–11), p. 29.

ROTH-SCHOLTZ, F. *Thesaurus Symbolorum et Emblematum*. Nuremberg and Altdorf, 1730. A rare volume. Copy in Library of Congress. Reproduces 508 printers' and publishers' devices. At foot of Plate 50 appears "*Partis prima finis*," but according to the Library of Congress Catalogue no second part was ever published.

SAUGRAINE, C. M. *Code de la librairie et imprimerie de Paris*. Paris, 1744.

SHARPE, R. R. *Calendar of Wills Proved and Enrolled in the Court of Husting, London A.D. 1258–A.D. 1688*. 2 vols. London, 1889–90.

SILVESTRE, L. C. *Marques typographiques*. Paris, 1867.

STEELE, R. *Earliest English Music Printing* (Bibliographical Society, Illustrated Monographs, No. XI). London, 1903.

THOMPSON, S. B. "Peter Short, Printer, and His Marks" in *Trans-*

actions of the Bibliographical Society, London, vol. iv, p. 103. London, 1898.

TILLEY, A. A. "The Reformation in France," in *Cambridge Modern History*, vol. ii, pp. 280–304. New York, 1904.

UNWIN, G. *The Gilds and Companies of London.* London, 1908.

UPDIKE, D. B. *Printing Types, their History, Forms and Use.* 2 vols. Cambridge, 1922.

ZARETZKY, O. See Introd. to *Die Kölner Büchermarken* in Heitz's BÜCHERMARKEN series.

E. LITERARY, BIOGRAPHICAL, CURRENT ECONOMIC AND MISCELLANEOUS WORKS AND ARTICLES

AMERICAN STATE PAPERS. Vol. ix (Class iv, vol. viii). Washington, 1832.

BISHOP, J. L. *History of American Manufactures.* 3 vols. Philadelphia, 1864.

BOSTON GAZETTE. Dec. 26, 1791.

BRECK, S. *Genealogy of the Breck Family.* Omaha, 1889.

BRIGHT, M. *Diary and Correspondence of Samuel Pepys.* 10 vols. New York, 1884.

CAMPBELL, J. C. *Lives of the Chief Justices of England.* 6 vols. New York, 1873.

COPELAND, M. A. "The Economies of Advertising" — Discussion of, in *American Economic Review*, vol. xv (Supplement), p. 38. New Haven, 1915.

D'EWES, SIR S. Journal of, ed. W. NOTENSTEIN (Yale Historical Publications, vol. vii). New Haven, 1923.

DOBSON, A. *Diary of John Evelyn.* 3 vols. London, 1906.

DUNLAP'S. *American Daily Advertiser.* Philadelphia, Dec. 12, 1791.

GOLLANCZ, SIR I. *A Good Short Debate Between Winner and Waster* (Selected Early English Poems for Early English Text Society, No. III). London, 1920.

GOODALL, G. W. *Advertising: A Study of a Modern Business Power* (London School of Economics Monographs, No. 41). London, 1914.

HANSARD, T. C. *Parliamentary Debates*, 3rd Series, vol. 217. London, 1874.

HOTCHKISS, G. B. "An Economic Defence of Advertising" in *American Economic Review*, vol. xv (Supplement), p. 14. New Haven, 1925.

JEFFERSON, T. *Complete Works.* Ed. by H. A. WASHINGTON, 9 vols. New York, 1853–55.

KERSEY, J. *Dictionarium Anglo-Britannicum: or a General English Dictionary*, etc. London, 1715.

MURRAY, J. A. H. *A New English Dictionary.* Vol. vi, part II (Oxford, 1908), *s.v.* "marks."

PAGE, E. D. *Trade Morals, Their Origin, Growth and Province.* New Haven, 1914.

REPORT OF THE COMMITTEE ON THE DECAY OF TRADE. (House of Lords, Oct. 28, 1669) in *Historical Manuscripts Commission Report*, vol. viii, Appendix Part i, No. 215, 133–136. London, 1881.

RUSHWORTH, J. *Historical Collections of Private Passages of State*, etc. 7 vols. London, 1659–1701.

ST. JAMES' CHRONICLE. London, Dec. 4, 1777.

SCUDDER, H. E. *Recollections of Samuel Breck.* Philadelphia, 1877.

SKEAT, W. *Pierce The Ploughman's Crede* (Early English Text Society). London, 1867.

VEBLEN, T. *The Theory of Business Enterprise.* New York, 1904.

WEBB, S. *Industrial Democracy.* New York, 1920.

WRIGHT, T. and HALLIWELL, J. O. *Reliquae Antiquae. Scraps from Ancient Manuscripts.* 2 vols. London, 1845.

YARRELL, W. *History of British Birds*, 4th ed. 4 vols. London, 1884.

YORKE, P. C. *Life and Correspondence of Philip Yorke, Earl of Hardwicke.* 3 vols. Cambridge, 1913.

INDEX

A.B.C. with a little cathechisme, 74–76
Abbott, C. J., 137
Abridgements, classification of trade-mark infringement by, 9
Admiralty courts, *see* Maritime courts
Advertisement, self-, repression by gilds, 46
Advertising, development of after Industrial Revolution, 130; Dr. Johnson on, 130; posters for, 130 and n. 3; economic justification of, 159 n. 2; protection of, in equity, 167 and n. 3, 168
Agnus dei, as merchant's mark, 24
Aldus, Manutius, complaint of infringement by, 63–64; forgery of italic of, 76 n. 2
Alverstone, L. J., quoted, 143 n. 1
American writers on trade-mark law, 13
Apprentices, enticement of, 42 and n. 3
Aquinas, Thomas, "Just Price" and, 42 n. 1
Arber, Edward, *Transcript of Registers*, of, 73 and n. 2
Arbitration: gild ordinances compelling, 16, 17 and n. 1, 2; statute forbidding, ineffectual, 18
Archæological societies, records of, 16
Archæology, trade-marks in, 11, 19, 20 and n. 4.
Armstrong, Clement, quoted, 85
Ascensius, Josse Badius, device of, 64 and n. 1
Ashley, quoted, 40, 80, 81
"Asperin," 168
"Asset mark" *see* Compulsory mark
Assisa Panis et Cervisiae (Assize of Bread and Ale), 49–50, 52, 56, 57
"Aunt Jemima," 169

Bacon, V. C., 9
Badius, complaint of, 64; devices of, 67–68; use of others' devices by, 68 n. 5
Baillet, *Jugemens des Savans* of, 69
Baize, seals on, 88–100
Baker, Judge, quoted, 155–156
"Baker's Chocolate," 148, 150
Bakers' marks, forms of, 39 and n. 7
Barack, cited, 66
Bargain, loss of, action for, 15 n. 1
Barrington, Daines, quoted, 48
Basel, printers of, 65
"Beehive," 134 n. 1

Lynn, merchants' marks in, 23; weavers of, 84 n. 2
Lyons, printers of, 68; Milanese armorers at, 105 n. 2

Madan, Falconer, 67
"Madeira wine," 79 n. 1
Mainz Psalter, 65
Majorca, merchants of, 26
Malynes, definition of merchant of, 15 n. 4; on merchants' marks, 124,
    147
Manchester, Leet Court of, 52
Mansfield, Lord, on plea of wreck, 31; on trade-mark infringement, 137
Maritime courts, no trade-mark cases in, 15; merchants' marks in, 15,
    31–34; law developed in, 15 n. 4
Marks and other trade symbols of:
  Ale-sellers, 56
  Armorers, 105 n. 2
  Arrow-head makers, 16, 105 n. 1
  Bakers, 14 and n. 2, 15, 48–56
  Barber-surgeons, 44
  Bladesmiths, 60, 61, 94 n. 1
  Bottle-makers, 56
  Brewers, 50 n. 1, 55 n. 1, 57
  Candlemakers, 39
  Cloth makers, 7–10, 16, 83
  Coopers, 14 and n. 2, 15, 57, 58 and n. 2, 59
  Cordwainers, 62
  Cutlers, 14, 79 n. 1., ch. V. *passim*
  Founders, 62
  Fullers, 61
  Goldsmiths, 16, 59 and n. 4, 60, 73
  Hatmakers, 62
  Heaumers (helmet-makers), 61 and n. 6
  Joiners, 61
  Merchant-adventurers, 45 and n. 1
  Painters, 39 and n. 4
  Paper makers, 77 n. 3, 94 n. 4
  Pewterers, 45, 61 and n. 10, 102 n. 1
  Printers, 63–77
  Publishers, 63–77
  Sail-cloth makers, 130–133
  Scriveners, 60
  Shoemakers, 62
  Silversmiths, 39
  Soap-maker, 94 n. 4
  Tapermakers, 39
  Tilers, 61
  Tinsmiths, 39
  Torchmakers, 39

Sacon, Jacques, device of, 70

Sail-cloth industry, Massachusetts bounties for, 130 and n. 5, 6, 131; trade-marks on, 130–131; petition for protection of, 131; Jefferson's Report on, 131–132; "Philadelphia manufacturer" on, 132–133

St. Albans Press, 70

St. Andrews, Baxter Books of, 48–49

Salisbury, cloth seals of, 82

Salmond, Judge, quoted, 151

Salop, Court of Earl of, 14

Sample, sale by, 15 n. 1

Sargent, L. J., quoted, 158

Sancius, goods of, 28

Schoeffer, colophon of, quoted, 65; device of, 68

Scienter, need not be proven, 161

Scotland, merchants' marks in, 22

Scottish linen, marks on protected, 128

Seaford, swan mark in, 37

Sebastian, quoted, 11

Select Essays in Anglo-American Legal History, trade-mark law ignored in, 13

Seligman, on relation of gild rules to common law, 125

Sellars, M. quoted, 17 n. 2

Seville, high court of, merchant's mark in, 26–27

Sheffield cutlery *see* Cutlery Trades

"Sheffield steel," 79 n. 1, 101 n. 1, 107 n. 1

Ships, merchants' marks in registers of, 26

Shoreham, piracy in, 30

Short, Peter, devices of, 70 n. 5 and illustration facing p. 70

Sign-boards, 71 and n. 4, 5; no copyright in, 71 n. 4, 72; imitations of, Lord Hardwicke on, 134; in London, 134 n. 1; in early New York, 134 n. 1

Silk trade, abuses in, 94 n. 2

Smith, Toulmin, cited, 50

Sources,unorthodox, used, 13

Southampton, Sheriff of, 28; Leet Court of, 59; cloth-making in, 82

Southern v. *How*, various reports of, 6–10; subsequent history of, 9–10, 123; Holdsworth on, 123; as link with modern law, 123–124; no contemporary reliance on, 124; further research into history of, 126

Southwark, prejudice against, 54

Spain, printers of, 67

Spanish trade-marks, compulsory, 39

Specialization in medieval industry, 102–103

Stanhope, Richard de, goods of, 29

Star Chamber, regulation of printing by, 75–77; protection of trade-marks by, 126–127

State Courts, first trade-mark litigation in, 133–134

"States Rights," and Federal trade-mark legislation, 141 and n. 2